THE ART OF
PERFUME

Frontispiece
Dépinox bottle no. 6047, 1925.
This bottle was used to represent
the company at the Exposition
Internationale des Arts Décoratifs et
Industriels Modernes, Paris, 1925.
H. 11.0 cm (4⅜ in.).

THE ART OF
PERFUME

Discovering and Collecting Perfume Bottles

Christie Mayer Lefkowith

PHOTOGRAPHS BY SKOT YOBBAGY
with 370 illustrations, 220 in colour

Thames and Hudson

To my husband, Ed, and to our children,

David and Samantha

&

James, David and Ann

© 1994 Christie Mayer Lefkowith

First paperback edition 1998

British Library Cataloguing-in-Publication Data
A catalogue record for this book is available from the British Library

ISBN 0-500-28044-4

Printed and bound in Singapore by C.S. Graphics

CONTENTS

Acknowledgments

My grateful thanks to Janine Bloch-Dermant for her support and encouragement for this project. Special thanks to Max Dépinoix, son of Maurice Dépinoix, for information on his father and grandfather, on the Dépinoix glassworks, on Société Parisienne de Verreries and on other glassworks; to Madame Jeannine Dépinoix, daughter of Julien Viard, for information on her father and grandfather and about their work; to Perrine de Wilde, daughter of Paul Poiret; to France de Brunhoff, daughter of Jacques de Brunhoff; to Marion de Brunhoff, daughter of Michel de Brunhoff; to Marie-Claude Vaillant-Couturier, daughter of Lucien Vogel; to Gilbert Fornells, son of Eduard Fornells; to François Rateau, son of Armand Albert Rateau; to Chrystiane Charles of Charles, Bronze d'Art; to Edouard Leroy, son of Andrée Leroy, Isabelle Leroy and their daughter, Martine Barère, for information on Fourrures Max and on couture; to Raymond Peynet, for information on Schiaparelli; and to Becky Kaminski, for information on Paquin and on couture.

I wish to thank the following individuals for providing information on the art of glassmaking, glass artists and their respective glassworks: from Verreries Brosse, René, Catherine and Patrick Barré, as well as Christian Taté and Jean Mettétal; from Verreries et Cristalleries de la Bresle, Gilbert Dubreucq; from Verreries Pochet et du Courval, Hubert Varlet; from Verrerie de Romesnil and Verrerie de la Nesle Normandeusc, Raymond Guignard and Elisabeth Guignard (née Evrard); from Saint-Gobain Desjonquères, Jacques Grolleron and Alain Trophardy; and from Baccarat, Véronique Nansenet.

I am also grateful to all those at many perfume and fashion houses for providing background information on their respective companies, especially: Jean de Moüy (Jean Patou); Daniel Damask (Henri Bendel); Jean-Alain Lelorrain (Cadolle); Joanne Feeney (Colgate-Palmolive); Natalie Scott (Chesebrough-Pond's for Prince Matchabelli); Alessandra Ruggieri (Borsari 1870); Caroline Eversfield (Rimmel); and Robert Dressler (Merle Norman).

I owe special thanks for their friendship to Liliane and Christopher Fawcett; Francis Touyarou-Grabe and his sister, Marie-Geo Touyarou-Grabe; Dr Jean and Dominique Blanchard; Juliette Bogaers; and Annette Green of the Fragrance Foundation. My deepest appreciation to Skot Yobbagy for his long hours and for his outstanding talent in photography, reflected in the colour plates and illustrations in this book.

Thanks are also due to the staffs of many libraries and museums in France, England and the United States, who have helped in my search for accurate documentation. I must also express my appreciation to all those – too numerous to mention individually – who share my passion for collecting perfume bottles and presentations and for studying the art associated with them: they include the members of many perfume clubs; the auction house staffs; and dealers and collectors in the United States, France, England, Germany, Austria, Switzerland, Belgium, Holland, Italy, Spain, Canada, South America and Japan.

My warmest thanks to Régine de Robien for her friendship, for her willingness to share her immense knowledge, and for her love and appreciation of flacons. I also owe my thanks and appreciation to the entire team at Thames and Hudson for contributing their enthusiasm, dedication, scholarship and professionalism to my project. And finally thanks and love to my husband Ed, who has been my partner in every meaning of that word.

C. M. L.

Note on dimensions
The sizes of objects shown in the captions to illustrations are given in centimetres and inches. Unless otherwise stated, the height (h.) refers to the bottle and its stopper; in a few examples, such as boxes, the width (w.) or depth (d.) is given.

Introduction

Analyzing the Art of Perfume

A new form of artistic expression associated with perfume first emerged in the late 19th century, but is essentially a phenomenon of the 20th century. Modern perfume packaging was originally designed to help an ephemeral product achieve commercial success by providing each brand with a unique identity and appeal; and, when detached from the perfume it was created to serve, it could transcend its initial purpose and become significant in its own right. When the commercial role of its first life is no longer relevant, its second life is that of an art object. Thus, perfume presentations can now be appreciated like other art forms which reflect the people, the events and the spirit of their time.

AN IMPORTANT DISTINCTION

Perfumes have been used for thousands of years, as have containers made specially for them. Excellent examples come from all over the world, and new designs are still being produced. However, decorative perfume bottles are created independently of individual products and should not be confused with modern perfume packaging developed to contain and market specific perfumes. This important distinction is well illustrated by two containers, both designed by René Lalique, but each intended for an entirely different purpose. The first is a traditional decorative perfume bottle (pl.63) called 'Fougères' ('Ferns'). It was also designated '489', both the name and the number being used in the catalogue of René Lalique & Cie. The name was simply descriptive of the design motif, and for this reason the name did not appear on the bottle, and no label was used (1, 2). This bottle's main feature was a double-sided central medallion with silver overtones, showing a different female figure depicted on each side. Around this medallion was the hollow space for the liquid. The stopper and bottle were both decorated with fern foliage, but the box did not complement the bottle, having been designed simply for presentation and safe transportation, and as a result was usually discarded. This bottle would have been purchased empty from René Lalique & Cie as a decorative object, either to be filled with perfume or to be displayed empty. While 'Fougères' is a high-quality decorative art object, the important distinction from the art of perfume presentation becomes clear when it is compared with the Houbigant perfume 'La Belle Saison' ('The

1, 2 René Lalique & Cie, 'Fougères'.

3, 4 Houbigant, 'La Belle Saison'.

Summer Months'). While this second example (pl. 128) was also designed by Lalique, and while the bottle's design concept was like that of 'Fougères', the similarity ends there.

The complex, multi-media presentation for the Houbigant perfume 'La Belle Saison' (which included name, bottle, label and box) could only be acquired when the perfume itself was purchased. While the French name literally means 'The Beautiful Season', it is a poetic phrase which signifies 'summer', with a hint of romance at a particularly pleasant time of year. This name worked with the other elements to create a unique identity and a compelling image for the perfume. Unlike 'Fougères', the medallion for 'La Belle Saison' had only a front figural design showing a young person enjoying a flower's scent – a pleasing experience associated with summer. From this central medallion radiated a floral motif resembling shafts of sunlight. The perfume's golden colour was visible through the sienna leaf motif on the clear-glass bottle, providing a sunny, warm effect. The reverse of the medallion was left smooth for the gilded paper label, an integral element of this presentation, on which the perfume name was printed in an elegant style (3). The box enhanced the design of the bottle. When closed, with the bottle inside, it was not immediately obvious that this was a perfume presentation (4). The box, which framed the front of the bottle as if it were a picture or an open window, was covered with paper printed in green and gold to simulate reptile skin, and was lined with yellow silk. Even the small pear-shaped pulls for opening the box were appropriately designed. This unusual box carried the Houbigant name and was designed as an integral part of the presentation, with the result that many examples have survived. This integrated multi-media presentation of 1925 today provides us with a valuable insight into the era in which it was created.

THE CONTRIBUTING ELEMENTS

The five contributing elements in perfume art are: name, bottle, label, box and, sometimes, additional ornaments. In order to achieve optimum artistic effect these elements should complement each other. Their individual roles have varied since the mid-19th century as part of a complex evolution, directly related to changes in society and the arts.

THE PERFUME NAME

The most unconventional element is the name given to a perfume. Unlike the title of a work of art, which is generally not integral to the work itself, the name of a perfume is an essential element in creating its unique identity. During the 19th century, most perfume names were simply those of flowers. The development of synthetic fragrances, known as aldehydes, created complex bouquets not found in nature. The naming of perfumes thus had unlimited possibilities, including real words, fabricated words, even punctuation marks. Names could be very short or very long, and many examples have been romantic, humorous, provocative, exotic, sensuous or enigmatic in tone, while some have had clever double meanings or were puns which cannot be adequately conveyed in translation.

Perfume names have frequently followed trends. After Chanel 'No. 5', Molyneux introduced 'The Number Five'. Then Alice Choquet named a perfume 'Le Double Cinq' ('The Double Five'), and Henri Bendel carried this numerical fashion to its ultimate, even absurd, limit by calling a perfume 'Cinque, Triple Cinque' ('Five, Triple Five'). Almost at the same time, the Parisian couturière Madeleine Vionnet used the letters 'A', 'B', 'C', 'D' as perfume names, while Lucien Lelong also used 'A', 'B' and 'C'. The names chosen for perfumes and for perfume companies have sometimes had a personal significance for those involved. Elsa Schiaparelli preferred names beginning with 'S', to be alliterative with her surname. In the case of a company named Lionceau, founded by Michel Schasseur, a special relationship becomes clearer.when it is understood that the French word *lionceau* means 'lion cub', and that 'Schasseur' is a homonym of the French word *chasseur*, meaning 'hunter'. The Lionceau shop in Paris was in rue Demours. Schasseur later formed another company, named Demours, and re-used a graphic design similar to the one developed for Lionceau, replacing lion cubs with 'angels' (pl.119).

The perfume name takes on a graphic form when presented visually on the label, bottle and box – thus integrating this verbal element into the presentation. Its treatment can make an adequate name stronger, and can make a very good name even better. A large question mark and the perfume name 'C'est?' ('It's?') were moulded on the front of a Silka bottle, while on the back of the bottle 'Silka' was moulded in minuscule, distorted letters (pls. 92, 93). The perfume and company names were thus presented like the question and answer of a perfume riddle. Later Silka used an avant-garde logotype for 'Ombre du Soir' ('Evening Shadow'), to make a charming perfume name visually dramatic (5).

THE PERFUME LABEL

During the 19th century, the label was the dominant element, covering almost the entire bottle, and often presenting a significant amount of information about the perfume company. At that time perfume, toiletry and medicine bottles and labels were very similar. When René Lalique began working with François Coty, *c.* 1907, he changed the label's role dramatically. He began by designing labels, but soon turned his attention to the perfume bottle itself – and a major breakthrough followed as Lalique incorporated much of the role associated with the label into the bottle design. When he did retain the use of labels, they were smaller than before, simply presenting the perfume name. Frequently, however, Lalique used no labels, preferring to integrate the name into the design of the bottle or of the stopper. Subsequent to this innovation by Lalique, other designers experimented with label shapes

5 Silka, 'Ombre du Soir', 1928, Baccarat bottle no. 506. H. 7 cm (2¾ in.).

6 Avenel, 'Le Bonheur Existe', 1921, Julien Viard design, Dépinoix bottle. H. 9.7 cm (3⅞ in.).

7 Sauzé, 'Prestige de Paris', 1947. H. 9.4 cm (3¾ in.).

8 Bryenne, 'Chu Chin Chow', bottle and figural perfumed card.

9 Gueldy, 'Le Prestige', c. 1922, Julien Viard design. H. 15.4 cm (6 in.).

10 Roger & Gallet, large presentation boxes for perfume-toiletry sets, c. 1925. W. (largest) 28.5 cm (11¼ in.), (smaller) 20.7 cm (8⅛ in.).

11 Eduard Fornells, three Bakelite boxes for perfume presentations, c. 1925. H. 9.0 cm (3½ in.).

and sizes, as well as with their placing and the materials used. While paper was the preferred material, labels were also made of Cellophane, celluloid, leather, metal, etc. Delettrez selected a most unusual material, greenish mother-of-pearl, surrounded by gilded paper, for 'Oryalis' (pl.33). Avenel used pewter, in the form of a realistic horseshoe studded with seven red glass beads, for 'Le Bonheur Existe' ('Happiness exists') – symbolizing good luck (6). In a few cases, the label was directly related to the stopper, as with 'Prestige de Paris', a Sauzé perfume, for which an elongated trapezoidal label of gilded paper was used, placed below a stopper shaped like the Arc de Triomphe (7). The label served to present a symbolic perspective view of the Champs-Elysées, as seen from the Place de la Concorde looking towards the Arc de Triomphe.

THE PERFUME BOTTLE

The bottle, which plays the indispensable functional role of container, can also – as a potential 'sculpture' – be the dominant element of a perfume presentation. The earliest bottles and stoppers were simple and standard, but they became more complex as glass-making techniques evolved. René Lalique and other innovators, such as Clovis and Julien Viard, brought a sculptor's approach to bottle and stopper design.

In many designs the bottle has a strong relationship with the accompanying stopper. All complete figural bottles, such as Bryenne's 'Chu Chin Chow' (8; pl.84) are integrated designs. Some bottles, such as that for Gueldy's 'Le Prestige', function as simple pedestals for figural stoppers – a style pioneered by Clovis and Julien Viard (9). Sometimes the stopper was reduced to a secondary role, as in the case of 'La Sirène' ('The Mermaid'), a perfume by de Burmann (pl.61).

Perfume bottles have been made from glass in qualities ranging from fine crystal down to ordinary industrial glass, and in all colours, clear or opaque. Even metal and Bakelite have been used for bottles and stoppers. The 'ground glass' technique was used for high-quality bottles and their stoppers. The stopper's stem and the neck of the bottle were both hand-ground so as to fit together perfectly – then the matching bottle and stopper were marked with the same number. Industrially produced bottles were provided with metal or plastic caps which were screwed on. A special class of bottles, 'miniatures', featured the thread-screw system for technical reasons – they were simply too small to permit the use of ground-glass stoppers effectively or economically.

THE PERFUME BOX

In the early years, the box was not designed to be either an integral or even an important element. It protected the bottle during handling and transportation and served as a gift package. Many boxes did not even carry the name of the perfume or of the company. During the latter part of the 19th century, the paper covering on the box began to be integrated into the overall presentation, by being given a design that was similar or identical to that of the label on the bottle. As the 20th century progressed, interesting and complementary boxes were developed in greater numbers, though some of the best-designed boxes often became separated from their bottles, because they were intended to be used afterwards for other purposes. Thus, Roger & Gallet created large beautiful boxes for perfume-cosmetic sets, discreetly marked on the inside only. They were meant to be kept and re-used for storing personal items (10).

Eduard Fornells, a noted artist working mostly in Bakelite, designed and produced some very innovative boxes for perfume presentations (11). These unmarked rare and beautiful objects in Bakelite have been put to numerous other uses, and became separated from their perfume bottles. After the first creations by Paul Poiret for many of his Rosine perfumes, the potential contribution of the perfume box began to be better understood. Singular and imaginative box designs soon appeared as integral features of the entire perfume presentation. Some boxes were conceived to function differently, by providing an element of surprise not only when closed, but also when opened. An outstanding example of this type of box was provided by 'Qui M'Aime?' ('Who Loves Me?') from Best & Co. (12, 13).

12, 13 Best & Co., 'Qui M'Aime?', c. 1925. Box closed; open box with bottle. H. 5.7 cm (2¼ in.).

ADDITIONAL ORNAMENTS

'Ornaments' include a wide variety of decorative items that have been used to enhance a perfume presentation. The earliest examples in this category were the silk cords or ribbons that served the functional purpose of keeping the stopper in place. Whenever these closures went beyond this primary purpose and were used to decorate the bottles, they became ornaments. The ornament is an 'optional' element – rarely found in perfume presentations. A wide range of materials has been used for ornamentation. Ribbon, cord, lace, fabric, metal, Bakelite, even feathers and simulated gemstones have decorated and completed perfume presentations. The first edition of 'Astris', an L. T. Piver perfume, incorporated a classic Baccarat bottle embellished with complex metal ornamentation that included a label area for identification, an elegant use of metal for more than one purpose (14).

14 L. T. Piver, 'Astris', 1912. Box and Baccarat bottle no. 169. H. 12.2 cm (4¾ in.).

Paul Poiret often used ornaments as reminders that he was primarily a fashion designer, and that the Rosine perfumes were closely related to his fashions. Other perfume companies understood that ornaments could enhance their presentations. In the case of Marquay's 'Prince Douka' several ornaments were used to complete an elaborate presentation (15). A simple perfume bottle was topped by a stopper in the form of a turbaned Indian maharajah. A simulated gem and feather were embedded in the stopper, and the entire bottle was concealed under variously coloured ornate satin capes, which were sewn together with a fabric label reading 'Marquay, le couturier de parfum' ('Marquay, the fashion designer of perfume').

15 Marquay, 'Prince Douka', 1951. H. (large) 16.5 cm (6½ in.); medium 9.5 cm (3¾ in.).; (small) 7.5 cm (3 in.).

10 Grand Concepts

The ten perfume presentations selected for special attention were chosen because the name, bottle, label, box and ornaments complement each other harmoniously to express a particular theme. Each was an innovative grand concept, an outstanding design achievement representative of the time in which it was created, though most of the individual designers are now unknown or forgotten.

16 'Cœur en Folie'.

'CŒUR EN FOLIE', LES PARFUMS DE ROSINE, 1925

Paul Poiret was the first fashion designer to establish a perfume company, which he called Les Parfums de Rosine. 'Cœur en Folie' ('Mad Heart'), introduced at the 1925 Exposition Internationale des Arts Décoratifs et Industriels Modernes in Paris, was based on an original idea of Jacques de Brunhoff – editor of *Comœdia Illustré* and designer of artistic Folies Bergère programmes. *Cœurs en Folie* had been the title of a show put on at the Folies Bergère in 1924 with romantic scenery and costumes. The presentation for 'Cœur en Folie' was a whimsical and romantic fantasy. Its bottle, made of red glass, resembled a heart-shaped cabochon ruby – more like a human heart than a stylized heart (16; pl.6). The neck was nothing more than an unobtrusive opening concealed below the stopper, which took the form of a pair of wings in clear and frosted glass. The French verb *battre* can mean 'to beat' both in the sense of the beating of a heart and the flapping of a bird's wings. Hence the juxtaposition of heart and wings suggested the idea of this beating heart being about to take flight. The red heart-shaped box was in perfect harmony with the bottle, even the form of the 'o' in 'Cœur' was adapted to suggest a heart. The base of the box was adorned with a delicately pleated ruffle, as a reminder that Poiret was a fashion designer. Since the French phrase *en folie* also meant 'in heat', as applied to an animal, the perfume name certainly carried a very expressive and daring implication.

17 'Folle Maîtresse'.

'FOLLE MAÎTRESSE', BLANCHE LEBOUVIER, 1925

Parisian night life, with its theatres, music halls and cabarets, engendered a very seductive atmosphere. Many female performers, famous then, forgotten today, owed their success more to their beauty and the dazzling clothes they wore than to real talent. They were often associated with wealthy men who indulged their needs and whims. 'Folle Maîtresse' ('Mad Mistress') was introduced at the height of this period by a company named after Blanche Lebouvier, a fashion designer who had won a gold medal at the 1900 International Exhibition, and whose shop near the Paris Opéra catered to this theatrical group.

In this perfume presentation the stopper of the bottle depicted a woman posing motionless, proudly displaying her appealing figure and her extravagant gown (17; pl. 7). Her Egyptian-style costume resembled those created by Erté for shows at the Folies Bergère and the Ba-ta-clan in Paris. While Erté might have inspired the design for 'Folle Maîtresse', it was an original idea of Lucien Willemetz, founder and artistic director of Robj. The floral motif of the box enhanced the bottle and stopper, and provided a charming and feminine backdrop. The outrageous name given to this perfume was obviously associated with the figure represented on the stopper – an exciting but probably untalented mistress.

'GARDEZ-MOI', JOVOY, 1926

'Gardez-moi' was a perfume presentation which appeared at first to be one of those stylish feline sculptures which were so popular in the modern interiors of the 1920s. This creation did not look like a perfume bottle at all (18; pl.8). However, when this black cat was lifted up, the stopper was revealed between the animal's legs. This Baccarat bottle was therefore presented upside-down, and relied on the base of its box to stay vertical.

18 'Gardez-moi'.

Since 'Gardez-moi' means 'Keep me', this presentation was clearly meant to be kept and treasured by its owner. This name could also have had two other interpretations. If this feline was seen as a lovely lost cat, then the expression 'Keep me' added a compelling dimension to its appeal. However, this perfume bottle could also have been considered a black panther. In ancient Greek literature, the panther was believed to be the only animal to exhale an appealing odour, capable of luring other animals with its sweet breath. The panther, therefore, symbolized the power of female beauty and cruel seduction. In ancient Greek *pardalis* meant both 'panther' and 'courtesan'. When associated with a perfumed black panther, the phrase 'Gardez-moi' acquired a provocative air combined with a hint of treachery.

'JE, TU, IL', LOUIS VUITTON, 1927

'Je, Tu, Il' was a rare perfume presentation from a company specializing in luxurious luggage, a firm always in the forefront of catering to new developments in travel needs and social trends. This was actually a set of three different perfumes, each in a separate but identical bottle (19; pl. 4). The three bottles, made to fit one into another, could be stacked in any order inside their cylindrical gold paper box. The name 'Je, Tu, Il' was printed in a circular fashion on the box, therefore, it had no beginning, no end, and could be read in any order. This box was placed in a sturdy outer box, which in turn was wrapped in paper bearing the Louis Vuitton symbols of ships and trains.

19 'Je, Tu, Il'.

This enigmatic presentation could have had several meanings. Maybe 'Je' ('I') was a perfume to be used when one travelled alone. Maybe 'Tu' ('You') was a perfume to be used when one travelled with 'you'. And maybe 'Il' ('He') was a perfume to be used when one travelled with 'him'. While 'He' was obviously male, the gender of either 'I' or 'You' is indeterminate, and interpretations of this most unusual perfume name must depend upon the fertility of one's imagination.

20 'Nuit Etoilée de Bagdad'.

'NUIT ÉTOILÉE DE BAGDAD', DIAMANT BLEU, c.1927

'Nuit Etoilée de Bagdad' ('Starry Night of Baghdad') represented the continuing interest in the Middle East prevalent in France during the 1920s. *Schéhérazade*, a choreographic drama based on 'The Thousand and One Nights', was brought to Paris by Diaghilev's Ballets Russes in 1910, and had a major impact on French audiences. The scenery and costumes designed for the production by Léon Bakst remained a source of inspiration for artists and designers. The 'Nuit Etoilée de Bagdad' perfume presentation alluded to ancient Babylon and Assyria. From Baghdad it was possible to see Nebuchadnezzar's great hanging gardens in Babylon, the massive terraced structure comprising three monumental steps covered in blue enamel tiles being one of the seven wonders of the ancient world.

The design of the bottle (20; pl. 9) probably represented these hanging gardens, with their basic outlines gilded, as if highlighted beneath a starry night sky. Two scalloped parallel lines, also gilded, were symbolic of the Tigris and Euphrates rivers. Rather than showing actual stars, this bottle suggested their reflected light – a very restrained design. The cover of the box was in the form of a classic Assyrian stele (ceremonial pillar), on the front of which the perfume name was inscribed. The stark shapes of this presentation were not only typical of 1920s geometric designs, but also representative of the architecture and symbols associated with Babylon and Assyria.

'PRÉSENCE', MARTIAL ET ARMAND, 1930

This perfume presentation from a long-established couture house was created by André Bonnet and related directly to the 'Machine Age' or the 'Metal Revolution'. 'Présence' was probably influenced by the Russian avant-garde operatic drama *Victory over the Sun*, produced in St Petersburg in 1913 with scenery and costumes designed by Kasimir Malevich. The libretto was written in 'Zaum', an alogical language in which sounds and words were apparently randomly mixed, yet feelings were expressed in a clear and powerful manner. The black square on a white backdrop for one stage set was the artist's first Suprematist work. In this futuristic drama, a small group of powerful men imprison the sun inside a square box – symbolizing the triumph of man over nature, since life could be sustained with the help of machines, and the sun's energy was no longer needed.

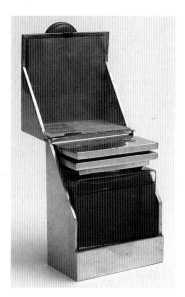

21 'Présence'.

The bottle's simple geometric shape (21; pl. 10) was reinforced by a harsh cover, consisting of four layers of steel held together by two large screws. Two parallel labels, with stark typeface, echoed the construction of the cover. The only decoration on the matching steel box was a round, red Bakelite knob suggestive of the sun's shape, captured by the square box. 'Présence' was an assertive name, expressed by an austere object, a 'Purist' design in keeping with 'L'Esprit Nouveau', the new modernist spirit. There is nothing feminine or even human about this presentation – it could even be perceived as the perfume intended for a robot.

'CAP À LA VIE', MURY, 1940

The name 'Cap à la Vie' (roughly translatable as 'On Course for Life') was based on the nautical expression *mettre le cap* ('to set course, or head for'). The bottle itself took the form of the bow of a ship parting the water, while the stopper represented a 16-point compass rose (22; pl.3). This astonishing bottle was designed by Georges Schwander and produced by Verreries Brosse. The labels were placed high on each side of the bottle, like the name painted on the bow of a ship. The box, with a miniature metal anchor as its closure, opened in the middle of its semicircular front, as if parted by the momentum of the ship. To complete the nautical references, even the inside of the box resembled mural paintings similar to those designed for ships' interiors by Max and Paule Ingrand.

'Cap à la Vie' was a sweet floral perfume intended for a young woman; its name also implied setting out on the course of adult life, and the luxury ocean liners of the day were the perfect place for wealthy débutantes to present their stylish clothes, as well as for seeking romance. This entire extravagant perfume presentation was youthful, whimsical and great fun; however, its timing, shortly after the declaration of war in September 1939, was unfortunate.

22 'Cap à la Vie'.

'DRIFTING', LILLY DACHÉ, 1941

With this perfume Lilly Daché, a Parisian milliner *extraordinaire*, introduced the perfect surreal metaphor. Surrealist artists were determined to destroy all conventional beliefs in art, philosophy and society. They created absurd, erotic, comical, enigmatic, ugly and poetic imagery – using bizarre juxtapositions of words and objects, giving rise to a new concept of reality set free by the subconscious. The bottle for 'Drifting' (23; pl.2) appeared to have no stopper, but of course it had to have one. It appeared to be the headless torso of a woman, an obviously perverse idea for a milliner. In the context of perfume, as in Surrealist art, the word is an integral part of the artistic expression. Here the all-important word 'Drifting' was symbolized by the feather, with its ability to be carried on the wind. Another more subtle suggestion was the passive or vegetative state, symbolized by the plant-like area, which appeared to be growing out of the box.

If a woman was depicted here, she was so lethargic that she needed neither legs nor arms; but even in such a truncated form this creature still appeared young and chic. The torso, trapped in leaves, seemed transformed, as if into an exotic bird. The only human feature was the curvaceous bust. Dressed in this way, the creature was ready for a Surrealist ball. 'Drifting' could have been seen as the symbol of what all other women dreamt to be like, or hated to be like. Or maybe this is not a woman at all, but a flying plant, or a rooted bird, or a strange flower-bird of a new kind – passive and powerful. A mysterious life? A mysterious toy? Perhaps this was just a beautiful dream. Or perhaps not . . .

23 'Drifting'.

24 'Insidia', pendent label.

25 'Le Roy Soleil'.

Facing page
1 Schiaparelli, 'Le Roy Soleil', 1946.
Salvador Dali design. Box and
Baccarat bottle no. 798.
H. 17.8 cm (7 in.).

'INSIDIA', GI. VI. EMME, 1945

'Insidia' ('Ambush') was an Italian perfume presentation that conjured up the image of cruel and treacherous romance; it was subtitled 'Il profumo che turba', meaning 'the perfume which drives you wild'. Italian history is especially rich in tragic figures, both real and imaginary, and in Machiavellian intrigues. Such ideas were symbolized in the presentation of 'Insidia' as a realistic representation of a dagger in its case (pl.5). The hollow, clear-glass handle formed the bottle, with its stopper at the top. The smoky glass blade was an essential, but not functional feature of the whole. The label, which was suspended from the handle by a gold cord, depicted an eye-mask surrounded by confetti and streamers, evoking Venetian masked balls (24).

The bottle was placed inside a sumptuous, blood-red velvet casket with no external markings, hence it had to be opened to reveal its contents. And if one expected to find some precious jewelry within, what a rude surprise to discover a dagger-shaped perfume bottle! This extraordinary concept for a luxury perfume would nevertheless have had an appeal to the kind of woman who might be regarded as the deadlier version of the species. The man giving such a present would be her kindred spirit. 'Insidia' was not a perfume for sweet young lovers.

'LE ROY SOLEIL', SCHIAPARELLI, 1946

'Le Roy Soleil' ('The Sun King') was created by Salvador Dali. This presentation's centrepiece was a Baccarat crystal bottle, a three-dimensional seascape, with blue enamelled waves and gilded rocks (25; pl. 1). The stopper's large cover depicted the blazing sun, fully risen over the horizon. Black sea-gulls in flight gave the sun clearly defined facial features. This magnificent and imposing sun had a vulnerable expression, a naive and tender quality. When the bottle was full, it resembled a golden reflection of the sun on water. Another dimension of fantasy was added by the box, in the form of a gilded metal scallop shell, lined with ivory-coloured satin, suggestive of mother-of-pearl. A gold-foil medallion, attached to two blue taffeta ribbons, served as the label, with 'Le Roy Soleil/Schiaparelli/Paris' printed inside a sunburst; on the reverse was a stylized figure of Elsa Schiaparelli.

Earlier, in the summer of 1938, Elsa Schiaparelli had presented her landmark Astrology collection. Horoscopes, stars, the moon and the sun were its chosen themes. For this series Christian Bérard designed a Medusa head as a splendid sunburst, embroidered in gold on the back of several evening capes. These 'Medusa' capes were also known as 'Roi Soleil' capes. The perfume 'Le Roy Soleil' celebrated the Allied victory in Europe in World War II and the re-opening of the Schiaparelli salons. It was named after Louis XIV, known as the 'Sun King', as a reminder of a glorious era in French history. By echoing the 'Roi Soleil' capes, it also represented one of the most glorious moments in the history of Schiaparelli's fashions.

Opposite
2 Lilly Daché. 'Drifting', 1941.
Bottle on base.
H. 15.2 cm (6 in.).

3 Mury, 'Cap à la Vie', 1940.
Open box containing Brosse bottle
designed by Georges Schwander.
H. 15.2 cm (6 in.).

4 Louis Vuitton, 'Je, Tu, Il', 1927.
Open box showing cover and inner
container for three stacking bottles.
H. of each bottle 4.7 cm (1⅞ in.).

5 GI. VI. Emme, 'Insidia', 1945.
Dino Villani design. Venini bottle
in box. Limited edition of 500 with
certificate.
H. 15.2 cm (6 in.).

6 Les Parfums de Rosine,
'Cœur en Folie', 1925. Bottle in box.
H. 3.8 cm (1½ in.); w. 8.9 cm
(3½ in.).

7 Blanche Lebouvier, 'Folle
Maîtresse', 1925. Robj design.
Bottle in box.
H. 8.9 cm (3½ in.).

8 Jovoy, 'Gardez-moi', 1926.
Baccarat bottle no. 601 on base.
H. 17.8 cm (7 in.).

9 Diamant Bleu, 'Nuit Etoilée de
Bagdad', *c.* 1927. Julien Viard
design. Bottle by Société Parisienne
de Verreries. Prototype presentation.
H. 8.9 cm (3½ in.).

10 Martial et Armand, 'Présence',
1930. Bottle and box, designed by
André Bonnet.
H. 10.2 cm (4 in.).

Chapter 1

Prior to 1900
The Formative Years

It was not until the second half of the 19th century that perfume packaging had clearly developed as a modern phenomenon which resulted from the fusion of art and science as a consequence of the Industrial Revolution. A necessary prerequisite for this alliance had been the numerous and complex interactions between various 'revolutions' – scientific, agricultural, commercial, and in the fields of transport and finance – which gave rise to major and far-reaching changes in society, not to mention the outcome of political revolutions which had taken place in America and France in the latter part of the 18th century. Without trying to establish exact causes and effects among these various 'revolutions', it is sufficient to conclude that by the beginning of the 19th century horizons and opportunities had expanded greatly.

As the century progressed, economic expansion moved from a local focus to a national and even international scope. Methods and systems of transportation improved, as did safety in travel, and trade flourished. New commodities and raw materials became more readily available, and agriculture became more scientific and efficient. As capital was accumulated, it was reinvested in further developments of production and distribution. The resulting demand for more and better consumer products intensified and stimulated additional industrial developments. Throughout Europe customs and manners were rapidly changing. A key factor was the dissolution and decline of the guild system, which gave way to free trade and, later, to the factory system. New social classes emerged and continued to develop. New sources of energy were required. The resulting changes interacted with each other to intensify the revolutionary trends. As far as the marketing of a product such as perfume was concerned, two vital developments were the emergence of the department store and the use of advertising.

In the 17th century, Louis XIV and his Minister, Colbert, imposed on industry a centralized system of regulations, along with high production standards. Since then France has specifically supported the expansion of *industries de luxe*, i.e. industries capable of manufacturing luxury products. The export of fine furniture, textiles, paper goods, ceramics, crystal, metalwork etc. would not only benefit the country's economy, but would also serve to enhance its cultural prestige. This development established what would become a tradition of French excellence in the decorative arts in general.

Facing page
11 L. T. Piver, 'Nijni-Novgorod
1896'. Box and bottle.
H. 10.5 cm (4⅛ in.).

As a result of Colbert's policies France was able to achieve an artistic superiority that was admired worldwide. Perfume was a product ideally suited to benefit from these policies, standards and official support, and the perfume industry as we know it today represents the embodiment of French culture.

Originally introduced to Europe from the Orient during antiquity, perfume disappeared during the Middle Ages before being reintroduced to France through Italy and Spain in the 16th century. At first scattered small-scale output was the norm, the main centres of production being Grasse (near Nice), where flowers – especially roses – were grown in abundance, and Paris, where many small shops made and sold fragrant waters, powders, salts etc. Perfumes were often sold in glove shops then, and scented gloves were to remain fashionable until the end of the 19th century.

As early as 1720, Fargeon, perfumer to Louis XV, patented his own secret formulas. These were passed on to his sons and were later purchased by L. Legrand and the Gellé brothers, whose respective acquisitions gave rise to the founding of two of the most important perfume companies, L. Legrand (later also known as Oriza-Legrand) and Gellé Frères. In 1774, Jean-François Houbigant and Michel Adam, the founders of two major perfume companies, Houbigant and L. T. Piver, opened their respective shops in Paris. In 1798, Pierre-François Lubin established his business in Paris. In 1828, Guerlain was founded, to be followed by Edouard Pinaud in 1839, Roger & Gallet in 1862 and Bourjois in 1869. These were among the first important names who contributed in significant ways to the establishment of French prestige in the area of perfume and luxury exports. Although industry generally was not as strong in France as it was in Germany, Britain or America during the latter part of the 19th century, France – because of its heritage – was better at producing luxury goods, which required the participation of a large labour force of skilled craftsmen, as well as the utilization not only of the nation's primary raw materials but of imports from overseas colonies. The perfume industry met all the requirements to qualify for support. The production of perfume utilized a primary resource of its horticultural industry – the large number of various flowers and herbs, notably those grown in the south of France, but also including the products of other areas. Rare and exotic essences from the French colonies could easily be imported, while the development of 'aldehydes' (synthetic scents) was a scientific breakthrough by chemists in the 19th century.

The manufacturing of perfume bottles in France drew its strength from the country's already advanced glass industry; the glass industry expanded as the demand for perfume grew. The traditional French excellence in the production of paper and printed materials favoured the creation of imaginative designs for labels and boxes, and as advertising developed the poster became an important medium, involving the talents of many artists. Finally, as consumer demand increased, large department stores flourished thanks to France's emphasis on products combining artistic and luxurious qualities.

The evolution of industrial art was enhanced by another important 19th-century development: the promotion provided by the many exhibitions (first national and later international), which would be mounted in Paris. The opening of the first public exhibition in Paris of French industrial products – the 'Exposition publique des produits de l'Industrie Française' – took place on 15 October 1798, on the Champ-de-Mars. The ancient guild system had recently been abolished by the Revolution, and the artists, craftsmen and manufacturers were now free to work and sell their wares independently. However, although this was the beginning of a situation which fostered originality through competition, the true merger between art and science did not occur until the second half of the 19th century. Despite numerous national exhibitions held in 1801, 1802, 1806, 1819, 1823, 1827, 1834, 1839, 1844 and 1849, there was a general artistic stagnation and, at least initially, members of the 'liberal arts' category did not want their works to be seen in the company of 'utilitarian' products.

The 'Great Exhibition of the Works of Industry of All Nations' held in London in 1851 changed those conditions. Inaugurated by Queen Victoria on 1 May in the spectacular 'Crystal Palace' (erected in only four months in Hyde Park), this exhibition was internationally acclaimed and more than six million admission tickets were sold. For the first time, products from the West and the East alike could be viewed side by side and compared. The potential for national pride was great, as was the potential for commercial exports. After the success of the 1851 exhibition in London, Napoleon III decided to undertake a major Universal Exhibition in Paris. It was held in 1855, from 15 May to 15 November, and more than five million visitors attended, including Queen Victoria. Among the 24,000 exhibitors were perfume companies. At that time fragrance was included in the 'Hygiène' ('Pharmacy and Chemistry') category, and such products were shown alongside medicines. The perfume bottles then in use were simple and generic. Paper labels were very large, and their overall aspect was similar to those used on patent medicine bottles. Both medicines and perfumes were sold without accompanying boxes. Generally, the elegant woman would decant fragrances into her own more suitable luxury containers, which formed part of her boudoir decoration.

An important 19th-century landmark in the context of perfume was a purse presentation by Antoine Chiris (pls. 16, 17). On one side, seen through a crystal plate, a pair of crystal bottles was housed in the recessed openings of an enamelled brass surface (26). The other side, a brown leather purse, with blue silk lining, was designed to hold various Chiris products. This luxury object would have been available for purchase from the Antoine Chiris stand, not only as a souvenir of the 1855 Universal Exhibition, but also to be filled exclusively with Antoine Chiris products. Its purpose was thus to promote sales and, at the same time, to create an image of luxury associated with the company.

26 Antoine Chiris, special purse presentation for the 1855 Universal Exhibition.

For the French perfume industry the 1855 exhibition brought about unprecedented opportunities, greater prestige and considerable exports. In 1860, in Paris alone, 197 different perfumers were registered, and by 1862 the value of French perfume exports reached the considerable sum of 20 million francs. Supported more than ever by the French government, helped by scientific and technological advances, and backed by the availability of numerous artists and craftsmen, the perfume industry became a dynamic force ready to meet the challenge of impending social change. At the next Universal Exhibition, held in Paris in 1867, perfume became an independent category, now divorced from 'Hygiène'.

During the second part of the 19th century, perfume presentations were becoming more sophisticated and more imaginative as a result of the growing competition between the now numerous perfume companies exhibiting side by side at these increasingly frequent Universal Exhibitions. The best perfume companies and their products would receive a prize, and the award would later be featured in each firm's catalogues, advertising and packaging in order to enhance its reputation and to broaden its sales. Improvements in machinery and manufacturing techniques and progress in transportation methods resulted in better-made perfume presentations that could travel further and in greater safety. The French perfume industry became so successful and so prestigious that towards the end of the century it became totally international, exporting its products in great quantities (especially to North and South America), despite the competition from developing perfume industries in other countries.

The social and economic changes of the 19th century were also a major contributory factor in the expansion of the perfume industry. In the past, the use of perfume had been associated mainly with members of the aristocracy, the theatre and also with women of dubious morals. As the century progressed, Victorian conventions slowly began to break down and fragrances became generally more socially acceptable. The middle class developed and grew, along with the newly rich, especially in the United States – and the members of both groups wanted access to privileges previously restricted to the aristocracy. As a result, luxury French products were in great demand.

With the evolution of perfume packaging, the appeal of this intangible product could be greatly enhanced when a complete image was successfully established thanks to the choice of an inspired name and the use of imaginative packaging for a luxury product. The high price it fetched enabled makers to attract, and afford, the best artists, the most competent artisans and craftsmen, using materials of the highest quality. The second half of the 19th century was unique in that it was the first period in which artistic creations could be produced by industrial means; all the necessary conditions to allow the birth of modern perfume packaging were now present.

An early, rudimentary perfume presentation, with bottles, box and company identification, was introduced c.1865 by L.T.Piver (pls.12, 13). This small ebony chest was embellished with brass trimmings and a white silk lining. It strongly resembled the popular machine-made Second Empire style of furniture. When opened, this chest revealed two perfume bottles, characteristic of this period, with miniature Paris scenes (the Palais Bourbon and the Place Vendôme) on their tops (27). Although much smaller in scale, this object was similar in style to a liquor cabinet. On the exterior of the lid were engraved the initials 'L. T. P.', and on its lining was the full name 'L. T. Piver, Paris, London'. Under the base of the box was a generic label with the Paris addresses of L. T. Piver and of Gants Jouvin (Jouvin Gloves), where the perfumes could also be purchased. Nothing in the overall style of this object's design indicated that it was specifically and carefully created for a perfume company, or for the presentation of two of its products. This chest was still a decorative object – it did not yet amount to a complex perfume presentation.

27 L. T. Piver, chest with crystal bottles, c. 1865.

It soon became apparent that the prevalent style in the arts and decorative arts would also dominate the style of perfume presentations. Madame Girard et Cie. Ltd was a London shop at 182 Regent Street with a French-sounding name, which enhanced its prestige. A Girard perfume presentation displayed 'Violette de Parme' and 'Opoponax', two classic, cut-crystal bottles in an impressive purple-lined box in the English Aesthetic style (pls. 14, 15). It was, no doubt, in perfect harmony with interiors in the same style which were fashionable in Great Britain around 1890. Equally interesting and representative of its times was a perfume by C. Amiel et Cie called 'Violette de Parme', created specifically to be sold in England. Since the London International Exhibition of 1862 and the Paris Universal Exhibition of 1878, the West had become infatuated with Japan and its decorative arts. So positive was this influence that Siegfried Bing, a leading art and antiques dealer based in Paris, published a magazine, *Le Japon Artistique*, from 1888 to 1891. The Japanese influence on Western art would prove to be an enduring one. This sumptuous Amiel presentation, although unmistakably a Western object, was not merely inspired by Japan, but also attempted to reproduce a classic Japanese scene quite literally (pls. 19, 20).

Several significant breakthroughs occurred as a result of the commercial and cultural dialogue which was established between various nations, particularly those of East and West. Many different kinds of commercial products were exhibited alongside each other and many different types of cultures, customs and art became more widely understood. The 1889 Universal Exhibition in Paris, an event commemorating the centenary of the French Revolution, witnessed the inauguration of the Eiffel Tower as well as the International Congress of Women's Rights. Only recently had women been allowed to receive secondary education, to open a savings account in their own name, or to seek a divorce. The use of cosmetics and fragrances, but only by married women, was becoming slightly more acceptable, providing that they were perceived as being beneficial to health. Alphonse Gravier, a maker of soap and fragrance, with a modest shop at 83 rue du Temple in Paris, was

28 Gellé Frères, 'Le Mikado', 1889;
Erasmic, 'La Reine d'Egypte' (with
box), c. 1900. H. 11.3 cm (4½ in.);
11.0 cm (4⅜ in.).

29 Ed Pinaud, 'Bouquet du
Président J. L. Cuestas', 1899.
H. 10.7 cm (4¼ in.).

on his way to becoming a major perfume company, while making medicinal claims for his products, which included a very successful line called 'Salutine', coined from the word *salut* ('health').

At the 1889 exhibition Dorin, a prestigious cosmetics company founded in 1780, patronized by French aristocratic and theatrical clients, received the highest prize in its category for powder, pomade and rouge. Eye makeup, as we know it today, did not exist then, but soon thereafter Dorin introduced 'El Mesdjem', a kohl-powder, possibly the earliest Western product of this type. Kohl-powder had been used in ancient Egypt, and its use had been known among women of Arabia ever since. In order to become accepted by women in the West, it was necessary for kohl-powder to be promoted as indispensable for eye health. To emphasize its ancient pedigree, the 'El Mesdjem' powder was offered in a delicately crafted ivory container decorated with Egyptian hieroglyphs (pl. 18). Its luxurious leather and velvet case, which resembled a jewelry box, was also decorated with hieroglyphs. 'El Mesdjem' was an expensive luxury product – definitely not for general use.

Also at the 1889 exhibition, Gellé Frères introduced a perfume called 'Le Mikado', and later Erasmic developed 'La Reine d'Egypte' ('The Queen of Egypt'). Both these perfumes (28) displayed images which provided a very Western view of the Far East and Middle East. Another blend of West and East was 'Le Lys du Nil' ('The Lily of the Nile'), produced by Rallet, a French perfume company established in Moscow as perfumers to the Russian Imperial court (pl. 22). Although this presentation was typical of fashionable French illustrations of the day, the label and the box bore the name written in the Cyrillic alphabet as used in Russian. The stopper and two sides of the wrap-around label suggested the shape of the cross associated with the Eastern Orthodox churches. This mélange of French style and Russian design elements to depict an Egyptian theme gave this perfume a unique identity.

The growing curiosity in the West worked in two ways, for not only was there much greater interest in other, particularly exotic, cultures, but a very strong desire developed to export luxury products, such as perfume, to far-away places. Two perfume companies, Ed. Pinaud and L. T. Piver, were particularly prolific in directing their sales abroad. One concept that they both pioneered was to name a perfume after a foreign monarch, general or celebrity – and to portray that person on the label, as for example in the case of the Pinaud perfume 'Bouquet du Président J. L. Cuestas' (29), which portrayed that Chilean president and thus ensured its success in Chile.

Exhibitions and the pavilions of individual countries were also featured in perfume presentations. In 1896, L. T. Piver introduced a perfume specially developed for the trade fair held in Nijni-Novgorod, the Russian city (renamed Gorki after the revolution, but now known by its historic name once more) standing at the confluence of the Oka and Volga rivers. The area was noted for its long tradition of important summer fairs, which became known as the link between Russia and the Orient. In cultural matters France and Russia had developed a very strong relationship, for the Russian élite had, since the eighteenth century, shown a great affinity with French art and culture. They spoke French fluently, and often surrounded themselves with French artefacts. It was reported that Tsar Alexander III even took off his hat when he heard 'La Marseillaise' – a startling and unprecedented gesture of respect shown by a head of state for a foreign national anthem. Perfume as a souvenir product was not a new idea, since many examples had already been specifically developed to be shown and sold at exhibition pavilions. However, this particular perfume was named 'Nijni-Novgorod 1896' (pl.11), and that year was special, for it marked the culmination of the close political, economic and artistic ties that existed between France and Russia. In October 1896, Tsar Nicholas II and the Tsarina visited Paris to lay the foundation stone of the Pont Alexandre III, the new bridge over the Seine so named in honour of the recently deceased father of Nicholas II.

The design principles applied in 'Nijni-Novgorod 1896' were typical of perfume presentations of the late 19th century – a generic bottle in clear glass, its front almost entirely covered by an ornate paper label, and a corresponding box bearing a graphic design very similar to that of the label. While Ed. Pinaud's 'Parfum Cydalise' (pl.21) featured this characteristic relationship of bottle, label and box, it also illustrated some advances in presentation.

30 L. Legrand, 'Essence Oriza', 1879, Baccarat bottle, h. 15 cm (5⅞ in.); 'Orizine', c. 1890, free sample powder box, w. 3.7 cm (1½ in.).

31 Roger & Gallet, 'Peau d'Espagne', 1895, box and bottle, h. 9 cm (3½ in.); 'Vera-Violetta', 1892, presentation box for three sachet bottles, and powder box; 'Violette de Parme', 1880, bottle and box, h. 9 cm (3½ in.).

The perfume's name was among the earliest examples in a long line of specially fabricated words used for this purpose: 'Cydalise' sounded elegant, poetic and distinctive – which probably was the way that Ed. Pinaud wanted this perfume to be perceived. An allegorical scene on the label and box was the dominant element of this charming presentation. The graphics, including two flaming hearts, a torch and a quiver on the box and a Cupid with spear and arrow on the label, were classic Louis XVI elements reworked in a 19th-century style. Slightly earlier, the first name innovation may have been 'Jicky', a Guerlain perfume introduced at the 1889 exhibition. This concise English-sounding nickname (for 'Jacques') immediately became very chic, and a few other French companies began adopting short, evocative English words as perfume names. Ed. Pinaud introduced 'Flirt' only two years later.

Yet another pre-1900 development was the introduction of co-ordinated presentations, known as a 'parfumerie' or 'line'. A line comprises one specific perfume and the complete range of its related cosmetic and toiletry products. In each case the products all share the same name, the same graphics and colours. L. Legrand's 'Parfumerie Oriza' (30) of 1879 appears to have been the first such line, a trend quickly followed by Roger & Gallet and L. T. Piver. All products in the 'Oriza' line (the name was derived from Latin *oryza*, rice), featured a gilded grain motif. Roger & Gallet lines, such as 'Violette de Parme', 'Vera-Violetta' ('True Violet') and 'Peau d'Espagne' ('Spanish Leather'), displayed a sober style featuring a single colour and gilded typography (31). In complete contrast, L. T. Piver used exuberant floral designs for the 'Floramye', 'Azurea' and 'Safranor' lines (pl. 23), similar to the Art Nouveau motifs of Eugène Grasset and Paul Berthon. The 'Essence Rosiris' line was one of the rare examples of a woman being portrayed – the subject obviously inspired by the Alphonse Mucha poster designs of that period.

A major development in art and the decorative arts in the later years of the 19th century, the Art Nouveau style, would culminate at the 1900 Universal Exhibition in Paris. All the leading artists and artisans of the day were preparing for this landmark occasion, which presented perfume companies with an ideal opportunity to develop and present new perfumes and new presentations.

While it is not possible to establish an exact date for the emergence of the modern perfume presentation, nor to credit a specific company or artist with this innovation, it is clear that by the end of the 19th century the concept was fully developed and would be further exploited in decades to come.

12, 13 L. T. Piver presentation, *c.* 1865. Black ebony box in the form of a chest with brass ornament, shown closed and open revealing crystal bottles with caps decorated with Parisian scenes. H. 7.7 cm (3 in.).

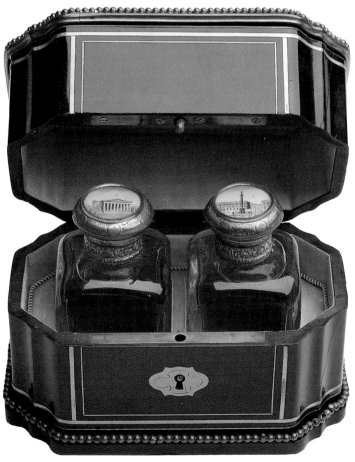

14, 15 Madame Girard et Cie Ltd,
'Violette de Parme' and 'Opoponax',
c. 1890. Presentation box, closed and
open. Richardson Crystal bottles.
H. 12.5 cm (4⅞ in.).

Opposite
16, 17 Antoine Chiris, special
presentation for the Universal
Exhibition, Paris, 1855. Back view of
leather-covered purse and front view
showing bottles seen through glazed
opening in enamelled brass case.
H. of bottles 6.0 cm (2⅜ in.).

36

Opposite below
18 Dorin, 'El Mesdjem', 1892. Open
box with carved ivory container for
kohl eye makeup.
H. 6.3 cm (2½ in.).

Above and opposite above
19, 20 C. Amiel et Cie, 'Violette de
Parme'. *c.* 1890. Bottle and box,
open and closed.
H. 14.5 cm (5¾ in.).

21 Ed. Pinaud. 'Cydalise', 1898.
Bottle and box.
H. 11.0 cm (4⅜ in.).

22 Rallet, 'Le Lys du Nil', *c.* 1890.
Bottle and box.
H. 12.2 cm (4¾ in.).

23 L. T. Piver presentations (from
left to right): 'Floramye', bottle and
box, 1895; 'Rosiris', bottle and box,
1899; 'Azurea', sachet bottle,
perfume bottle and box and powder
box, 1901; 'Safranor', bottle and
box, 1904.
H. of perfume bottles: 12.0 cm
(4¾ in.); 10.0 cm (4 in.); 11.7 cm
(4⅝ in.); 11.7 cm (4⅝ in.).

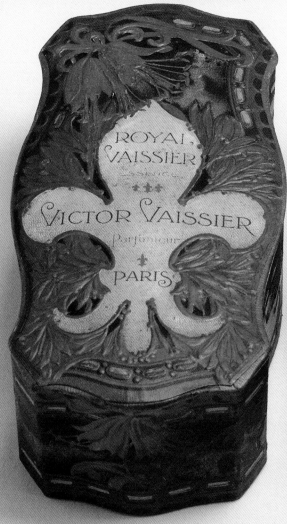

From the opening of the Universal Exhibition on 14 April 1900 until its closing on 13 November more than 47 million admission tickets were sold. Paris was the place to be. The entrance to the exhibition, the Porte Binet (so named after its architect), consisted of a monumental arch flanked by a pair of tall, slender pillars. On the low walls linking the arch and these pillars, a frieze of artisans and workmen engaged in various trades was the main decorative theme, representing the broad range of France's capabilities, but the overall design and flamboyant ornamentation were clearly inspired by the Orient. Surmounting the arch was a gigantic statue entitled *La Parisienne* ('The Parisian Woman'), depicting an elaborately attired figure wearing a high-fashion evening gown and coat designed by Jeanne Paquin. This symbolic figure, 6 m (20 ft) high, represented a radical departure from previous practice whereby such an official statue would almost certainly have portrayed a mythological figure. Now *La Parisienne*, the symbol of the New Woman and of the New Century, as well as of Art Nouveau, was given the place of honour.

The idea of the 'New Woman' had been born in the years after 1880, when women began to be granted certain legal rights. No doubt, for most women in France and abroad, these new rights meant very little in terms of their daily lives, but it was a beginning. Nevertheless, the 'New Woman', with her longing for equality and independence, was perceived as constituting a grave threat to all established institutions in society, and not surprisingly the French press and its cartoons made continuous fun of her. However, the importance of the 'New Woman' was officially recognized when it was decided that the statue of *La Parisienne* would form the summit, quite literally, of the Universal Exhibition. However, this was the new *Parisian* woman, and she was different. Although obviously modern, she would pose no threat to men and society; independent and elegant, she would become the trendsetter, admired the world over, and thanks to her innate good taste and informed choices she would make all the crucial decisions that would be so vital to the national economy and artistic prestige of France. The pool of workmen would look up to her.

At that time it was clear that France's heavy industrial output and exports still lagged far behind those of Germany, Great Britain and the

Facing page
24 Victor Vaissier, 'Royal Vaissier', 1900. Soap box and Baccarat bottle no. 10 in open box.
H. of bottle 10.6 cm (4⅛ in.).

32 Roger & Gallet, 'Bouquet Nouveau', *c.* 1900.

United States. As a defensive measure new protectionist laws were introduced to restrict foreign imports into France, but most of all, an intensified policy aimed at encouraging a return to the standards of craftsmanship of the 17th and 18th centuries was pursued. All traditional French luxury industries received official government support for the production of artistically crafted objects in a new modern style, thus placing the decorative arts on a par with the fine arts, painting and sculpture. This effort also rejected the international interest in pseudo-luxury bourgeois taste, which was satisfied with mostly machine-made, nondescript, ornate decorative objects, lacking in innovation. Once the French government had announced its intention to stage the Universal Exhibition, as early as 1892, it seemed that all artists and artisans immediately began to prepare for it. All these new developments greatly enhanced the prospects for the success of the perfume industry in the 20th century.

During the exhibition, a number of startling innovations were seen by the public. The newly built automobiles, called 'road engines', caused quite a stir. The 'Fairy Electricity' displayed her power throughout, and especially in the Palace of Electricity. And even Sarah Bernhardt was associated with these new technological advances, when she silently portrayed Hamlet in one of the first motion pictures ever produced.

In 1900, Art Nouveau was at its apogee, dynamic and unconventional, with its exaggerated asymmetry and sinuous curves, reminiscent of plant life and the female form. This exhibition marked not just the crowning of Art Nouveau, but also the beginning of its demise, for the high level of creativity could not be sustained for long, and too many poorly executed objects flooded the market afterwards. Although the perfume section at the 1900 Universal Exhibition achieved a huge success, high-style Art Nouveau did not inspire perfumers in general. The only extreme Art Nouveau presentations were those designed by Hector Guimard – one of the leading figures in the Art Nouveau movement – for the F. Millot perfumes and soaps: 'Kantirix', 'Primialis' and 'Violi-Violette'. In each case the bottle, box and graphics were stylistically in keeping with all the other works by Hector Guimard in various media around the turn of the century, including his entire F. Millot pavilion and its decoration.

An interesting Art Nouveau concept was 'Bouquet Nouveau' ('New Bouquet'), a Roger & Gallet perfume, the square green-glass bottle and stopper for which retained a very classic overall shape (32; pl.25). Only the surface ornamentation could be considered Art Nouveau in style, as parts of the glass seemed to overflow out of the most unusual perforated, gilded brass casing, signed by Louis Chalon. Chalon was one of the exhibition's artists whose work as a sculptor found great favour with both critics and the public. Before turning to sculpture, Chalon had worked as a painter, illustrator, costume designer and jeweller. However, the metalwork element of 'Bouquet Nouveau' was mostly representative of his work as an illustrator, which was a wonderful mixture of Art Nouveau plant motifs, carefully controlled by the use of repetition and symmetry.

In general, various Art Nouveau elements, mostly floral motifs, were reproduced on the paper used for perfume labels and for covering boxes, while the shape of bottles and boxes remained fairly traditional. These Art Nouveau design elements were, therefore, incorporated essentially as surface decoration. Victor Vaissier, a prestigious soap and perfume company, had already been awarded 22 gold medals at earlier exhibitions during the 19th century; now 'Royal Vaissier' (pl. 24), created for the 1900 exhibition, displayed its magnificent Art Nouveau style paper motifs in the form of a fleur de lys, and was considered a most desirable presentation. Meanwhile, a small and humble Lorenzy-Palanca powder box, 'Cri du Cœur' (literally 'Cry from the Heart', though also having overtones of an 'irresistible impulse'), displayed an extraordinary lyrical and avant-garde name, along with a 'woman-flower' image (pl. 28), truly one of the rare high-style Art Nouveau icons produced for a perfume company.

The preferred style for perfume presentations at this 1900 exhibition, and throughout the ensuing decade, was that of the 'Belle Epoque'. This was nothing new, since it had been prevalent in France throughout the last thirty years of the 19th century and was evident in everything from architecture to simple knick-knacks – traditional, cluttered, but nonetheless elegant and very French. It was the accepted style and, because it was uncontroversial, perfectly suited to the turn-of-the-century era. Examples included 'Coronis', by Monpelas, which featured a delicate floral motif on a powder box of unusual shape (pl. 27), and Roger & Gallet's 'Gloire de Paris' ('Glory of Paris'), which was a sumptuous, but classic perfume line (pl. 31). Both presentations were certainly quintessential Belle Epoque symbols, as were their names. At the time most perfume names still included those of flowers or were fabricated to sound flowery, poetic and sweet: examples like 'Floramye', 'Rosiris', 'Azurea', 'Safranor', 'Coronis' and 'Vera-Violetta' were still the norm.

Some perfume companies used bottles which were deliberately designed to resemble the luxurious crystal bottles fitted with elaborate gold caps made by master goldsmiths in the 17th and 18th centuries. These new versions were classic designs with smooth surfaces, and had standard inner glass stoppers concealed under elegant gilded brass caps which matched their ornate gold labels. The bottles, their brass caps, labels and boxes were all very similar, with only minor variations. Seven perfume presentations from this period illustrate this tendency. All these items featured standard bottles and metal caps, with different kinds of labels. 'Rose Ispahan' and 'Prince Igor', both Rigaud perfumes, had labels resembling bronze plaques. 'Rose de Chiraz' ('Rose of Shiraz'), by the German company F. Wolff & Sohn, was given a tooled and gilded leather label (pl. 32), probably intended to reflect the beauty of Persian leatherwork. 'Stylis' by Delettrez was presented in a luxurious rococo style, with a gold paper label depicting an allegorical scene typical of the Louis XV period. Richard Hudnut, an American company, introduced 'Eros' in a French-made bottle, similar to the examples already noted, but in this case three sides of the bottle were moulded with a woman-floral motif – a very innovative idea. Two of the very few surviving perfume samples of this period – Rigaud's 'Le Lilas' and Vivaudou's 'Mavis' – were actually miniature replicas, resembling the larger capped bottles (pl. 32). This style remained popular for many years, gradually evolving to take on a more streamlined appearance.

Although these types of presentation were the norm throughout the first decade of the 20th century, two very different and major developments of the previous century made a significant impact between 1905 and 1910: the continued development of man-made fragrances, and perceptions arising from the emergence of the science of psychology. Many synthetic fragrances had been produced after the discovery of the first aldehyde in 1837, but the 20th century brought even greater diversity and greatly enhanced differentiation among perfumes. Single-flower perfumes, known by their simple descriptions such as 'Rose' or 'Violet', were all but abandoned in favour of more complex bouquets, unlike anything found in nature. The marketing of these increasingly complex and unusual blends called for increasingly sophisticated and unusual names, the ideas they evoked being interpreted by more expressive and imaginative packaging.

The important psychological findings of the late 19th century, such as the revelation of the unconscious, the power of suggestion and the importance of dreams, had an immediate impact on society, on literature and on the visual arts. Because olfactory sensations are powerful and can trigger memories, emotions and dreams, it became increasingly clear that in commercial terms new complex perfumes would benefit from more evocative names and distinctive identities. Soon, perfume presentations were enhanced by unusual visual renderings of the more imaginative names through co-ordinated designs for graphics, bottles, labels and, later on, boxes. When this individual identity was expressed well, the presentation greatly enhanced the appeal of the perfume, and together they became for many people an attractive, if not irresistible combination. The possibilities for new perfumes were limitless, whether conceived for sophisticated women or for young girls, for blondes or brunettes. Perfumes could be marketed for daytime or nighttime use and for different seasons of the year. From this decade forward, perfume imagery would be drawn from a multitude of new sources, including nature, literature and the visual arts.

In 1900, Guerlain introduced a perfume at the Universal Exhibition which broke new ground in exploring these possibilities. It featured a most unusual name and an innovative presentation. The perfume name was actually a sentence: 'Voilà pourquoi j'aimais Rosine' ('That's why I loved Rosine'), and the presentation included what was probably the first 'representational' perfume bottle. This bottle itself resembled a vase, its plain stopper being concealed under a prominent imitation begonia with silk flowers (pl. 26). Because of its novelty, this presentation caused an immediate sensation, and the bottle shape was later retained for another Guerlain perfume, 'Muguet' ('Lily of the Valley'), which had been marketed successfully since the 19th century and was re-introduced in an all-white presentation, with a white ribbon replacing the silk floral decoration (33). The design of these bottles was perfectly suited to display the magnificent Guerlain label depicting the Place Vendôme column as seen from the rue de la Paix, where the Guerlain shop was then located. At about the same time, Guerlain introduced 'Le Mouchoir de Monsieur' ('The Gentleman's Handkerchief'). Its bottle had a triangular section and on each of its three sides it bore a moulded spiral motif; it had a matching stopper and a conforming three-sided box (pl. 30). This avant-garde name and presentation was another example of the increasingly imaginative approach adopted by perfume companies and the artists they commissioned.

Two other early examples of representational bottles introduced by perfume makers were enhanced by the choice of foreign words as perfume names. Both displayed a great sense of humour in the manner in which the name was related to the imagery of the presentation. (This concept would flourish especially from the 1920s on.) 'Rediviva' (Spanish for 'Revived'), a perfume introduced by La Compagnie Française du Lysogène c. 1908, was a fanciful rendition of a Limoges porcelain coffeepot, in which the stopper was inserted at the end of the spout (34). In 1908, Dralle, a German perfume company based in Hamburg, introduced 'Illusion', using a word adopted from French or English for the perfume name; this special luxury edition featured an elaborate silver case, shaped like a lighthouse, to house the bottle. The sample bottle for the 'Illusion' perfume, which was also housed unusually in a metal case, had a ground-glass stopper – an amazing achievement in the context of a bottle only 3 cm (less than 1¼ in.) high. Also, the word 'Illusion' (35) was presented in an imaginative manner, the initial I being adapted to appear as a reversed capital L – an illusion in itself.

Without doubt, the single most significant advance in the presentation of perfume during this first decade of the new century resulted from the extraordinary collaboration between two great innovators: René Lalique and François Coty. The first Lalique creations for Coty occurred around 1907-8, and these entirely novel perfume presentations were just the beginning of a business relationship that would continue to flourish into the next decade. In addition, as Lalique became involved with many other perfume companies, his innovations would abound and his influence would broaden.

René Lalique, the leading and much-acclaimed Art Nouveau genius, was already well known before the turn of the century. Sarah Bernhardt and Calouste Gulbenkian were among his patrons, along with other leading members of European society, and his *objets d'art* and jewelry were among

33 Guerlain, 'Muguet', 1905. H. 9.5 cm (3¾ in.).

34 La Compagnie Française du Lysogène, 'Rediviva', c. 1908. H. 16.5 cm (6½ in.).

35. Dralle, 'Illusion', 1908, bottle and luxury silver case, h. 8.4 cm (3¼ in.); miniature with metal case, h. 3.0 cm (1⅛ in.).

the highlights of the 1900 Universal Exhibition. Early in his career, he had started to experiment with the use of glass when he needed unconventional materials to bring unusual colours and fluid shapes to his jewelry designs. In 1905, he opened his first shop in Paris at 24 place Vendôme. The year before, François Coty had opened his first perfume shop in the capital, at 61 rue La Boétie. This small shop would be the location at which Coty (already experienced in making perfume) formulated, displayed and sold his perfumes. Coty's 'L'Origan' ('Oregano'), introduced there in 1905, was destined to become one of the century's most successful perfumes. Shortly afterwards, Coty expanded his business activities, selling his perfumes throughout France and abroad through other perfume shops and department stores. Then, in 1908, Coty opened a luxurious establishment at 23 place Vendôme. About that time Lalique started to design graphics for Coty, to be incorporated on paper perfume labels, packaging and displays.

An unusual perfume label designed by Lalique in 1909 for 'L'Effleurt', a Coty perfume, consisted of a small rectangular glass plaque, its front moulded in relief and its back completely flat; this glass label was applied on the front of a standard Baccarat bottle of classic form. Very few examples of these glass plaques were used in this way, and the production of this original 'L'Effleurt' presentation must have been minimal. Three years later, in 1912, another version was introduced employing a similar bottle; the new stopper used the cicada design, another popular Art Nouveau motif. The label was now moulded as an integral part of the glass body, rather than being applied to the finished bottle. The thickness of the bottle's clear-glass walls was such that the perfume was contained in a rectangular space with exactly the same shape as the label, but slightly larger overall – thereby allowing the colour of the perfume to form a narrow frame around the label.

The name 'L'Effleurt' is a fabricated word and hence does not have a precise meaning, yet it poetically evokes the ideas of the softness of woman, the fragility of flowers and the intangibility of perfume. The closest word in French is *effleurer*, which means 'to touch lightly'; another close word in similar form is *effluve*, which means 'emanation', as a scent is exuded by a flower. And, of course, the word *fleur* or 'flower', is actually embraced within the name 'L'Effleurt'. The moulded glass label showed an elusive female apparition born out of swirls, seemingly surrounded by water, or perhaps flames or wind. She could even be considered to represent the perfume itself, rising, reaching out and bewitching. In this design Lalique created the quintessential Art Nouveau perfume label. Even though the Art Nouveau movement had reached a dead end by 1909, Lalique nevertheless chose to present 'L'Effleurt' with an unashamedly Art Nouveau image (pl.29).

Lalique and Coty must have been aware that 'L'Effleurt' was a significant work. For this reason, on the revised 1912 edition, the perfume name is phrased 'L'Effleurt de Coty'. The preposition *de* (meaning, in this context, 'by') had never been used before in perfume names. Company names and perfume names were shown side by side, but not directly connected or interrelated. Thus, the use of *de* implies a work of art, a masterpiece perfume created by Coty, and René Lalique also signed his own name on the image (front, lower right), just as a painter might sign his works.

While 'L'Effleurt' represented a major new departure, the earliest bottles designed by Lalique for Coty were fairly innovative in form, but not avant-garde. Only the surface motifs were in the Art Nouveau style. In 1909, three years before his redesigned presentation of 'L'Effleurt', the first bottle Lalique designed for Coty seems to have been 'Cyclamen'(pl.29). Although in retrospect this may not immediately appear to be a true design innovation, it was at the time. The bottle featured six identical panels depicting the same woman-dragonfly motif, but the stopper was meaningfully different in its design concept, since it bore the name 'Cyclamen, Coty, Paris' in moulded lettering – the first time that this important information identifying the perfume and its maker was placed directly on the stopper.

The second bottle that Lalique designed for Coty was 'Ambre Antique' of 1910, and the third was 'Styx' of 1911 (pl. 29). Of these bottles the one for 'Styx' was the closest to the Art Nouveau style. The Lalique signature again appeared on the front surface of these bottles. None of the corresponding boxes for these first four Coty-Lalique collaborations represented any design innovations and, consequently, very few examples have survived.

36, 37, 38 L. T. Piver, 'Scarabée', 1909: bottle; leather box for bottle; glass powder jar.

Another significant perfume presentation, introduced for Christmas 1909, was 'Scarabée' by L. T. Piver. Because of the absence of accurate records, and because this bottle was unsigned, it is difficult to ascertain exactly which artist designed, and which glassworks produced it. The entire 'Scarabée' presentation was an accurate rendering of the scarab beetle often used as a motif for jewelry, amulets and seals in ancient Egypt, where it had come to symbolize the sun, and was often depicted as rolling forward an incandescent sphere representing the sun. The sides of this bottle featured two moulded scarabs facing one another, as in a mirror image, supporting a spherical shape (the stopper) resembling a flower (36; pl. 34). The design was completely symmetrical, including the unusual feature of having identical labels front and back. The 'Scarabée' bottle and stopper must be viewed as a unit, for they complemented each other in such a closely integrated manner that it would be almost unimaginable to consider one without the other. Together they can be regarded as a sculpture or a three-dimensional work of art. In Egyptian art the scarab was often dark in colour, and therefore the elegant tooled leather box for the perfume bottle continued the theme of the scarab – accurately rendered in both shape and colour (37). All elements of the 'Scarabée' perfume presentation – the name, the bottle, and the leather box – were excellently co-ordinated, and even a related product, the 'Scarabée' powder, was presented in a glass jar with identical features continuing the excellence of design (38).

'Scarabée' has been attributed to René Lalique, which is reasonable, because his Art Nouveau designs, especially for jewelry, often depicted two identical figures (women, insects, reptiles, fish, birds, etc.) facing each other, as in a mirror image. A Lalique brooch of *c.* 1903 in the Gulbenkian Museum depicts two identical dark scarabs, facing each other in a confrontational manner, but separated by a sphere of colour; this brooch resembles the 'Scarabée' box. However, Lalique was not alone in creating such striking and disquieting Art Nouveau images. His good friend Lucien Gaillard, another jeweller, was simultaneously exhibiting his own almost identical jewelry creations, based on the same principles of design. It is therefore also possible that Gaillard designed 'Scarabée' or that the two artists collaborated on this design, itself a landmark in the art of perfume presentation.

In this decade new cultural and artistic developments were accompanied by rapid technological progress, especially in glass production. The seeds were now sown for even faster growth and greater prosperity in the field of perfume, and numerous original and imaginative perfume presentations would blossom during the next two decades – clear evidence that this new art form was fully established.

25 Roger & Gallet, 'Bouquet
Nouveau', *c.* 1900. Bottle with
gilt-brass ornament by Louis Chalon.
H. 10.7 cm (4¼ in.).

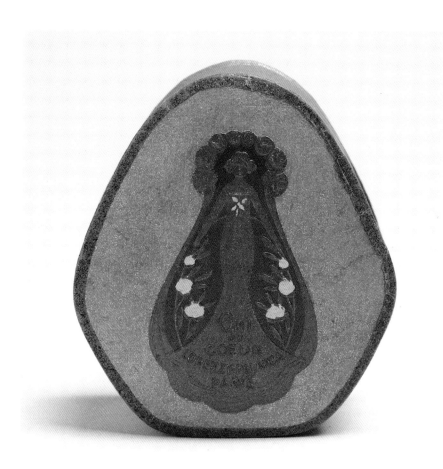

Opposite
26 Guerlain, 'Voilà pourquoi
j'aimais Rosine', 1900. Bottle with
silk flowers concealing stopper.
H. 9.5 cm (3¾ in.).

27 Monpelas, 'Coronis', 1905.
Powder box.
H. 8.0 cm (3⅛ in.).

28 Lorenzy-Palanca, 'Cri du Cœur',
c. 1905. Powder box.
H. 6.0 cm (2⅜ in.).

Right
29 Four bottles designed and made by René Lalique for Coty perfumes (from left to right): 'L'Effleurt', 1912 edition; 'Cyclamen', 1909; 'Styx', 1911; and 'Ambre Antique', 1910.
H. 11.2 cm (4⅜ in.), 13.8 cm (5⅜ in.), 12.5 cm (4⅞ in.), 15.4 cm (6⅛ in.).

Below
30 Guerlain, 'Le Mouchoir de Monsieur', 1904. Three-sided box and bottle.
H. 11.5 cm (4½ in.).

Opposite, above
31 Roger & Gallet, 'Gloire de Paris', 1907. Bottle and box.
H. 11.5 cm (4½ in.).

Opposite, below
32 Bottles in classic style with brass caps over inner glass stoppers (from left to right): Delettrez, 'Stylis', 1910 (Baccarat bottle no. 79); F. Wolff & Sohn, 'Rose de Chiraz', *c.* 1910; Rigaud, 'Prince Igor', 1909, and 'Rose Ispahan', 1910 (with box); Richard Hudnut, 'Eros', *c.* 1910. Sample size bottles in foreground: Rigaud, 'Le Lilas', *c.* 1910, and Vivaudou, 'Mavis', 1915.
H. of bottles 9.4–10.3 cm (3¾–4 in.); miniatures 4.0 cm (1⅝ in.) and 4.4 cm (1¾ in.).

33 Delettrez, 'Oryalis', *c.* 1908.
Box and Baccarat bottle no. 30 with
stopper no. 25; greenish mother-of-
pearl labels.
H. 11.7 cm (4⅝ in.).

34 L. T. Piver, 'Scarabée', 1909.
Glass powder box, bottle in open box,
and lid of box, all with scarab motifs.
H. of bottle 8.5 cm (3⅜ in.).

In the spring of 1909, the first season of Sergei Diaghilev's Ballets Russes had just opened in Paris, and France was captivated by the exotic and colourful energy of the company's productions. The time had come to accept a new artistic movement. It had probably been too early for this to happen in 1905, when the first Fauvist paintings, with their 'wild' colours and unfamiliar style, were shown at the Salon d'Automne and had been so vehemently rejected. Now the Ballets Russes would have a determining influence not only on the decorative arts generally, but on painting, sculpture, literature, music, theatre and dance, and would contribute to the beginning of the Art Deco movement, as it later became known.

In June 1910, Paul Poiret attended the opening of *Schéhérazade*, a choreographic drama written by Léon Bakst, who also designed the costumes and the scenery. That evening, Poiret's wife Denise wore an elegant neo-classical gown designed by him for his collection. This dress model, called 'Lavallière', which caused a sensation, was named after the famous actress Eve Lavallière, the leading lady in *Le Bois Sacré*, a great Parisian stage success of 1910. In fact, Poiret had designed her costumes for that play, one of many stage productions to which he contributed. Intrigued, Diaghilev and the Nijinsky would visit the Poiret salons the following autumn to view his fashions. Later Diaghilev, Bakst and Poiret were to become mutual admirers, though the two Russians never worked in collaboration with Poiret.

Poiret, the fashion innovator, was now established and was generally considered the foremost designer of his time. He had liberated women from their corsets and constraints. His neo-classical, high-waisted and elongated styles allowed the wearer a much greater degree of comfort and freedom of movement, but by the end of 1910 he was ready for a change, and 1911 would see three major new developments: the beginning of his oriental-style fashions, featuring 'at home' harem pants and Turkish-style turbans (Poiret always insisted that his own use of colour and oriental themes had not been influenced by the Ballets Russes, but was simply coincidental); the establishment of his interior design firm Atelier Martine (named after his infant daughter), the first of its kind to be founded by a fashion designer; and the advent of Les Parfums de Rosine (named after his eldest daughter), the first perfume and cosmetics company to be founded by a couturier.

Facing page
35 Les Parfums de Rosine, 'Nuit de Chine', 1913. Box and bottle. H. 8.5 cm (3¾ in.).

To understand the background to these three simultaneous developments, one has to be aware of the preceding events in Poiret's life. Since 1906 Poiret had been travelling constantly around Europe, eager to discover new styles and avant-garde artists. At the end of 1910, he visited Berlin and Vienna. While in Vienna, he met the painter Gustav Klimt and Josef Hoffmann, one of the founders of the Wiener Werkstätte, a community of artists and artisans, and fell in love with his work. According to the Wiener Werkstätte philosophy, its members, completely attuned to the public's needs, would create and produce a wide range of artistic, simple, logical and good-quality utilitarian objects – in short they aimed to bring art into everyday life. This community would also produce textile designs and fabrics, fashions, accessories and jewelry. Poiret was captivated by this philosophy.

After his return to Paris, the style of Poiret's fashions started to evolve towards the Orient. Even his lifestyle, already sumptuous, acquired a new oriental magnificence. In June 1911, his lavish ball, which he called 'The Thousand and Second Night', was an event of unsurpassed splendour. Poiret soon became known as the 'Pasha of Paris'. His newly founded Atelier Martine included a small group of about fifteen talented but previously untrained girls, some less than twelve years old, who designed motifs to be painted or printed on textiles and paper. Furniture and home accessories were also produced there – in fact, complete and co-ordinated interior designs could be ordered through the Atelier Martine, in keeping with the Wiener Werkstätte philosophy.

For the woman who wore Poiret fashions and who lived in a Poiret interior, a Poiret perfume produced by Les Parfums de Rosine would be the indispensable and ultimate touch. Those who could not afford either a Poiret dress or any other substantial Poiret or Martine creations might still be able to afford a Rosine perfume. Poiret had been quoted as saying to his clients, 'This dress fits you wonderfully, but put one drop of my perfume on its hem, and the dress will make you ravishing.' His Rosine perfumes could travel far, throughout the world, and should have served to promote Poiret's name and style, but by choosing to use the name Rosine, rather than his own, he did not fully accomplish this objective.

Another workshop, Atelier Colin, named after Poiret's eldest son, was also founded in 1911, mainly to produce boxes and packaging materials, some for perfume. Even the Rosine perfumes were created in a Poiret laboratory. And although the glass bottles involved the production of various glassworks (Dépinoix and Lefèbure among them), most of the other packaging elements were designed and some were produced by Atelier Martine or Atelier Colin. In this way Poiret was directly involved in every stage of the perfume production process. Of course, the artists who collaborated with Poiret – such as Paul Iribe, Georges Lepape and Raoul Dufy – influenced and participated in the imagery of the Rosine perfumes, which represented the synthesis of Poiret's philosophy of aesthetics. For the next eight years Poiret remained the only fashion designer producing perfume, until Maurice Babani followed his example in 1919.

'Chez Poiret' ('At Poiret's') was among the first Rosine perfumes in 1912, and the same name was also given to a Poiret outfit presented that year. The perfume bottle and stopper (pl. 41) resembled three wine carafes as seen in a Lepape drawing, *Fête chez Paul Poiret* ('Paul Poiret's Banquet'). The combination of a coloured-glass stopper with a clear-glass bottle was a very novel idea – as was the inclusion of four gold tassels, which were an allusion to Poiret's fashions and home accessories. Lepape also designed an elegant 'R', which would be used for many Rosine labels. The box, similar in form to a hat box, bore a reproduction of a drawing originally executed by Lepape for the fashion album 'Les Choses de Paul Poiret vues par Georges Lepape' ('Paul Poiret's Things as seen by Georges Lepape'), which also appeared on the fashion house's invoices. The box was also decorated with a colourful floral print with an innocent quality, characteristic of Atelier Martine's drawings. Martine designs would be used for many Rosine presentations. Simple toilet-water bottles and hookah-shaped vaporizers were given an original appearance by being hand-painted at Atelier Martine with many colourful motifs (pl. 40). The hat-shaped Rosine powder boxes were covered with Martine fabrics or with inexpensive printed cottons of the kind normally used for making little girls' dresses.

Back in 1908, Paul Iribe had drawn a distinctive full and round rose for use with the advertising of Lubin toilet waters. The motif was so highly acclaimed that it became known as the 'Iribe rose'. Poiret loved it, and had a very similar rose embroidered next to his name on his fashion labels; this in turn came to be associated with Poiret as his symbol. 'La Rose de Rosine' ('The Rose of Rosine') was another Poiret perfume introduced in 1912. When viewed frontally, the bottle and stopper were large and wide, but when seen from the side, they appeared extremely thin and narrow (39). Their flat front and back served as a background for surface decoration consisting of a series of gold roses alternating with vertical gold stripes. This neo-classical motif was reminiscent of wallpaper and textile designs used in France for interior decoration or fashions during the Directoire, Consulat and even the Empire periods. Poiret had also used similar designs for his fashion fabrics in neo-classical style. The bottle and stopper were not only avant-garde because of their overall shape, but also because the gold designs were hand-painted directly on the smooth glass surfaces, with no moulding or engraving. The elegant logo by Lepape – an 'R' within a gold oval – identified this bottle as a Rosine perfume. 'La Rose de Rosine' was a quintessential Poiret creation, totally French in style.

At that time Poiret was enamoured of the 18th century, and had purchased Le Butard, a distressed hunting lodge near Paris. Assisted by Raoul Dufy, he was involved in its restoration, while also working on his new collection which featured his favourite Directoire style. The name 'Fan Fan la

39 Les Parfums de Rosine, 'La Rose de Rosine', Georges Lepape logo, 1912. H. 10.9 cm (4¼ in.); profile, w. 2.0 cm (¾ in.).

Tulipe' (loosely translated as 'The Tulip Child') referred to a fantasy character – a good-humoured and kind-hearted French soldier, with a penchant for glory, women and wine, and always ready to fight for a just cause. The subject of songs and plays, Fan Fan la Tulipe was the idealized French man, seemingly frivolous, but also capable of profound care. Poiret's perfume presentation was equally deceptive, apparently simple, while brilliantly avant-garde and sophisticated. The bottle was a reproduction of a typical 18th-century model, with tricolor enamelling by Atelier Martine (pl. 37). Two identical labels, one on the reverse of the bottle, the other on the box, reproduced as their main motif the Phrygian cap, symbol of the French Republic. High on the box, which was entirely covered in tricolor cloth, was a military *cocarde* (rosette). The box resembled the elongated striped Poiret dresses, which were often adorned by a circular cloth 'rose' near the bosom. This presentation was rendered dramatic by the use of humble materials and a 'home-made' appearance – poor-quality glass containing air bubbles and having a rippled surface, inexpensive metal, rough paper with archaic printing, and modest fabric reminiscent of the French revolutionary flag. The box even had a resemblance to a draped coffin. The character Fan Fan la Tulipe was the symbol of the Revolution and of hard-won freedom – an unlikely theme for a perfume presentation, something which only Paul Poiret would have attempted, and which only he could have achieved.

In spring 1913, Poiret and his two new assistants, Zamora and Erté, created the costumes for the play *Le Minaret*. Its leading lady, Cora Laparcerie, wore a grand outfit made of tulle, which seemed to glow in the stage lights. The simple elongated bottle for the Rosine perfume 'Le Minaret', also of spring 1913, was entirely and tightly covered with tulle, which had been hand-embroidered with reflective gold thread, the first time a textile had been used to cover a glass perfume bottle (40). Another innovation was the absence of a traditional paper label or of any information directly engraved on the bottle or stopper. Instead the identification appeared on a gilded brass medallion in the form of a stylized minaret suspended from the bottle's neck; the perfume name 'Le Minaret' was moulded on one side and 'Rosine' appeared on the other.

Later in 1913, the perfume presentation 'Nuit de Chine' ('Night of China') was introduced as a completely integrated design. In general the form of the bottle resembled that of a classic Chinese snuff bottle, interpreted in a very modern and streamlined style (41; pl. 35). The shape of the label, placed in an unusually low position on the front, echoed the outline of the bottle. The perfume name appeared both in Chinese characters and in French. From a moulded glass ring on each of the bottle's shoulders hung a dark-blue Bakelite ring – probably the first time Bakelite was used in conjunction with glass in a perfume presentation. The shape of the box resembled that of the bottle and label, and its design motif was also classically Chinese. However, despite all these Chinese elements, the presentation

40 Les Parfums de Rosine, 'Le Minaret', 1913, h. 11.4 cm (4½ in.); 'Borgia', 1914, h. 9.5 cm (3¾ in.).

looked very Western, very French. Poiret's genius lay in his ability to adopt styles from other cultures or periods and transform them into his own.

Although Poiret's couture house was temporarily closed during World War I, Martine and Rosine continued some operations. 'Borgia', introduced in 1914 in an elegant amphora-shaped bottle (40), was a very small production. The black glass bottle featured swirls of gold inclusions – possibly the first time that this glass technique had been seen in the context of perfume bottles, most likely the work of Georges Dumoulin. The advertising for 'Borgia' claimed that *une seule goutte rend fou* ('a single drop will drive you mad'); the same idea was later used in 1945 when 'Insidia' was subtitled 'Il profumo che turba' ('the perfume which drives you wild').

The name 'Le Fruit Défendu' ('The Forbidden Fruit') was trademarked in 1915, the same day as 'Le Sang Français' ('French Blood'), though it is unlikely that the latter perfume was ever produced, whereas 'Le Fruit Défendu' was probably introduced after the war. The body of the apple-shaped glass bottle (pl. 38) displayed a multitude of tiny air bubbles, another major innovation, again possibly attributable to Georges Dumoulin. The bottle and its large cover of grey metal resembled an eccentric apple-shaped box produced by Dagobert Peche at the Wiener Werkstätte in 1918-20. The elongated leaves, which formed part of the design of both label and box, were almost identical to those adorning the silver box by Dagobert Peche. Even the unruly creeper which completed the cover of 'Le Fruit Défendu' was somewhat reminiscent of the ornament on Dagobert Peche's silver box; this presentation was an excellent example of the affinity that Paul Poiret had with contemporary Viennese design.

The silver paper covering the box for 'Le Fruit Défendu' resembled the silvered finishes on some items of furniture produced by Atelier Martine around that time. Fruit was then one of Poiret's favourite decorative motifs. A Martine interior presented at the Salon d'Automne of 1919 featured melon-shaped and melon-size cushions strewn everywhere, even on the floor. In 1916, Iribe and Atelier Martine collaborated in the interior decoration of the home of the famous actress Mademoiselle Spinelly, who not only endorsed 'Le Fruit Défendu', but in a later photograph was shown facing her salon wall, on which was painted a fruit tree, and making believe that she was biting into one of the painted fruits. This photograph was reproduced in the Rosine catalogue with the caption 'Mademoiselle Spinelly prefers The Forbidden Fruit, a Poiret perfume.'

Another wartime introduction, 'La Coupe d'Or' ('The Golden Bowl'), dated from 1917. Poiret must have hesitated over this name, as it was trademarked together with 'Les Fruits d'Or' ('The Golden Fruits'). The bottle, which was in the form of a classic pedestal, was topped by a metal-covered glass stopper – literally the golden bowl (42). The centrepiece of this whole presentation, which reflected Poiret's interest in neo-classical designs, was a gilded metal ornament representing various fruits piled high and spilling out

41 Les Parfums de Rosine, 'Nuit de Chine', 1913. H. 11.0 cm (4⅜ in.); 8.5 cm (3¾ in.).

42 Les Parfums de Rosine, 'La Coupe d'Or', 1917. H. 13.3 cm (5¼ in.).

of the bowl. So realistic was the effect that a large label would have been distracting, therefore only a small label bearing the 'R' logo was used, very high on one side. On the opposite side, a sliver of gold paper, marked 'La Coupe d'Or' in tiny letters, was placed near the base of the bottle. Previously, both Lepape and Iribe had used the overflowing fruit bowl as a design motif.

The first Rosine perfume introduced after the war was 'Pierrot', in a simple frosted bottle which represented a stylized Pierrot coat, while the enamelled stopper was reminiscent of Pierrot's black cap (pl. 36). Around the neck of the bottle was a realistic gauze ruff – a clear reminder that Poiret was primarily a fashion designer. The label, placed low on the bottle, was a masterpiece of abstraction, yet totally descriptive. The design, which could have been a vignette by Iribe, consisted of an upright oval evenly divided across the middle; the upper part was black, depicting Pierrot's cap, and the lower part was white, representing his face – but an abstract face, since it showed only the lips, from which dangled the Poiret rose. The cap bore the name 'Pierrot', unconventionally separated into two lines, while the subtitle 'Parfum Frais' ('Fresh Perfume') appeared in small letters below the mouth. The 'Pierrot' box, now exceedingly rare, was a splendid object, stylistically close to the Iribe aesthetic. The sharp contrast of black and white, though refined and delicate, was nevertheless powerful and disquieting. The box illustrated Pierrot's song 'Au Clair de la Lune' ('In the Moonlight'), composed in 1646 by Jean-Baptiste Lully, musician to Louis XIV. A distant fairytale landscape was shown, glowing in the moonlight, dwarfed by an overwhelming star-filled sky. No more poetic imagery was ever expressed on a perfume box. 'Pierrot' could be considered to represent one side of Poiret's character – his innocence and vulnerability.

Another new introduction of 1919 was 'Aladin' (pl. 39). This perfume inspired by the possessor of the magic lamp in *The Thousand and One Nights*, might have represented another side of Poiret – the 'Pasha of Paris'. Poiret viewed himself as a modern-day Aladdin, and this bottle was his magic lamp. This most unusual metal bottle, with a Bakelite stopper simulating old ivory, could be lifted like a portable lamp by means of an attached chain – all original features in perfume presentations. A luxury edition of 'Aladin' was offered in a pink-stained crystal bottle.

All Rosine creations displayed at least one innovative feature. All were avant-garde, departing from traditional design principles, and were so different one from another that, as a group, they provided excellent proof of Poiret's versatility. Not only was he the first fashion designer to produce his own perfumes, but he also changed dramatically the creative potential for the presentation of perfume. His innovations would be a source of inspiration for other designers for many years to come. The Rosine perfume presentations may prove to be the most enduring examples of Paul Poiret's genius.

The Orient, as seen through Poiret's eyes, influenced fashions and lifestyles, and certainly influenced perfume presentations. As Lalique broadened his involvement with many perfume companies, he was influenced by new trends in the fine and decorative arts. The sculptors Clovis and Julien Viard and the glass artist Maurice Dépinoix also emerged as major innovators, but most significant of all was the impact of World War I. Not only did it bring the Belle Epoque to an abrupt end, but it delayed the development and public recognition of the new style in the decorative arts – Art Deco. This decade was not the first time that France, and especially Parisian women, had fallen in love with exotic oriental themes. In the 18th century, Turkish and Persian styles had become fashionable, giving rise to two new words: *Turqueries* and *Perseries*. In 1910, however, it seemed as if the women of Paris were actively seeking a Persian identity, first at masked balls, then at home, and finally in the style of their street clothes.

The year 1910 saw the introduction by Guerlain of 'Quand vient l'été' ('When Summer comes'), a luxury presentation for which an 18th-century French bottle, similar to a bottle of Middle Eastern origin in the Guerlain collection, served as the model; this presentation (pl. 82) was also used for other Guerlain perfumes. Around the same time, the trans-European Orient Express, providing a direct rail link between Paris and Istanbul, encouraged a revival of interest in Turkey. The city of Konya (ancient Iconium) in Anatolia, historically a major centre of art and literature, now found its name brought back to the attention of Europeans through the introduction by Silka in 1919 of a dream-like perfume presentation with the name 'Ikonia'. The label suggests the mythical character of ancient Iconium, while the stopper in the shape of a crescent-moon completed the Turkish symbolism (pl. 83).

One Middle Eastern personality with whom Paris became fascinated was Bichara Malhamé, founder of Bichara perfumes and cosmetics. Originally from Syria, Bichara became an immensely successful perfumer in Paris at the turn of the century, with Sarah Bernhardt as his muse. Bichara perfumes were her favourites, and the playwright Edmond Rostand called Bichara 'the poet of perfume'. His famous label, placed on most of his perfumes and cosmetics, showed a vignette with the inscription 'Comment Bichara saisit la fortune' ('How Bichara grabs good fortune'). The vignette portrayed Bichara seizing a mythological figure of Fortune by the hair – an appropriate image, since his original fortune was made with 'Le Henné Bichara', a hair product. Not content with portraying himself on the label, he also appeared on a Baccarat stopper of 1913. Probably wanting to look like a pharaoh, he had himself represented wearing a curious wig, which gave him more the appearance of an English judge (pl. 42). Another Syrian perfumer, Henriette Gabilla, a friend of Colette, provided Bichara with plenty of competition after 1910, and in the course of the next decade many superb presentations would be created for Gabilla perfumes.

Throughout the century since Napoleon's expedition to Egypt, France had also been fascinated by that country and its culture. Egyptian styles thoroughly infiltrated French decorative arts. This love was reciprocated,

43 Ramsès, soap box, 1918. H. 10.5 cm (4⅛ in.).

44 L. Plassard, 'Une Femme Passa', 1910, Baccarat bottle no. 146. H. 12.3 cm (4⅞ in.).

since educated Egyptians were attracted to French culture and French perfumes. Ahmed Soliman, who called himself 'Cairo's Perfum [*sic*] King', introduced exotic perfumes in luxurious bottles made of coloured crystal with enamelled decoration using motifs from ancient Egypt (pl. 43). The usual shape for Ahmed Soliman's bottles was long and narrow (pl. 46), and his perfumes appealed to French and Egyptian buyers alike. Perhaps the best perfume rendering of an Egyptian theme was 'Ramsès IV', a Ramsès perfume of 1919; produced by Baccarat, the bottle was completely sculptural and perfectly formed from every angle (pls. 44, 45). A head with aristocratic features and a sphinx-like quality was crowned by a stopper symbolizing the solar disc and two ostrich plumes, the headdress associated with Amun-Re, god of Thebes and supreme deity under the New Kingdom, as well as with certain pharaohs. The Ramsès graphics on powder boxes (pl. 47) and soap boxes (43) were equally intricate and sumptuous.

As this decade began, the Parisian theatre was at its apogee, and would serve as a major source of inspiration for perfume creations, a trend which would continue for many years to come. In 1910, Paris could boast over forty theatres, including the Opéra and the Comédie-Française, and many more music-halls and cabarets. The city attracted leading artists and its night life held a special magic, even for those who only heard of it. This was the time and place where all nationalities met, and where all classes of society mingled – where all could experience and enjoy the many spectacles on offer, as well as the spectacle of Paris itself.

Perfume companies regularly borrowed the titles of successful plays for use as perfume names. This strategy was clever, since in addition to the many people who saw a fashionable play, even more would read about it. The perfume's image could, therefore, benefit by association with the story, costumes, sets, performers and even the play's success. *La Vierge Folle* ('The Mad Virgin'), the title of a play about a young girl who fell in love with an older man, was adopted by Gabilla for one of her first perfumes. The same year, Gueldy introduced the perfume 'Le Bois Sacré' ('The Sacred Woods'), also with a current theatrical success in mind. This perfume's extraordinary label, resembling a miniature landscape painting, depicted a sacred stone in the middle of the woods (pls. 50, 51). 'Une Femme Passa' ('A Woman Passed by') was used in 1911 for a perfume by L. Plassard, the name in this case having been borrowed from another play, about a short-lived extra-marital affair, staged in 1910. Its bottle (44) was a landmark Baccarat model, showing Lalique's influence, in which both bottle and stopper were entirely covered in an intricate and precise frosted floral design – a significant departure from Baccarat's previous well-polished classic designs.

The play *La Phalène* by Henry Bataille was the theatrical scandal of Paris in 1913; the plot of this erotic and morbid work about sex and suicide concerns a young woman, a talented sculptor, who learns that she is terminally ill. She breaks off her engagement, abandons her art and decides to live a life of debauchery, and then to commit suicide to avoid suffering. The stage sets, designed by Paul Iribe, which reproduced the interior of a modern apartment with avant-garde furniture, marked a major step forward for the Art Deco movement. The name 'Phalène' ('Moth') was given to a perfume presentation introduced by d'Héraud several years after the play. The bottle (pl. 56) depicted a central female nude, surrounded by draped veils, in the shape of a moth. The unique colour gradation of the Lalique bottle, from red to orange to yellow, symbolized the moth's attraction to the glow of the flame, into which it would fly in a self-destructive act. This use of graduated colours was unprecedented in perfume presentations.

Chu-Chin-Chow, which established a new record as the longest-running musical play, enjoyed enormous success in both London and New York. Not only was the title used for a Bryenne perfume of 1918, but the bottle (pl. 84) was a figural portrayal of the mandarin disguise used by the protagonist-thief in the story from *The Thousand and One Nights* on which the musical was based. This bottle, created by G. K. Benda (well known for his posters of Mistinguett), was complemented by a perfumed card with the same outline and features (8). Some perfume companies chose to use the names of successful performers for their products. Thus, 'Mary Garden', 'Marthe Chenal' and 'Geraldine Farrar' were three Rigaud perfumes named after famous opera singers of the day. A music-hall performer could also lend a fascinating personality to a perfume, such as 'Sahary Djeli', introduced by Delettrez in 1910, which was named after a famous exotic dancer of the period, who had become extraordinarily successful by introducing a dance that only she seemed capable of performing: 'La Danse Prohibée' ('The Forbidden Dance'). She was in fact more a contortionist than a dancer, and was often shown in photographs of the period performing bizarre movements. To emphasize the seemingly impossible positions she was capable of achieving, one issue of *Comœdia Illustré* even included a photograph of her accompanied by an artist's rendition of how she would appear in an X-ray taken while she was holding that pose. She performed in many music-hall revues, and danced a riveting 'Salomé' at Le Casino de Paris, Les Variétés in Brussels and the Hippodrome in London.

Sahary Djeli was clever in self-promotion, and created an entire legend about her origins. She claimed to belong to a strange sect from the Orient, and that her name meant 'La Sorcière du Siècle' ('The Sorceress of the Century'). Although everyone was delighted with her charming tales, there were also reports suggesting that in reality she might have been born on a French farm. While the 'Sahary Djeli' bottle is typical for this period, it is the detailed and attractive label (pls. 54, 55) that tells the story, showing the dancer in movement, wrapped in her veils (possibly her Salomé costume), with a slave kneeling in front of her as he presents a tray, perhaps laden with the head of St John the Baptist. Although the palatial interior decoration created an impression of ancient history, certain inaccuracies together with a mixture of design elements suggested a stage set. In any event, it is remarkable that a small perfume label, which with the patina of age looks like a bronze plaque, could so faithfully record a moment in history.

The name 'Gaby', which became very fashionable, probably because of the popularity of Gaby Deslys, who was one of the most idolized French music-hall artistes of her time and who was particularly successful in London, was used for an Avenel perfume. It was presented in an exquisite floral bottle and a uniquely constructed box with a pair of curved doors which, when opened, disappeared inside the cylindrical sides of the box – recalling a stage (pl. 58). It was the world of fantasy associated with the theatre which led to the use of names of legendary characters in perfume presentations. 'Laïs', a Delettrez perfume, was based on a mythical Greek courtesan from Thessaly, so threatening a figure that all the wives of that region co-operated in murdering her. The heart-shaped perfume label – one of the most important ever produced – depicted the reclining figure of Laïs against an idyllic classical landscape (pls. 52, 53).

Hygiènof began in 1915 as a household soaps company, adopting as its symbol the figure of Pierrot in a spotless white coat. Among Hygiènof's first perfumes was 'Pierrot Vainqueur' ('Victorious Pierrot'), in which he is depicted being kissed by Pierrette (pl. 74). In 1918, a French company, Parfumerie Brissac, recently founded in Argentina, introduced 'Lune d'Amour' ('Moon of Love') in a French-produced presentation (pl. 62). Its poetic name, inspired by Pierrot, was expressed beautifully on the very unusual crescent-moon label.

René Lalique, like Poiret, was a great innovator whose style showed great versatility and continued to evolve throughout his career. As this decade progressed, Lalique's style became more modern in feeling, and the overall shapes of his designs became more abstract and geometric. However, he had a preference for using surface motifs inspired by nature, and c. 1912 he designed for Coty an Art Nouveau bronze plaque to be affixed inside the lid of sumptuous wooden cases containing 12 tester bottles, all with Lalique paper labels (45). Lalique also began working with many other perfume companies, one of his creations being a glass sign (pl. 59) for the Roger & Gallet shop in the rue du Faubourg-Saint-Honoré, Paris. Among the Art Nouveau flowers on this sign, the name Roger & Gallet appeared in elegant moulded letter forms which Lalique had originally designed for his personal letterhead in 1886.

An iridescent blue bottle and a stopper in the form of a bee collecting pollen from a flower distinguished a new Coty perfume of 1912 called 'Au Cœur des Calices' ('At the Heart of the Calyx'). Created by Lalique, this presentation was a masterpiece of design and technique, in which the bee and the calyx were realistically emphasized by the use of a brown patina, while droplets of dew clearly visible on the flower suggested early morning (pl. 57). In order to convey realistically the translucent quality of water, these

45 Coty, Tester, *c.* 1912, bronze plaque and labels by René Lalique, twelve Dépinoix bottles no. 136. W. of box 15.5 cm (6⅛ in.); h. of bottle 5.7 cm (2¼ in.).

dewdrops were moulded in relief on the inside of the bottle, the outside surface being left smooth. This inner relief was a unique feature, very difficult to achieve technically, which brought about a shimmering quality produced by the play of light on the surface of the bottle.

Two years earlier, another Art Nouveau masterpiece had been either created or strongly influenced by Lalique. Although unsigned, 'Cigalia', a Roger & Gallet perfume, is attributed to Lalique, because it resembled the design for 'Quatre Cigales' ('Four Cicadas'), the first bottle which Lalique designed for his own company, also in 1910. The design principle adopted for 'Cigalia' was the same as that used for 'Scarabée' (L. T. Piver, 1909). The identical front and back of the bottle, each featuring two upright cicadas, formed a mirror image (pl. 79). In 1903, Lalique and Gaillard had exhibited very similar brooches, each depicting two cicadas. The 'Cigalia' box motif with its two confrontational cicadas was identical to Gaillard's brooch. It may never be possible to establish who designed 'Cigalia' or what was the exact nature of the collaboration between Lalique and Gaillard.

The Art Nouveau movement made frequent use of motifs derived from nature, often featuring creatures that are considered by many people to be unattractive, for example insects and reptiles. Baccarat adapted this influence perfectly to its own style, notably in the bottle produced in 1914 for 'Champs-Elysées' ('Elysian Fields'), an existing Guerlain perfume. Modelled to represent an upright turtle, almost identical front and back, it was faceted overall (pl. 87). To reinforce the Art Nouveau spirit, the earliest versions of the 'Cigalia' and 'Champs-Elysées' perfumes were both coloured green. 'Au Soleil' ('In the Sun'), was an avant-garde creation introduced by Lubin some time between 1909 and 1912. This presentation was most likely designed as early as 1909, the same year as 'Scarabée', in which case the concept would have been even more avant-garde. The bottle and stopper depicted a lighthouse, with a lizard crawling towards the light to catch a fly (pl. 85). This sculptural group was designed as an integrated unit, representative of the perfume name, by Maurice Dépinoix, an early exponent of perfume presentations whose genius has yet to receive proper recognition. Dépinoix introduced his own unique perspective to interpretations which often blended and streamlined floral and vegetal motifs into abstract shapes.

In the course of this decade many other completely new bottle shapes were introduced. One innovation by Lalique was a design for a circular bottle with flattened body, technically difficult to produce. He used this new model in 1912 for 'Misti', an L. T. Piver perfume continuing the Art Nouveau tradition by decorating the surface of the bottle with moulded flowers and butterflies (46). However, this bottle also incorporated a rare feature – in the form of a convex base which allowed the bottle to be rocked, so creating the impression of fluttering butterfly wings. 'Auteuil', a perfume by Lalo, was introduced in 1919 in an extremely flat, circular Lalique bottle (47). Lalo was an exclusive leather goods company which introduced a few of its own

46 L. T. Piver, 'Misti', 1912, René Lalique design and bottle. H. 5.0 cm (2 in.).

47 Lalo, 'Auteuil', 1919, René Lalique design and bottle. H. 4.0 cm (1⅝ in.).

perfumes, the names of which suggested elegant places, like 'Ritz' (the famous hotel) or 'Auteuil' (the fashionable racetrack in the Bois de Boulogne). All Lalo perfumes were presented in the same Lalique model, but the special edition of 'Auteuil' had a stopper of black glass and black enamelling on the upper portion of its clear-glass bottle.

Another very important artist, whose work in the field of perfume presentations also deserves greater recognition, was the sculptor Julien Viard. After the war, Julien and his father, Clovis, also a sculptor, opened a workshop specializing in glass creations. While there are doubts as to whether Clovis was directly involved in designing perfume bottles, it is probable that some of his sculptures may have served as models for figural stoppers in perfume presentations. Julien Viard exhibited extensively, and seems to have begun designing perfume bottles shortly after being awarded the prestigious Prix de Rome in 1907. One of his first creations must have been 'Isadora', an extremely rare Caron perfume of 1910. The opalescent bottle (pl. 60), in the shape of an ancient Greek amphora, combined a very avant-garde concept with a classical form. It was decorated with a circular frieze, highlighted with brown patina, in which the American dancer Isadora Duncan, then at the height of her success, is shown in three poses, barefoot and wearing a loose Grecian-style tunic. It is also likely that Julien Viard designed 'Parfum Précieux' ('Precious Perfume') for Caron: an elongated opalescent amphora-shaped bottle with a scarab-shaped stopper (pl. 60).

Isadora Duncan's role in reviving interest in ancient Greece also served as an influence on Lalique, who in 1911 created 'Ambre d'Orsay', perhaps the first use of an all-black glass bottle, featuring four caryatids. Then, in 1912, he designed a circular silver-gilt frieze depicting a group of Grecian dancers, which was placed on a bottle in the form of a simple frosted cylinder made by Baccarat (possibly a first for that company) that was used for another version of 'Ambre d'Orsay' (48).

The most important contribution made by Viard to perfume presentations was his development of stoppers in the form of human figures. Here, an exquisite sculptural stopper became the featured element, with the bottle serving as its pedestal. Such stoppers were conceived to be disproportionately small vis-à-vis the bottle, so producing a very elegant relationship. One of the first stoppers of this type was designed by Viard before the war, and then used c. 1919 for 'Blue Lagoon', an early Dubarry perfume, inspired by the title of a romantic novel by Henry de Vere Stacpoole (pl. 64). The frosted glass stopper, which portrayed a young Egyptian princess, had a multicoloured patina and gilding to emphasize the most minute details, while the bottle had a lotus flower as its motif. This romantic composition expressed the poetic name beautifully, without any literal interpretation.

Many other sculptural stoppers were designed by Viard, often in the form of exotic Grecian or oriental figures (pls. 65, 66, 68, 69). One of the most beautiful examples, however, was a replica of a bronze seal by Clovis

48 D'Orsay, 'Ambre d'Orsay', 1912, Baccarat bottle no. 173, silver-gilt frieze designed by René Lalique; another version, 1911, René Lalique design and bottle. H. 13.5 cm (5¼ in.); 13.2 cm (5¼ in.).

Viard depicting Pierrot. This model (pl. 67) was originally used in 1919 for the Dubarry perfume 'A Toi' ('To You') and was later adopted by other companies, for example by Gilot for 'Chypre de Fleur'. Julien Viard also created representational stoppers featuring floral motifs, butterflies etc. (49). The influence of this style on Lalique was evident in the latter's delicate draped figure designed for use with d'Orsay 'Roses', for which Lalique also designed the rare leaf-shaped perfume card, both of 1919 (52).

Another innovation by Viard was the moulding of full landscape views on perfume bottles – a considerable technical feat. He created the first such model in 1912 for 'Gai Paris', a T. Jones perfume. The bottle featured two popular images of Paris: on the front the Champs-Elysées and the Arc de Triomphe (pl. 88), much visited by day, and on the back the Moulin Rouge, a night-time attraction. The stopper presented an eye-mask, as worn at costume balls, thus reinforcing the concept of having fun in Gay Paris (50). Later that year, Viard created 'Désir Princier' ('Princely Desire') for Lenthéric, but instead of being moulded, two different detailed landscapes were exquisitely enamelled on the front and back of the bottle (pls. 89, 90). These striking miniatures depicted two views of Touraine, a region of France rich in important historical associations with princes and Renaissance castles.

Early in this decade, a new artistic tendency was being felt in France, known as the 'harmony of contrasts'. The author and painter Jacques-Emile Blanche called it the 'folly of black and white', and traced it to the work of the English illustrator Aubrey Beardsley. This 'harmony of contrasts' first became fashionable in England before conquering the United States and then Paris. Perfume presentations introduced this concept by juxtaposing black glass and clear glass. 'Narcisse Noir' ('Black Narcissus'), a Caron perfume of 1911, may have been the first example of this combination (pl. 70). Its silk-covered box also displayed a harmony between light shades and black. Two perfumes by F. Wolff & Sohn of c. 1913, 'Narcissus' and 'Jasmin', were

50 T. Jones, 'Gai Paris', 1912.
Back of bottle, stopper removed.

51 Bourjois, 'Mon Parfum', 1919, Baccarat bottle no. 421. H. 9.3 cm (3⅝ in.).

52 D'Orsay, 'Roses', 1919, René Lalique design and bottle, and rare perfumed card designed by Lalique. H. of bottle 10.0 cm (4 in.).

53 T. Jones, 'Veni-Vici', 1911, Baccarat bottle no. 368; L. T. Piver, 'Floramye' and 'Pompeia', 1919, Baccarat bottle no. 411; L. T. Piver, 'Volt', 1922. H. 10.5 cm (4⅛ in.); 6.5 cm (2½ in.); 8.7 cm (3⅜ in.).

offered in clear-glass bottles designed by Julien Viard, combined with black stoppers in the form of a six-pointed star with a mythological scene (pl. 72). Black crystal and clear crystal were juxtaposed for two perfumes by Bourjois: 'Talis' of 1912 (pl. 73), a creation of Cristalleries de Saint-Louis, and 'Mon Parfum' ('My Perfume') of 1919 (51). Other companies displayed this 'harmony of contrasts' by applying black enamelling in a dramatic way on the upper portion of the bottle, as in 'Chypre' by Alphonse Gravier (pl. 71) and the special edition of 'Auteuil' by Lalo (47).

The last major influence on this decade's perfume presentations in France was the early Art Deco style, a simplification of the Louis XVI and Louis-Philippe styles. However, this return to tradition was infused with a dazzling sense of colour and energy derived from the Ballets Russes. The illustrators who worked for fashion magazines, *La Gazette du Bon Ton* in particular, were at the origin of the Art Deco movement: Georges Barbier, Georges Lepape and Charles Martin were among those who replaced classic rigid elegance with whimsical and youthful grace in their drawings of fashions and interiors, simplifying ornate details into basic shapes and using bright, often unconventional, colour combinations.

This new style soon became the preferred choice of many perfume companies, and was particularly successful when used on paper graphics, as seen in the early Gabilla floral designs on bottles and labels. Such Gabilla perfumes included 'Violette', in a tall graceful bottle, and 'Pour Changer' ('For a Change'), in much simpler bottles (pl. 75). A powder box for Ernest Coty (no relation of François Coty) depicted the current concept of ideal feminine beauty, as conveyed in illustrations of the time (pl. 77). Co-ordinated Art Deco graphics were used on bottles and boxes, and the Lubin perfume 'Bouquet de Papillons' ('Bouquet of Butterflies') was an exquisitely delicate and playful presentation (pl. 78). Another playful presentation in the early Art Deco style was 'Un Peu d'Ambre' ('A Little Bit of Amber') by Houbigant (pl. 76). A simple Baccarat bottle was used, but here, for the first time, the narrow side of the bottle was treated as the front, and the label was placed there, as if to emphasize 'a little bit'. The box opened, unusually, on its narrow side; on it were depicted baby whales leaping from the ocean waves – a reference to ambergris (obtained from sperm whales), the traditional ingredient used in so-called 'amber' perfume formulations.

A new version for 'Le Triomphe' ('The Triumph'), a Gueldy perfume dating from 1912, was introduced immediately after the war. The striped bottle with a floral stopper was also a typical early Art Deco object, and the avant-garde label showed the Arc de Triomphe inside the 'O' of the word 'Triomphe' (pl. 48). Another Gueldy perfume, 'La Feuilleraie', was given a new presentation in 1919. The name 'La Feuilleraie' was a fabricated word, implying 'the place of leaves'. The surface of the bottle was appropriately moulded, the leaves being coloured sienna-red, and the large gold paper label depicted a landscape with windswept leaves (pl. 49). The outer covering of the box was printed with a leaf pattern in autumnal colours. All the elements of this presentation were perfectly in tune with decorations of the period.

Arys was a perfume company which emerged during the war. Georges Lepape created all its early advertising, and the simple design of the Arys bottles (pl. 81) was inspired by the delicate Lepape drawings. 'Un Jour Viendra' ('A Day Will Come') displayed a pattern of circles. 'L'Heure Heureuse' ('The Happy Hour') had vertical stripes with a rose pattern and 'Un Jardin la Nuit' ('A Garden at Night') featured a trellis pattern. The motifs used on all three boxes were familiar Lepape designs.

This decade witnessed the increasing popularity of modern representational perfume bottles, the stopper and bottle being designed as an integral unit to form a recognizable shape. Among the first examples of such bottles was the very advanced T. Jones perfume presentation 'Veni-Vici' ('I Came, I Conquered') of 1911. The Baccarat bottle had a metal cover, and the entire presentation was shaped like a cartridge, with the cover in the shape of a bullet. Using two-thirds of Julius Cæsar's famous phrase was quite restrained; it gave the perfume a briefer and more distinctive name while stimulating recall of the entire phrase. In 1919, L. T. Piver introduced a purse perfume bottle in the shape of a cigarette lighter, associated with the fact that after the war liberated women were even smoking in public. Shortly thereafter, L. T. Piver introduced the perfume 'Volt', appropriately housed in a bottle shaped like a light bulb – yet another example of the whimsical presentations stimulated by Art Deco (53).

In 1917, Grenoville introduced 'Le Beau Masque' ('The Beautiful Mask') in a bottle that was both eccentric and fanciful, a very advanced design (54). It portrayed an androgynous figure, a small masked face over a disproportionately large robed body, maybe a puppet. The eye-mask and physical

54 Grenoville, 'Le Beau Masque', 1917. H. 16.0 cm (6¼ in.).

55 De Vigny, 'Golliwogg' lotion, 1919. H. 16.5 cm (6½ in.).

56 De Vigny, 'Golliwogg', 1919: tester bottle; small round bottle and box and larger round bottle, both Baccarat no. 378; cylindrical bottle, Baccarat no. 524; large bottle with fur hair and box, also medium, small and smallest sizes in open boxes; red and yellow powder boxes; enamelled bronze pin in front. Figural bottles and all labels designed by Michel de Brunhoff. H. of bottles 5.7 cm (2¼ in.); 5.8 cm (2¼ in.); 8.7 cm (3⅜ in.); 7.5 cm (3 in.); 17.0 cm (6¾ in.); 10.0 cm (4 in.); 8.0 cm (3⅛ in.); 7.0 cm (2¾ in.).

proportions of this figure resembled those of a group of marionettes for which Lepape designed costumes in 1917, and also resembled other Lepape works dating from between 1911 and 1915. This historically important bottle may have been the first rendering of a full-length figure.

Perhaps the most influential figure in the propagation of the Art Deco movement in general was Lucien Vogel, who through his fashion magazines would change the style of a whole epoch. Vogel founded *La Gazette du Bon Ton*, *Jardin des Modes* and French *Vogue* in collaboration with his wife Cosette and her brother, Michel de Brunhoff. Their high standards and creativity attracted the best artists and illustrators. Lucien Vogel also started de Vigny perfumes, though his involvement with the company lasted for only a short time. One of the first de Vigny perfumes was 'Golliwogg', introduced in 1919. The graphics for 'Golliwogg' and its basic bottle design were by Michel de Brunhoff. It was an appropriate moment for the Golliwogg – originally a character (based on an American rag doll) in children's books by Florence and Bertha Upton published in England – to become popular in France, as the Jazz Age had just begun in 1917, when Gaby Deslys returned from her American tour accompanied by the first black jazz band to visit Europe. The rare first edition of the 'Golliwogg' perfume had a black-glass stopper which portrayed the character's face and hair (55), whereas the next edition used real fur to simulate hair (56). Charles Martin designed all the early de Vigny advertising in *La Gazette du Bon Ton*. The three Lalique bottles used for early de Vigny perfumes, 'Musky' (de Vigny's first perfume), 'Ambre' and 'Jamerose', were directly inspired by Martin's ethereal style (pl. 86).

In 1919, Maurice Babani became the second fashion designer to produce his own perfume. Very little is known about Babani except that he had a predilection for oriental fashions and gold embroidery. Babani must have had Poiret in mind when he introduced his first perfumes, since the box for 'Jasmin de Corée' ('Korean Jasmine') was covered with a less delicate rendition of the 'Nuit de Chine' pattern, the Babani signature being printed on the underside. However, unlike Poiret, who created so many different models, Babani used bottles made of clear glass decorated with gilding and imaginative black designs for all his luxury presentations. As a result, all these Babani perfumes had clearly recognizable features in common (pl. 80).

The decade from 1910 to 1919 witnessed major advances in the style of perfume presentations. Leading designers such as Paul Poiret, René Lalique and Julien Viard created outstanding presentations, as did other less well documented figures like Maurice Dépinoix and Lucien Gaillard. Following a period of inevitable restraint during World War I, many new presentations appeared in 1919. This amazing growth in both the artistic quality and the variety of designs would accelerate further during the 1920s, a decade in which creativity was clearly in its full flowering stage.

36 Les Parfums de Rosine, 'Pierrot',
1919. Bottle with ruff, and box.
H. 11.7 cm (4⅝ in.).

74

The aura of Ancient Egypt

Left
42 Bichara, 'Myrbaha', 1913.
Baccarat bottle no. 228.
H. 15.0 cm (5⅞ in.).

Below
43 Ahmed Soliman, unidentified
perfume, *c.* 1919. H. 9.5 cm
(3¾ in.).

Opposite above
44, 45 Ramsès, 'Ramsès IV', 1919.
Baccarat bottle no. 403 with stopper
in imitation of the double-plumed
crown worn by certain deities and
pharaohs.
H. 12.0 cm (4¾ in.).

46 Ahmed Soliman, group of
bottles, *c.* 1919 (from left to right):
'Attar of Roses'; 'Antique Ambar';
'Royal Ambar'; unidentified.
H. 19.0 cm (7½ in.) and (smaller
size) 15.0 cm (5⅞ in.).

47 Ramsès, powder box, 1918.
D. 7.7 cm (3 in.).

48 Gueldy, 'Le Triomphe', 1919.
Julien Viard design. Bottle with label
incorporating the Arc de Triomphe.
H. 9.0 cm (3½ in.).

49 Gueldy, 'La Feuilleraie;, 1919.
Julien Viard design. Box containing
bottle with moulded decoration and
prominent label.
H. 9.6 cm (3¾ in.).

Top
50, 51 Gueldy, 'Le Bois Sacré',
1910. Detail of label, and box with
bottle.
H. of label 3.8 cm (1½ in.); of bottle
11.5 cm (4½ in.).

Centre
52, 53 Delettrez, 'Laïs', *c.* 1914.
Detail of label, and box with
Dépinoix bottle. H. of label 3.6 cm
(1⅜ in.); of bottle 11.2 cm (4⅜ in.).

Right
54, 55 Delettrez. 'Sahary Djeli',
1910. Detail of label, and bottle with
brass cap over inner stopper.
H. of label 4.0 cm (1⅝ in.); of bottle
12.6 cm (5 in.).

Opposite
56, 57 Bottles designed and made by
René Lalique: d'Héraud, 'Phalène',
c. 1919; Coty, 'Au Cœur des Calices',
1912.
H. 7.8 cm (3⅛ in.) and 6.6 cm
(2⅝ in.).

Above
58 Avenel, 'Gaby', *c.* 1913. Julien
Viard design. Box with bottle.
H. 9.5 cm (3¾ in.).

Right
59 Glass sign designed and made
by René Lalique for Roger & Gallet,
c. 1913.
W. 25.0 cm (9⅞ in.).

Opposite
60 Caron, 'Isadora' (standing) and
'Parfum Précieux', both 1910. Julien
Viard designs.
H. 16.6 cm (6½ in.) and 15.2 cm
(6 in.).

Above
61 De Burmann, 'La Sirène'. Bottle
designed *c.* 1912. and made by René
Lalique; introduced *c.* 1935.
H. 10.5 cm (4⅛ in.).

Above right
62 Brissac, 'Lune d'Amour', 1918.
Bottle in open box.
H. 12.5 cm (4⅞ in.).

Right
63 A decorative perfume bottle by
René Lalique et Cie: 'Fougères' or
'No. 489', 1912.
H. 9.5 cm (3¾ in.).

Julien Viard designs, Dépinoix bottles.

64 Dubarry, 'Blue Lagoon',
c. 1919, bottle in open box.
H. 10.5 cm (4⅛ in.).

Below
65, 66 Félix Boissard, 'Madelon',
c. 1919, front and back views.
H. 10.0 cm (4 in.).

Opposite above
67 Dubarry, 'A Toi', 1919; and
Gilot, 'Chypre de Fleur', *c.* 1922.
H. 17.0 cm (6¾ in.); 12.0 cm
(4¾ in.).

Opposite below left
68 Dubarry, 'Fantôme d'Orient',
c. 1919, box and bottle.
H. 8.0 cm (3⅛ in.).

Opposite below right
69 Dubarry, 'Garden of Kama',
1919, box and bottle.
H. 10.0 cm (4 in.).

Right
70 Caron, 'Narcisse Noir', 1911.
Large and medium-size boxes and
bottles and small bottle; and (right)
the rare 'Narcisse Blanc', 1923,
medium size.
H. large 8.5 cm (3⅝ in.), medium
5.5 cm (2⅛ in.), small 4.0 cm
(1⅝ in.).

Below
71 A. Gravier, 'Chypre', *c.* 1919.
Box and bottle.
H. 10.8 cm (4¼ in.).

Below right
72 F. Wolff & Sohn, 'Jasmin' and
'Narcissus' (in box), both *c.* 1913.
Julien Viard design.
H. 5.5 cm (2⅛ in.); 4.5 cm (1¾ in.).

Above
73 Bourjois, 'Talis', 1912. Bottle
by Cristalleries de Saint-Louis.
H. 11.3 cm (4½ in.).

Left
74 Hygiènof, 'Pierrot Vainqueur',
1918. Julien Viard design. Dépinoix
bottle.
H. 11.5 cm (4½ in.).

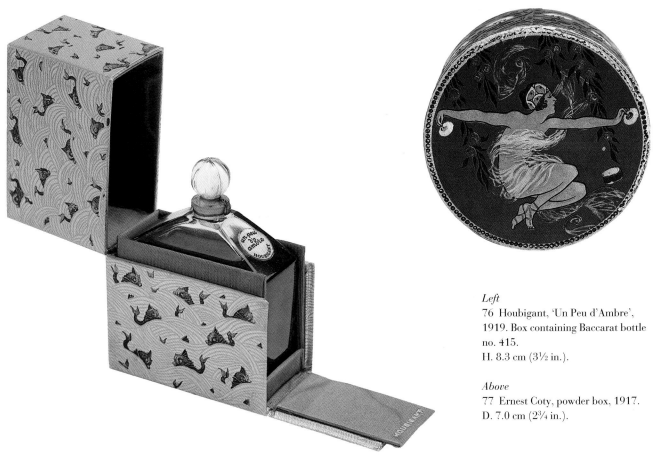

Left
76 Houbigant, 'Un Peu d'Ambre',
1919. Box containing Baccarat bottle
no. 415.
H. 8.3 cm (3½ in.).

Above
77 Ernest Coty, powder box, 1917.
D. 7.0 cm (2¾ in.).

Opposite
75 Gabilla perfumes: 'Violette'
(left), enamelled green and clear
bottles, *c.* 1912 (possibly designed by
Julien Viard), h. 13.5 cm (5½ in.);
'Pour Changer' (right), 1917, in two
sizes (smaller example Baccarat no.
372), h. 17.8 cm (7 in.) and 9.5 cm
(3¾ in.). First three bottles made by
Société Parisienne de Verreries.

Right
78 Lubin, 'Bouquet de Papillons',
1918. Box with bottle designed and
made by Maurice Dépinoix.
H. 7.6 cm (3 in.).

Below
79 Roger & Gallet, 'Cigalia', 1910.
Box and bottle containing earliest
green perfume.
H. 13.2 cm (5¼ in.).

80 Babani perfumes (from left to right):
'Ambre de Delhi', 1919, medium (back view)
and large (front), both Dépinoix bottle no.
218, and small size in foreground, Dépinoix
bottle 129; 'Chypre Egyptien', 1919, back
and front of oval Dépinoix bottle no. 5718,
and small size Dépinoix bottle no. 129 in
foreground with box; 'Abdulla', 1926;
'Nandita', 1925.
H. of largest bottle 18.5 cm (7¼ in.),
smallest 6.6 cm (2⅝ in.).

81 Group of Arys products with sign in
foreground (from left to right): 'Un Jardin la
Nuit', 1919, bottle and box (green flowers);
box of similar design (yellow flowers)
containing 'Parlez-lui de Moi', 1919; 'Le
Chypre', 1917, Baccarat bottle no. 327;
'L'Amour dans le Cœur', c. 1920, bottle with
figural stopper, Julien Viard design; 'Un Jour
Viendra', 1918, bottle and box; 'L'Heure
Heureuse', c. 1920, bottle and box; 'Le
Chypre', 1920, bottle designed and made by
René Lalique; 'Le Jasmin', c. 1920 (in back-
ground), and 'L'Amour dans le Cœur', 1920
(in foreground), both designed and made by
René Lalique; 'L'Heure Heureuse', 1918,
Julien Viard design, bottle and box; and
'L'Œillet' powder box.
H. of largest bottle 14.0 cm (5½ in.),
smallest 6.5 cm (2½ in.).

Left
82 Guerlain, 'Quand vient l'été',
1910. Box and bottle.
H. 22.5 cm (8⅞ in.).

Above
83 Silka, 'Ikonia', 1917. Baccarat
bottle no. 352.
H. 10.5 cm (4⅛ in.).

84 Bryenne, 'Chu Chin Chow',
1918. Figural bottle designed
by G. K. Benda.
H. 6.2 cm (2½ in.).

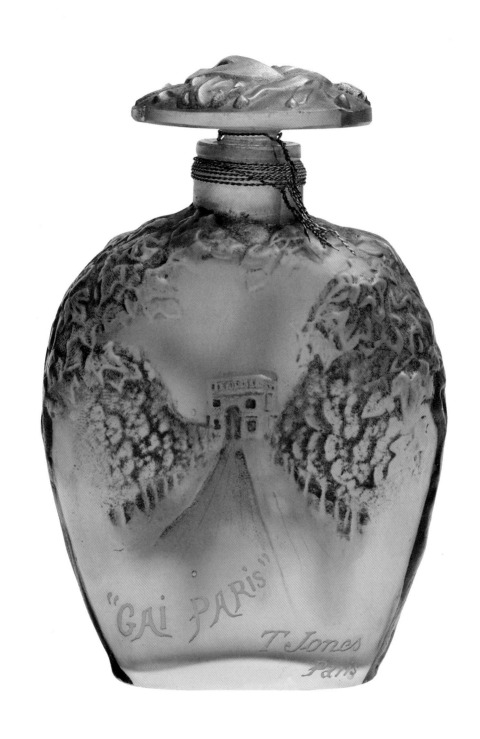

Opposite
88 T. Jones, 'Gai Paris', 1912.
Julien Viard design. Front of bottle,
incorporating view of the Arc de
Triomphe and the Avenue des
Champs-Elysées.
H. 9.8 cm (3⅞ in.).

89, 90 Lenthéric, 'Désir Princier',
1912. Julien Viard design. Front and
back of bottle.
H. 11.3 cm (4½ in.).

When accounts were settled after World War I, the losses in terms of human lives and permanent injuries were staggering. This unprecedented disaster left no winners, but for those still fortunate enough to have survived unscathed it seemed as if life would be better if lived to excess, and so the 'Roaring Twenties' began. In France a large proportion of the new generation of young adults had been destroyed, and industry, agriculture and commerce had suffered greatly. There was now a new class of impoverished people, and owing to the general disorganization and confusion there were all kinds of shortages, including a dearth of workmen and skilled artisans. The activity of luxury industries, including of course perfume production, had been placed on hold.

Out of this chaos a 'new woman' was emerging as the 1920s began. While her husband had been away at war, she had been obliged to manage family and business affairs by herself. If, as so often happened, he did not return, she remained in charge. The social conventions of the 19th century were gone forever. This new woman had gained her freedom inadvertently, and now was active and busy. She looked around in search of role models, and discovered one in Suzanne Lenglen, the French tennis player who, in 1919, at the age of only twenty, had won the first of her six women's singles titles at the Wimbledon championships. Initially, her tennis-court fashions were considered daring and risqué, but before long they were being adapted for everyday wear, as major fashion innovators such as Chanel and Patou started to create sporty, comfortable, yet elegant women's clothes. Although Suzanne Lenglen was no beauty, she was muscular, tanned and athletic. It was not long before she emerged as an important symbol of this decade's fascination with fast action and speed. Consequently, when Victor Marguerite published his novel *Une Garçonne* (literally 'A Boyish Woman') in 1922, it proved a great success. The new woman was called 'la garçonne', which was also the name given to the new short hairstyle, known in English as the 'urchin cut'.

Fashions changed accordingly. Women went to jazz clubs, and no longer dressed like Persian queens. The British sporting life, the relaxed and understated elegance of British clothes became the latest influence on Parisian attire and lifestyle. The city's night life revived, and a new group of visitors

Facing page
91 Marcel Guerlain, 'Rolls Royce', 1926. Bottle with decorative mascot stopper (replacing utilitarian glass stopper used when packed for distribution) and Bakelite base. H. 13.7 cm (5⅜ in.).

from abroad, mostly well-to-do Americans, came to Paris to see the spectacular music-hall revues and nude shows.

France had not only benefited from military intervention by the United States during the war, but the economic gains continued throughout this decade. When they returned home from Europe, countless American soldiers took back such luxury goods and perfumes as were available, and in this way these symbols of French culture reached a new, broader and increasingly affluent market. In the 1920s, the economic expansion in the United States was unprecedented, and business in general flourished, including the beauty business. Three enterprising women – Harriet Hubbard Ayer, Elizabeth Arden and Helena Rubinstein – contributed to this development by establishing international cosmetics empires. Their timing was opportune, for women had become very independent, particularly in the United States. Not only did they now smoke in public, but they drove fast cars and wore makeup and perfume. The perfume industry in post-war France expanded rapidly, with countless new perfumes being created in the hope of finding an export market in the United States. Many new perfume companies were established, all dreaming the same dream. Trends in new perfume presentation styles were as varied and excessive as life in general became during the 1920s.

Early Art Deco was now prevalent – an appealing style that caused the decorative arts to thrive. It became the focal point of the Exposition Internationale des Arts Décoratifs et Industriels Modernes, a major international exhibition, originally scheduled for 1915, but delayed by the war until 1925, when it had a widespread impact. There was evidence of influences from many artistic movements. Paris was a centre for the development of avant-garde ideas in the arts. Around 1909, for example, Cubism had been born in Paris with Braque and Picasso – at exactly the same time as Lalique and Coty were collaborating; these events took place the same time and in the same place, but were worlds apart. Before the war, perfume presentations had generally ignored other artistic currents. Cubism had been rejected by critics and by the public, just as foreign movements, such as the Wiener Werkstätte, Constructivism, De Stijl and the Bauhaus, had initially been rejected in France. However, these influences, as well as African art, would eventually affect the Art Deco style and the design of perfume presentations. Throughout the 1920s, there were creative opportunities in abundance, and the new world demand for perfume encouraged diversity in its presentation which, as a result, appears in retrospect to have had no clear sense of direction in style during this decade.

Some companies, such as L. T. Piver and Roger & Gallet, primarily continued with their established styles, and only developed more modern designs after 1922. Some companies were influenced by Lalique, others by Poiret and the artists around him. Many couture houses introduced perfumes in association with their fashion designs. As the 1925 exhibition approached, the applied and decorative arts in general had an increasingly important effect on perfume presentations, while the music-hall entertainment continued to exert a major influence through the display of elaborate sets and costumes which fuelled a wide variety of perfume fantasies. The multiplicity of styles associated with this decade can best be understood by reviewing the many individual themes used for perfume presentations.

In this golden age of music-hall, many important fashion illustrators became involved with the 'grandes revues', which were unlike anything seen on stage before, displaying elaborate sets and sumptuous costumes. Each revue stimulated design creativity through the sheer variety of the themes presented and through its magic fantasies. Balls, romance and legends became popular perfume themes, as did the Orient, Venice, jewelry and gems. And nudity was everywhere.

The 'Carnaval de Venise' atmosphere was a familiar aspect of Paris night life, as were balls and masquerades. In 1925, Marcel Guerlain (unrelated to Guerlain perfumes) introduced 'Masque Rouge' ('Red Mask'), in a very modern bottle (which now appears standard), with a box on which the superb red-mask motif was prominently featured. The lower part of the label bearing the initials MG had been deliberately designed to look 'cut off', partially 'disguising' the company's identity. The title 'Masque Rouge' referred not only to fashionable masked balls, but also, obliquely, to the newly accepted custom of women wearing lipstick, rouge and makeup, any time, anywhere. The popularity of masquerades was reflected in the names of two perfumes: 'Mascarades', by Cherigan, in a standard black bottle but with a most unusual front decoration – a golden face under a rain of gold dust, suggesting a black eye-mask blending into the night; and 'Mascarade', by L. T. Piver, in a gilded red glass bottle shaped like a crinoline. Ciro 'Maskee' and Colgate 'Piquante' also used the masked-ball theme. (Pl. 96)

Closely related to the masquerade theme was 'Arlequinade', a Rosine perfume featuring a superb rendering of the Harlequin costume – gilded and clear triangles on the bottle, a dark-green Bakelite stopper in the form of Harlequin's hat and an orange wool tassel (pl. 96). This perfume name was almost identical to a Russian ballet entitled *Harlequinade*, which was seen in Paris in 1922 – a Commedia dell'Arte melodrama in which reality was hidden by masked characters. This sombre concept was probably appropriate to Poiret's own mood in 1923, when he gradually began to lose control of his business. He loved the Harlequin persona, and owned one of Picasso's paintings on the Harlequin theme (now in the Museum of Modern Art, New York) – a work which he was soon forced to sell as his financial condition worsened. The Dubarry perfume 'The Heart of a Rose' also featured baroque masks (pl. 105), and could have referred to the 13th-century allegorical poem, 'Le Roman de la Rose'. The music-hall stage was perfectly suited to such elaborate and romantic fairy-tale productions, in which the hero and heroine customarily 'live happily ever after'. They provided many appealing themes for perfumes. In the case of 'Contes de Fées' ('Fairy Tales'), a Violet

57 Marques de Elorza, 'Marche Nuptiale', 1929, Julien Viard design, bottles and boxes. H. 10.3 cm (4 in.); 7.0 cm (2¾ in.).

58 Robertet, 'Boîte à Mouillettes', c. 1920, Julien Viard design, Dépinoix box. W. 18.5 cm (7¼ in.).

perfume, the treasure-chest box was decorated with scenes from five classic French fairy tales, and opened to reveal a turbaned bottle within (pl. 135).

'Marche Nuptiale' ('Wedding March'), the name of a Marques de Elorza perfume, was adopted from the title of a stage play. The bottle displayed a scene with a bride, holding hands with Cupid, ascending to the temple of love, while the box resembled a Gothic arch over a stepped base (57). All elements worked together to evoke a romantic feeling with religious overtones. By contrast, 'Nuit de Mariage' ('Wedding Night') by de Paul was an abstract presentation in which a melon-shaped clear-glass bottle and its needle-sharp stopper were covered in a multitude of tiny green-glass dots (pl. 106). This fragile and graceful model expressed femininity and vulnerability, while its steeple-shaped box suggested Gothic religious architecture. The presentation for 'Le Chevalier de la Nuit' ('The Knight of the Night'), one of the first Ciro perfumes, was a superb modern interpretation by Viard of the theme of a medieval knight in armour (pl. 95).

Specific theatrical productions continued to lend their titles to perfumes during the 1920s. Lubin introduced 'Magda' in 1921, its name derived from a successful play in which the role of the eponymous heroine had been portrayed by Sarah Bernhardt, Eleonora Duse and Mrs Patrick Campbell since 1892. This was another superb Viard presentation, with a stopper in the form of a charming sculpted head of a young girl surmounting a gracefully sloping bottle (pl. 103). Similarly, in 1924 'Le Miracle' took its name from a successful operatic drama first staged in 1910 with spectacular scenery. The story, about a miracle involving a saint and a courtesan, was set in Burgundy in the 15th century, and provided Marthe Chenal with her greatest role. In this presentation by Lenthéric the black-glass bottle had gold-dust inclusions below the surface (pl. 141), and since an infinite variety of swirls could be produced, each bottle was different. This technique, developed by Georges Dumoulin, was difficult to execute and may have been used only in this case and for 'Borgia', a Rosine perfume.

Following the appearance of a completely nude woman on the French stage for the first time in 1919, nudity became a regular feature of the music hall. In the 1920s, total nudity also made its first appearance in the context of perfume presentations, very different from the previous use of partially draped mythological figures. One of the first such presentations was the '*boîte à mouillettes*' ('box for cotton swabs') designed by Viard to sample various Robertet perfumes (58). Another Viard design – 'Nuit Fleurie' ('Flowery Night') for L'Institut de Beauté – created a theatrical atmosphere by depicting a sleeping female nude watched over by Cupid (59). These nude figures were definitely 20th-century women.

The Franz Lehár operetta *Eva* may have inspired the name of a Bertelli perfume. The front of the Viard bottle for 'Eva' showed a classic portrayal of Eve in a very theatrical Garden of Eden (60), while the sides were decorated with a European landscape (61) identical to that on the Lenthéric 'Désir

Princier' bottle (pls. 89, 90). Another 'Eva', also in a Viard bottle, was a Lubin perfume which presented all the biblical symbols: the bottle was fruit-shaped, and the stopper depicted a naked Eve on a coiled serpent (pl. 98). This finely moulded nude figure could have been a contemporary showgirl.

In Parisian society of the 1920s, entertaining and being entertained was a serious affair. One of the greatest figural perfume presentations of the decade was 'Guili-Guili' by de Vigny. This striking creation of 1926 looked like and was named after a real-life character, an Egyptian magician and illusionist from Alexandria. The 'Guili-Guili' bottle had a head and foot of carved mahogany (62). The head covered the inner stopper, while the foot enabled this fragile and most unusual crystal bottle to stand upright. The bottle was shaped like one of the elements from the sculpture *Endless Column* by Brancusi. In *La Gazette du Bon Ton* of April 1924, the poet Léon-Paul Fargue recalled their first meeting, when he was strolling one evening in the Place Blanche, '. . . a tall lanky fellow asked me for a light . . . "What do you do in life?", I asked him. "Me?" he replied, "I do Guili-Guili." Now it was one of those evenings when I needed some Guili-Guilism myself . . . So I followed the lanky fellow who had asked me for a light. It is then that he showed me some wonderful things . . .'

Fargue took his new acquaintance everywhere, and soon Guili-Guili was in great demand in Parisian society. He performed at parties given by Paul Poiret's sister Nicole, married to the artist André Groult. Marie Laurencin was intrigued by him. He knew Jacques-Emile Blanche, Edouard de Rothschild and J. C. Mardrus (who had translated *The Thousand and One Nights* into French in 1900). Guili-Guili also went to London, where he performed for King George V and Queen Mary.

Now, other perfume companies were ready to catch up with Poiret's use of oriental themes. The style of the still successful Ballets Russes company was now much more international, thanks to the participation of many avant-garde artists, like Balla, Picasso, Derain, Matisse, Survage, Gris, Laurencin, Braque, etc., and to the influence of Jean Cocteau on Diaghilev. For the 'grandes revues', however, oriental opulence provided the ideal background, and this new music-hall style influenced many perfume designs. As early as 1917, two major shows had started the music-hall craze for the Orient: *L'Orient Merveilleux* ('The Wonderful Orient') and *The Thousand and Second Night in Baghdad* (inspired by the Poiret's ball of 1911). While Turkey, Persia, China and Japan had been preferred sources of inspiration in the early years, the shows of the 1920s rediscovered the opulence of India as well. The first presentation to be inspired by India may have been 'Kismet', a Lubin perfume of 1921, in a superbly enamelled Baccarat bottle (pl. 97) in the form of an elephant with its mahout as the stopper – a concept which could have reflected real-life performances on the stage of the Folies Bergère.

Rénaud was a successful company known for its attractive, moderately priced presentations. Most of these were 'omnibus' bottles and boxes supplied

59 L'Institut de Beauté, 'Nuit Fleurie', *c.* 1920, Julien Viard design, Dépinoix bottle. H. 10.5 cm (4⅛ in.).

60, 61 Bertelli, 'Eva', *c.* 1920, Julien Viard design, Dépinoix bottle. Front view and profile of bottle showing landscape design almost identical to that of Lenthéric, 'Désir Princier' (pls. 89, 90). H. 12.3 cm (4⅞ in.).

62 De Vigny, 'Guili-Guili', 1926,
designed by Michel de Brunhoff.
H. 16.0 cm (6¼ in.).

by Cristalleries de Nancy (pl. 118). The term 'omnibus' meant not just that those models were always available in all colours, but that they were also used by other perfume companies. 'Ghedma', a rare Rénaud perfume introduced *c.* 1925, was an example of how surface decoration could transform an ordinary bottle into a luxury presentation. In this case, an omnibus bottle from Cristalleries de Nancy was produced in rare cobalt-blue crystal and covered with gold leaf, except for a rectangular area on the front which served as the label area, in which the perfume name and the 'Ghedma' elephant were enamelled on the blue crystal (pl. 99). A most remarkable feature was that the elephant's trunk extended onto the surrounding gold leaf, where it held a bouquet of flowers. In the context of perfume, this design concept may be unique. 'Ghedma' was advertised as the 'Indian flower of happiness'. It was probably inspired by Ganesha, the Hindu god of wisdom and good fortune. This deity was portrayed in white, with a human body and a sweet elephant head. Both 'Ghedma' and 'Kismet' (meaning 'destiny') were Indian themes with overtones of 'good luck'.

Honoré Payan, a Grasse perfume company, introduced 'Bakanir' in 1927. The understated bottle had an abstract geometric shape, while the gilded and enamelled stopper resembled an exotic headdress (pl. 94). An exquisite ceramic plaque, embedded in the top of a luxurious box covered with painted leather, most likely represented Lakshmi, the perfumed Hindu goddess of fortune, reputed to have been the most beautiful woman. The 'Bakanir' box was one of the most amazing and elegant objects ever produced for a perfume presentation. Another striking oriental creation, 'Ming Toy', was a Forest perfume with an anglicized Chinese name (pl. 100). Forest, a French company, often used English words – then a fashionable practice. 'Ming Toy' was a Western fantasy, not an accurate rendering – like a stage costume somewhere between Chinese and Japanese style. Entirely different, 'Chin-Li' was a very modern Dépinoix creation for Gabilla, a superb presentation using vivid co-ordinated colours – red, orange, yellow or green (green being the rarest) – for bottles and boxes, the latter shaped like a Chinese coolie hat (pl. 112). 'Le Jade', a Roger & Gallet line (pl. 113) also inspired by China, featured graphics designed by Lalique on all labels, boxes and packaging papers. The Lalique bottle, which resembled a Chinese snuff bottle, was made of opaque green glass – a rarely used colour. An exotic bird, seemingly carved into the surface, was in fact moulded in imitation of jade carving. The box and tassel, made of Chinese silk, were equally luxurious.

At this time, most of the Violet perfume presentations were inspired by Japan. Lucien Gaillard designed not only the bottles, but also all related graphics and advertising. Four different models were introduced *c.* 1922: 'Fleur d'Alizé' ('Trade Wind Flower'), 'Pourpre d'Automne' ('Autumnal Crimson'), 'Les Sylvies' and the basic Violet model for single-flower perfumes – ('Jasmin', 'Muguet', 'Rose', etc.). All these models had a tall and flat front with a thin profile, and while they were directly inspired by Japanese *inro* boxes, they were nevertheless unmistakably recognizable as Western products (pl. 132).

In France, ancient Egyptian themes and motifs have traditionally been featured prominently in the decorative arts, and especially so after the tomb of the Pharaoh Tutankhamen was rediscovered in 1922. Such motifs were well suited to the modern style, and L'Institut de Beauté introduced *c.* 1925 a presentation called 'Djavidan' (pl. 108), which represented a curious combination of many foreign elements, ranging from Turkey to Greece to Egypt. The name was Turkish-Armenian, and a coat-of-arms incorporating the crescent moon and star associated with Turkey was enamelled on a crystal bottle in the form of an ancient Greek amphora. A gilded tripod, on which the bottle stood, was decorated with the Egyptian motif of outstretched vulture's wings. The box, with its triangular section, was a totally Egypt-inspired concept. The front panel depicted an Egyptian princess assisted in her beauty rituals by two attendants, and similar decoration continued onto the other two panels. The 'Djavidan' presentation taken as a whole was one of the more sophisticated and unusual creations of the 1920s. In another interpretation of an Egyptian motif, Lalique introduced 'Canarina' in 1928. The pattern on the cobalt-blue glass bottle and on the box (63) was the *udjat* of the sky god Horus. That all-seeing eye was considered to have the power to bestow prosperity and to protect against the 'evil eye'.

A Lubin perfume, 'Enigma', first introduced in 1898, was given a new presentation in 1921. The pyramidal bottle (pl. 110) displayed on one side a sphinx that was partially Greek in form (the body of a lion with a woman's head and bust), and partially Egyptian (the headdress and the absence of wings – the Greek sphinx was winged). The 'Enigma' sphinx was thus an ambiguous creature, an elegant Symbolist interpretation, reminiscent of the smiling female leopard depicted in Fernand Khnopff's painting *Des Caresses* of 1896 (now in the Musées Royaux des Beaux-Arts, Brussels). The name 'Enigma' was written vertically within an Egyptian cartouche emphasizing the design's sculptural quality.

In 1928, Bichara introduced 'Ramsès II' in a tall obelisk-shaped bottle made by Cristalleries de Saint-Louis (pl. 109). This bottle was decorated overall with hieroglyphs, as on the obelisk still standing at Luxor in Egypt (its pendant pair adorns the Place de la Concorde in Paris). Everything about Bichara was taken to excess, just as everything had been in the case of the Pharaoh Rameses II who reigned for 67 years, had six 'Great Wives', fathered more than a hundred 'Regal Children' and lived to be almost 100 years old. Through this presentation, the memory of this great pharaoh of ancient Egypt encountered Bichara, the great Syrian perfumer of Paris.

Meanwhile companies from other countries had also been inspired by Egypt (pl. 111). The German company Dralle introduced its 'Sphinx' in a very unusual bottle – up-to-date, yet classically Egyptian in style. In the United States, a Colgate perfume named 'Egypt' was presented in an

63 Canarina, 1928, bottle designed and made by René Lalique, with box. H. 5.2 cm (2 in.).

64 Cottan, 'Dacry', c. 1921, Julien Viard design, Dépinoix bottle. H. 14.7 cm (5¾ in.).

65 Myrurgia, 'Suspiro de Granada', 1922, Julien Viard design, bottles and boxes. H. 8.0 cm (3⅛ in.); 6.0 cm (2⅜ in.).

amphora-shaped bottle, with a superb Egyptian-style portrait on label and box, while La Ducale, an Italian company, used a stylized Egyptian woman with a contemporary face for the powder 'Egizia'. Other ancient cultures, such as that of Babylon, were also of interest both to music-hall artistes and to perfumers – as expressed in the Diamant Bleu presentation 'Nuit Etoilée de Bagdad', c. 1927 (see p. 14 and pl. 9).

In addition to the Middle East and the Orient, Venice was another special place, perfectly suited to music-hall revues. The Lido nightclub in Paris introduced its own, probably short-lived, perfume for its opening in 1929. The Lido perfume company was called 'Un Coin de Venise' ('A Corner of Venice'). A glimpse of Venice was shown on the label, and the box, with a lid shaped like a gilded cupola, featured Venetian scenes on all four sides (pl. 101). The presentation for 'Dacry', a Cottan perfume of c. 1921, was somewhat disquieting. This Viard bottle (64) suggested, in abstract form, a sombre, mysterious figure, seemingly taken from a Venetian masked ball.

In the 1920s black glass became fashionable as an appropriate medium related to night life. 'Fête de Nuit' ('Festive Night') by Agnel appeared in 1920. The six-panelled Viard bottle suggested movement and joy, and resembled the full skirt of a ball gown, with a Tam o'Shanter stopper (pl. 136). Both bottle and stopper were trimmed in red enamel – the first time that a vivid colour had been juxtaposed with black. Even the star-shaped label design was fanciful. A dramatic box covered with black velvet and embellished with a gold tassel and red lining had the elegance of an evening coat. 'Fête de Nuit' was one of the most successful presentations at the 1925 exhibition, even though the perfume had been in existence for five years. A directly related Viard creation (65) was 'Suspiro de Granada' ('Sigh of Granada'), a Myrurgia perfume, expressing Spanish dance and movement.

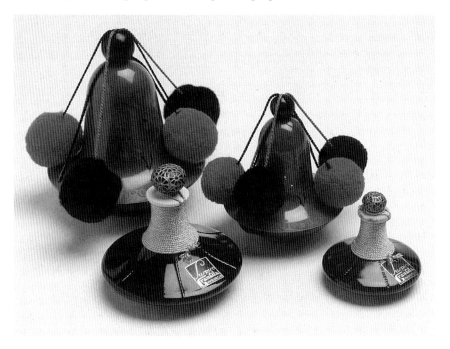

Other Viard black bottles were variously enhanced with colours: blue for A. Euzière 'Source Bleue' ('Blue Spring'); green for Rallet 'No. 1' and for Lemoine perfumes; and silver (with yellow Bakelite) for the Drialis presentation of 'Extracto Mariposa' (pl. 136). The combination of black glass and gilded decoration also became very popular; Cherigan (66) and numerous other perfumers (pl. 137) offered beautiful black-and-gold presentations. Another example was the very elegant 'Merry Christmas', a Benoît perfume of 1927, which may have been the only instance of a perfume presentation with a completely religious theme (pl. 142). Its stylish, flat black-glass bottle bore a gilded Nativity scene and the gilded sculptural stopper depicted the Virgin Mary and the infant Jesus. A box in the shape of a Gothic arch incorporated a pair of 'church doors' with green galalith facings.

Another feature of the decade was the influence of decorative finishes and coverings, such as lacquer and sharkskin, a trend that was especially prevalent around the time of the 1925 exhibition, when perfume presentations displayed a wide variety of elements derived from interior decoration. A favourite finish for wall-panels, furniture and accessories was lacquer in black or in a variety of colours. Opaque glass bears a close resemblance to lacquer finishes, and 'Vert Nil' ('Nile Green'), was then a fashionable pastel shade. In 1925, Rimmel introduced 'Art Moderne', an exciting presentation inspired by lacquer finishes. The heavy 'Vert Nil' crystal bottle, which had a hard geometric outline, was topped by a black-crystal cover with stylized floral ornamentation typical of the period, while placement of the label low and off-centre was reminiscent of Art Deco geometric asymmetry (pl. 121).

In 1927, Baccarat created two magnificent geometric models in pink crystal with silver ornamentation. The first was for Delettrez 'Silver Butterfly', a stretched vertical hexagon with an abstract, almost oriental motif (pl. 139). The second was for a new luxury edition of an existing perfume, 'Astris' by L. T. Piver. The root of the fabricated name 'Astris' was the French word *astre* ('star'). The bottle, an upright hexagon, featured a silvered six-pointed motif, expressing the perfume name in a very modern graphic way (pl. 138). Turquoise, a very rare colour for crystal or glass, was used for the Benoît perfume 'Lune de Miel' ('Honeymoon'). The bottle had a whimsical silvered crescent moon and stars motif, with a stopper in the form of a crescent moon (pl. 117). Cristalleries de Nancy made a wide variety of 'omnibus' bottles using opaque glass in various colours: red, green, blue, black and, rarely, yellow. These models, though intended for lower-priced presentations, were nevertheless very representative of the period (pl. 118). Opaque white was the rarest type of crystal or glass, and Baccarat produced a classic example of Art Deco design for 'Mon Talisman' ('My Talisman'), by Gabilla, using an opaque white crystal bottle highlighted with gilding (67).

Sharkskin, *galuchat* in French, a stylish Art Deco covering, was imitated in printed paper graphics for 'Galuchat', an L. T. Piver line, while the glass artist André Jolivet developed a bottle for 'Charme Caressant'

66 Cherigan, 'Chance', 1929.
H. 8.2 cm (3¼ in.).

67 Gabilla, 'Mon Talisman', 1926, Baccarat bottle no. 621 in two sizes. H. 27.0 cm (10⅝ in.); 9.0 cm (3½ in.).

68 Dalon, 'Charme Caressant', 1924, André Jolivet design and bottle; L. T. Piver, 'Galuchat', c. 1927, with simulated sharkskin box and rouge box; Silka, 'Ami', 1925, Baccarat bottle no. 552. H. 10.7 cm (4¼ in.); 8.5 cm (3⅜ in.); 10.5 cm (4⅛ in.).

69 Volnay, 'Fleurs Vives', 1920, bottle designed and made by René Lalique. H. 13.0 cm (5⅛ in.).

70 L. T. Piver, 'Rêve d'Or', 1925, bottles and graphics designed by Louis Süe: Baccarat bottle no. 550 in two sizes, with box for smaller size, two powder boxes and cardboard sign in foreground. H. 14.0 cm (5½ in.); 11.3 cm (4½ in.).

('Caressing Charm') by Dalon, in which he recreated sharkskin scales on opaque green glass. Similarly, the black-crystal Baccarat bottle for the Silka perfume 'Ami' ('Friend') had a moulded section which simulated silvered sharkskin (68). In addition, Art Deco architectural elements and motifs were influential. In 1920, Lalique designed an exceptional bottle for a Volnay perfume, 'Fleurs Vives' ('Living Flowers'), the overall shape of which was a cylindrical pillar, while the stopper was in the form of an overflowing bowl, a popular motif which became a classic Art Deco symbol (69).

'Le Présentoir' ('The Display Case'), a 1926 Lérys presentation for six perfumes, was a sumptuous object representative of the Art Deco style. Six bottles, each triangular in section, resembling pie wedges, were grouped to form a cylinder, with one metal tray as the base, and another as the top (pl. 146). The two trays were held together by a vertical metal rod which ran through the centre of 'Le Présentoir'. The individual perfume names and lace motif, which appeared on the bottles, were actually imprinted in gold on a clear Cellophane covering – an extremely fragile detail. The same year, L. T. Piver introduced 'Fétiche' ('Fetish'), for which the primary graphic decoration was a continuous line of alternating black and gold squares (pl. 140), representing the 'perfect harmony of contrasts' inspired by Beardsley. The accompanying perfumed card displayed a border of black and gold squares, similar to the border regularly used on the covers of *Art, Goût, Beauté*, one of the most famous magazines of that time in the field of the arts and fashion.

Among the most talked-about objects in the 1925 exhibition were the Lalique fountain and the monumental metal screen with geometric flowers, called 'L'Oasis', by Edgar Brandt. Both objects were reproduced as decoration on the blue and silver paper graphics designed for a presentation used by Guerlain for various perfumes (pl. 159). Meanwhile, Louis Süe and André

Mare had recently redecorated the L. T. Piver salons in Paris, creating the entire interior decor, including furniture and accessories. The colour-scheme they chose was a combination of blue and gold, and the ceilings were draped. The presentation of the L. T. Piver 'Rêve d'Or' ('Dream of Gold') line, which was also designed by Louis Süe, reproduced the colour contrast of the wall and ceiling coverings of the salons (70).

When Richard Hudnut opened a splendid new shop in Paris in 1927, four unusual blends of perfume, each called 'Le Début', were introduced in identical presentations (pl. 120), except for the use of glass of different colours to suggest four different moods: green for 'Le Début Vert' was associated with Adventure, white or clear for 'Le Début Blanc' with Gaiety, blue for 'Le Début Bleu' with Romance, and black for 'Le Début Noir' with Sophistication. The presentation as a whole was representative of the interior decor of the new Hudnut shop, with its sumptuous, ornate Art Deco style.

During the 1920s, many perfume presentations continued the long-standing tradition of using flowers and floral motifs as inspiration, now interpreted in a more modern style. However, because flowing shapes of flowers do not mix well with geometric forms, these perfume bottles had to be particularly well-conceived and stylistically evolved. Baccarat created a few exceptional pure geometric shapes, softened with floral decorations. For example, a bottle designed in 1921 was used for a number of Fontanis perfumes; and another created in 1928 was used for various Maudy perfumes. The Maudy model displayed a unique openwork design concept, the upper part of the bottle being actually a crystal cover which, when lifted, revealed a small inner stopper (71).

A Jolivet bottle for de Morny, an exclusive London perfume company, was used for various perfumes; it appeared to be a round glass jar with a prominent tassel through its flower-decorated cover (pl. 116). A hole in the top of the brown-marbled octagonal box allowed the tassel to be displayed on the outside when the box was closed. Another successful Jolivet model was cre-ted for Volnay. Its simple square shape was softened by moulded decoration on front and back, and the basic form produced in black or clear glass with various finishes was used for various Volnay perfumes (72, 73).

Another unusual Lalique creation for Roger & Gallet was a hexagonal glass sign, the front of which was transparent and devoid of ornamentation, except for the company name in bold. The stand, projecting from the rear, featured an overall floral representation, sculptural, opaque and delicately ribbed; the contrasting views when seen from the front and the side presented an intriguing juxtaposition of Art Deco and Art Nouveau (74, 75). Lalique was equally successful with geometric shapes which were made to appear very graceful through the use of floral surface decorations. 'La Belle Saison' (see p. 8 and pl. 128), one of the great successes of the 1925 exhibition. In the same year René Lalique also created an exceptional bottle for Houbigant – possibly for 'Celle Que Mon Cœur Aime' ('She Whom My Heart Loves').

71 Maudy, 'Jasmin' and 'Muguet', 1928, both Baccarat bottle no. 644; Fontanis, 'Eau de Toilette au Jasmin Fontanis' and 'Sous la Charmille', 1921, both Baccarat bottle no. 480. H. 5.5 cm (2⅛ in.); 6.5 cm (2½ in.); 15.5 cm (6⅛ in); 8.5 cm (3⅜ in.).

72 Volnay, 'Ambre' and 'Rose Brumaire' (with box), c. 1920, bottles designed and made by André Jolivet. H. 8.5 cm (3⅜ in.); 8.7 cm (3⅜ in.).

73 Volnay, 'Yapana', c. 1920, bottles designed and made by André Jolivet, with box. H. 8.6 cm (3⅜ in.).

74, 75 Roger & Gallet, glass display sign, 1925, designed and made by René Lalique, front and side views. H. 5.5 cm (2⅛ in.), d. 3.6 cm (1⅜ in.).

76 Houbigant, 'Celle Que Mon Cœur Aime'(?), 1925, René Lalique design and bottle. H. 10.5 cm (4⅛ in.)

Examples of this presentation are so rare that it is impossible to ascertain today if it was ever distributed. The bottle, in clear glass with identical decoration front and back, depicted an open dahlia flower, its petals outlined in blue enamel within a hexagon (76). This was a very modern floral design, of unparalleled perfection in this medium, one of the wonderful examples which illustrate Lalique's ability to move into the 1920s Modern Style while still retaining his own unique design perspective.

Another strong floral Lalique presentation was for 'Pavots d'Argent' ('Silver Poppies'), a Roger & Gallet perfume of 1927. The bottle's overall form displayed the flattened shape so fashionable during the 1920s, its profile being very narrow in proportion to its front (pl. 124). Lalique also designed the most extraordinary graphics for the packaging to match the bottle's floral design. A similar Lalique bottle design, enamelled in black, was produced for the luxury edition of a Colgate perfume, 'Night' (77). Other exceptional Lalique floral designs created for Gabilla included those for 'Jasmin' and 'Lilas' (pl. 114). The 'Jasmin' box was also a luxury object, echoing the bottle's floral pattern, while a pendent paper medallion, shaped like a flower, was attached to the box by a silk tassel.

The typical Art Deco motif, the flower-filled basket, was beautifully interpreted on an Elizabeth Arden rouge box, possibly designed by Lepape. The same floral motif was incorporated in the Arden logo on the label for her first perfume, 'Lilac', as well as those used for other products (pl. 122). The bottle for Lydès 'Narcisse' was a wonderful flower-shaped design (pl. 123), complemented by exceptional floral decoration on the box. Other outstanding floral designs (78) included: Nesly 'Chypre' (created by Daillet, a skilled glass artist, forgotten today) and Forest 'L'Origan' (a Viard creation). Viard also designed bottles for Biette 'Narciris' (pl. 104) – an original concept with moulded decoration of exceptional quality – as well as for 'Lys Noir' ('Black Lily') and other perfumes by Isabey, while Henri Hamm created an abstract floral design which was used by Isabey for several perfumes (pl. 107).

In 1929, George Baring, a wealthy Austrian, whose shop in Paris was located almost opposite the Elysée Palace, sold rare artefacts, fashions and his own perfumes; one of the decade's last major perfume creations was the distinctive floral bottle for his 'Le Comble' ('The Limit' in the sense of 'too much') – a rounded shape with fluted sides and two hollow triangular extensions protruding from the base (pl. 127). Unfortunately for Baring, however, the timing of his new enterprise resulted in his going bankrupt shortly after the American stock-market crash.

The new trend in perfume presentations, 'representational' bottles designed to depict a recognizable object, animal or human figure, developed after 1900, and included the L. T. Piver portable bottles in the shape of a cigarette lighter, the turtle for Guerlain 'Champs-Elysées' and the figure for Bryenne 'Chu Chin Chow'. By the 1920s, this style had been perfected, and many high-quality, witty representations were produced. Thus in 1923 – in a humorous twist on the classic combination of a bottle with a brass cap covering a glass inner stopper – de Vigny introduced 'Chick-Chick' for Easter. The bottle with gilded wings formed the body of the chick, while an oversized gilded cap served as its head (pl. 133). Since de Vigny had also developed 'Golliwogg' (1919) and later produced 'Guili-Guili', that company and the designer of all three bottles, Michel de Brunhoff, must be considered leaders in the introduction of whimsical representational bottles.

Two other innovators, Blanche Arvoy and Marcel Guerlain, went a step further in creating perfume-related items that could even be displayed as *objets d'art*. Arvoy, who had a penchant for animal subjects and clever names, founded both the Jovoy and Corday perfume companies. One of her first Jovoy perfumes was 'Allo Coco', the bottle for which displayed a colourful enamelled parrot – very popular as a house pet in France at the time – on the stopper (pl. 129). The name 'Coco' was frequently given to pet parrots and was sometimes also used as a nickname for a person, while 'Allo' had recently become a familiar telephone greeting. 'Allo Coco' was intended to make fun of the new Parisian habit of holding endless telephone conversations. The fact that Gabrielle Chanel was known as 'Coco' also suggested a joke at her expense. Blanche Arvoy's greatest artistic figural creation for a Jovoy perfume was 'Gardez-moi' (see p. 13 and pl. 8).

A new perfume company was founded in 1923 by Marcel Guerlain, who sold his perfumes internationally and opened a splendid shop in Paris opposite the Elysée Palace. Because Marcel Guerlain's name happened to be the same as that of a member of the well-known Guerlain family of perfumers, the Guerlain perfume company advertised the difference by stating: 'Nous n'avons pas de prénom' ('We have no first name'). The newcomer Marcel Guerlain was a great perfume innovator, his representational perfume creations being at once extremely luxurious and inventive. In its pointed use of archaic French orthography 'Le Roy le Veult' ('The King Wills It'), of 1923, recalled the formula used for the royal assent in the enactment of legislation, and the bottle was a reproduction of the former French royal crown (pl. 143). 'Pavillon Royal', of 1924, was another regal presentation in a luxurious box – the architectural features of the bottle (pl. 145) possibly inspired by the Pavillon Royal at Biarritz, where society balls and fashion shows were held. Perhaps Marcel Guerlain's most luxurious, grandest and completely outlandish presentation was 'Rolls Royce' of 1926 (pl. 91). The crystal bottle reproduced the classic grille of Rolls-Royce cars and rested on a black Bakelite base, realistically imitating the mudguards and tyres. Initially, the bottle was provided with a small, simple ground-glass stopper to facilitate safe handling, but an ornate stopper, simulating the familiar silver 'Spirit of Victory' mascot, was also included. Because this bottle had two stoppers, one functional, one ornamental, it must have been created with the intention of being kept and displayed. The 'Rolls Royce' perfume concept and design may represent most accurately the prevalent spirit of excess of this decade.

77 Colgate, 'Night', *c.* 1926, bottle designed and made by René Lalique. H. 8.5 cm (3⅜ in.).

78 Nesly, 'Chypre', *c.* 1920, bottle designed and made by Daillet; and Forest, 'L'Origan', *c.* 1922, Julien Viard design. H. 13.0 cm (5⅛ in.); 15 cm (5⅞ in.).

79 Salancy, 'Babillage de Fleurs', c. 1920, simulated book with three perfumes, 'Babillage de Fleurs', 'Le Roman de la Rose' and 'Le Secret de Dame Violette'; and (right) Robj, 'Entre Tous', 1925, Robj design, simulated book with bottle. H. 7.3 cm (2⅞ in.); 9.0 cm (3½ in.).

80 Pélissier-Aragon (trade name: Les Fontaines Parfumées, Grasse), 'Jasmin', 1924, Dépinoix bottle (also used for other perfumes). H. 12.7 cm (5 in.).

One particularly imaginative and humorous creation – 'L'Orange' – was introduced c. 1925 by de Marcy. In this presentation a group of eight segments of a simulated orange served as perfume bottles which were placed upside-down, each held in place by having its neck inserted into a metal frame concealed inside a simulated orange-skin (pl. 147). Without following the written instructions provided, the bottles could not be removed.

Lucien Willemetz, who in 1908 founded Robj, a company producing perfume-burners, lamps, curios etc., first became involved with perfumes for his Robj perfume-burners and later, in 1925, created one of the great figural stoppers, 'Folle Maîtresse', for Blanche Lebouvier (see pp. 12–13 and pl. 7). In one original Robj presentation called 'Entre Tous' ('Among All') the bottle was fitted inside a realistic imitation of a leather-bound book, complete with jacket (79). Earlier the Salancy perfume set 'Babillage de Fleurs' ('Chatter of Flowers') had also used a book format. However, in that case, the 'book' was only the box, which contained three standard perfume bottles (79).

Although René Lalique could not have been very fond of the purely figural or representational style, in the case of 'Le Parfum des Anges' ('The Perfume of the Angels'), produced for the opening of the Oviatt Building in Los Angeles (for which he also designed architectural motifs), he created a bell-shaped bottle and accompanying box decorated with the double-angel motif, symbolic of the City of Los Angeles (pl. 144).

Perfume bottles of unusual shape included one designated 'Les Fontaines Parfumées, Grasse' ('The Perfumed Fountains, Grasse'), a trade name adopted by Pélissier-Aragon in 1924. It was a replica of a fountain in Grasse dating from 1640 but no longer in existence (80), and was used for various single-flower perfumes (Muguet, Cyclamen, etc.). Another singular form was produced for Guyla, a short-lived perfume company, forgotten today, which in 1926 presented its 'Divin Narcisse' ('Divine Narcissus') perfume in a bottle shaped exactly like a champagne flute, with hand-painted decoration by Atelier Martine (pls. 125, 126). When the champagne flute stood upright, it was realistically hollow and deep, but when in this position, the perfume bottle was actually upside-down. In reality the base of the flute formed the stopper, and the stem was the neck, the perfume being contained in the narrow space between the extremely thin, fragile inner and outer walls of the elongated flute, the rim of which became the base when the perfume bottle was the right way up. 'Divin Narcisse' was such a fragile bottle that its very survival is remarkable.

In the 1920s luxurious, high-quality figural and representational designs became very popular in France. Later, especially in the United States, most representational bottles were lower-priced humorous knick-knacks of inferior quality, but often with clever names – a trend which might explain why some prestigious perfume companies were careful to avoid such designs. This decade also witnessed the fashion of perfume presentations simulating pearls and gems. After World War I, André Jolivet introduced a new pearlized finish using a substance derived from herring scales (which he called *laitance de hareng* – literally, herring roe). Although simulated pearl materials had existed before, this synthetic substance produced more realistic and resistant results and led to a surge of interest in such opaque finishes for perfume bottles. Volnay, founded in 1919, had an experimental and possibly unique bottle created for 'Lilas' ('Lilac'). This curious glass bottle, its overall outline similar to that for 'Divin Narcisse', was amazingly light in weight – almost like a Christmas-tree ornament. Its flame-shaped stopper was completely hollow, matching the bottle's weight. The pearlized finish, probably used for the first time on 'Lilas', was also a feature of many other Volnay bottles, stoppers or both (pl. 151). In 1925, Isabey introduced a simulated pearl model for all of its perfumes. This company won a gold medal in 1925, when it introduced 'Le Collier d'Isabey' ('The Isabey Necklace') at the Paris exhibition. Also known as 'Le Collier Parfumé' ('The Perfumed Necklace'), this presentation comprised a group of six pearlized bottles displayed in a semicircular box (pl. 154). Pleville, a short-lived company, introduced *c.* 1926 'Le Secret de la Perle' ('The Secret of the Pearl'), the box for which opened to reveal a large grey imitation pearl with a beige pearlized perfume bottle inside it. Other simulated-pearl presentations were created for Ota perfumes: either a single pearl presented in its box (pl. 148); or three bottles, two of which had indentations in their bases, so that they would all fit together and appear to form a single unit of three pearls (pl. 149).

Possibly the most extraordinary pearl presentation was a simulated necklace consisting of 13 graduated pearls, eleven of which were perfume bottles placed upside down, with the corked necks of each fitting into an opening inside the base of the box, while the two small end 'pearls' were nonfunctional. This model, created by Paul Heymann, was used by de Marcy perfumes for the aptly named 'Le Collier Miraculeux' ('The Miraculous Necklace') of 1927 (pl. 150), a rare presentation which was not produced for long, though the same model was also used for 'Parfum XXIII' by Delettrez. Another startling de Marcy creation was in the form of a simulated sapphire bracelet, in which five independent, removable bottles, each with a simulated sapphire as a stopper, were trapped inside the middle section of a box resembling a casket for jewelry (pls. 152, 153). When this middle section was closed, only the stopper tops – the simulated sapphires, apparently connected by a row of fixed simulated diamonds – were visible; the overall effect was a masterpiece of visual deception.

Louise Peszyñska, a *corsetière* with a Paris shop, also used the theme of gems when she introduced 'Le Secret du Diamant' ('The Secret of the Diamond') in 1929 in an avant-garde black-crystal bottle simulating the shape of a faceted diamond, housed in a magnificent black leather-covered box with an interior mirror, suitable for re-use as a cosmetic case for travel (82). Some years earlier, a glass perfume bottle inside a silver cicada (pl. 130) had served as a jewel-like presentation for 'Toute la Provence' ('All over

81 Pleville, 'Le Secret de la Perle', 1925, box, bottle on base, and pearlized cover. H. 8.0 cm (3⅛ in.).

82 Louise Peszyñska, 'Le Secret du Diamant', 1929, bottle in leather box containing mirror. H. 9.0 cm (3½ in.).

83 Fioret, powder box, 1920.
D. 7.5 cm (3 in.).

84 Fioret perfumes (from left to right): 'Jouir', 1919, Baccarat bottle no. 444; 'Prévert' in two sizes, smaller with box, 1919, Baccarat bottle no. 445; 'Prière', 1924, Baccarat bottle no. 543 with box; 'Le Muguet', 1924, Baccarat bottle no. 543; 'Jouir', 1919. Boxes feature glass medallions designed and made by René Lalique. H. 15.5 cm (6⅛ in.); 12.5 cm (4⅞ in.); 9.3 cm (3⅝ in.); 8.0 cm (3⅛ in.); 5.8 cm (2¼ in.); 8.5 cm (3⅜ in.).

Provence'), a Molinard Jeune perfume of 1923, which was appropriately named, since it was derived from various flowers grown all over Provence, in the south of France. The four-leaf clover, used as a medallion, and the cicada were also appropriate motifs, since both are encountered 'all over Provence'.

Although there are numerous examples of avant-garde and imaginative presentations in the 1920s, few perfume designers worked consistently in a modern abstract geometric style. A pioneering figure in this context was Simon Jaroslawski, the driving force behind three perfume companies: Fioret, Ybry and Mÿon. Not much is known about him, however, except that he was a respected 'nose' in the perfume industry, and held very strong artistic views. His companies developed high-quality, pure geometric presentations, but did not influence many others. Jaroslawski collaborated primarily with Baccarat for perfume bottles, but used Lalique for one Fioret creation. Both Fioret and Ybry perfumes were often embellished with luxurious Lalique medallions. The first Fioret bottles, produced in 1919, were rectangular, and made of clear crystal with gilded brass caps over inner ground-glass stoppers, the purpose of all the early bottles being to display the colour of the perfume to maximum advantage (84). 'Jouir' ('To Enjoy'), one of the first Fioret perfumes, was presented in a bottle in the form of a tall, stark rectangular column. The perfume names were romantic, and the understated bottles were enhanced by elaborate gilded paper labels with Symbolist or Art Nouveau motifs. The simple light-grey boxes were made to open like drawers, then a novel idea, and bore Art Nouveau glass medallions by Lalique. In contrast to the relatively stark appearance of the perfume

presentations, the Fioret powder box featured very elaborate overall Art Nouveau designs (83).

One of the great designs of the decade was created by Lalique for Fioret in 1924. Its classic Lalique stopper was married with a Baccarat-style bottle and presented the understated elegance of the Jaroslawski design requirements – a perfect blend of ideas contributed by two great innovators. The perfume in question was appropriately named 'Chose Promise' ('Promised Thing'). The relative proportion of the stopper to the bottle may, at first, seem odd (85). Even the juxtaposition of the Art Nouveau style stopper with the simple geometric Art Deco bottle may seem strange. However, therein lies the key to the meaning of 'Chose Promise', for in order to understand its intention completely, it is necessary to go back to 1911, when Lalique designed two small and similar seals, 'Figurines, Face' and 'Quatre Figurines'. The Fioret stopper, a combination of the two seals' designs, was about the same height, 5.5 cm, or slightly over 2 inches. The plain rectangular bottle served like a 'sheet of paper' on which were imprinted the two identical seal-like rectangles. However, the left-hand rectangle framed the perfume name, 'Chose Promise', while the right-hand rectangle bore the maker's name, 'Fioret, Paris' – each apparently the imprint of a different seal. The result was a striking juxtaposition of a very modern bottle with an object originally conceived in 1911.

Ybry, Jaroslawski's second company, founded in 1925, had an even more luxurious image than Fioret. Baccarat produced the classic Ybry model, a flat square bottle in coloured crystal. Variety was introduced by overlaying coloured crystal (green, red, purple, orange, black, etc.) on white crystal to create an opaque and luminescent quality (pl.157). Each different colour was related to a particular perfume, and to a different gem. In most cases the bottle had an enamelled and gilded metal cover in a co-ordinated colour-scheme, the cover being placed over an inner stopper positioned in one corner of the bottle (in an eccentric but harmonious manner). The Ybry boxes for individual perfumes were exquisite leather-covered creations, often featuring small triangular segments and silk tassels in co-ordinated colours. Perhaps the most spectacular examples were the large suede-covered cases created for multiple presentations, one model of which displayed three bottles and two atomizers (pl. 156). Another featured two bottles, one atomizer and a beautiful René Lalique medallion attached to the case by a silk tassel (pl. 155). The Ybry perfumes were advertised as being 'the most expensive in the world'.

The third company in which Jaroslawski was involved, Mÿon, was established in 1928. The first Mÿon model was reminiscent of a Chinese ginger jar, though the opaque body and gilded cover were angular rather than round (86). Mÿon luxury editions were offered in a variety of colourful Baccarat opaque overlaid crystal creations. These editions seem to have been very limited and were fairly short-lived.

Following the example of Poiret and Babani, many other leading fashion designers introduced their own perfumes in the course of the 1920s. It had become apparent that perfume presentations were the ideal medium to extend one's fashion philosophy to a larger, more global audience. It appears that twelve more couture houses introduced their perfumes in quick succession: 1921, Chanel; 1922, Boué Sœurs; 1923, Callot Sœurs, Lanvin and

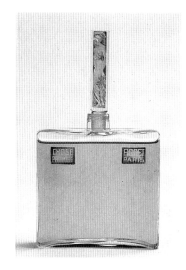

85 Fioret, 'Chose Promise', 1924, bottle designed and made by René Lalique. H. 12.8 cm (5 in.).

86 Mÿon, '1000 Joies', 1928, Baccarat bottle no. 667, with gilded and enamelled brass cover and label. H. 9.0 cm (3½ in.).

Louiseboulanger; 1924, Lelong, Martial et Armand, Premet, Vionnet and Worth; 1925, Molyneux and Patou. Luxury goods companies were next to introduce perfumes. These included three Parisian furriers: Max (1925), Weil (1927) and Blondel (1928). Cadolle Frères, the well-known lingerie designers, had entered the perfume business in 1926, while Louis Vuitton, the luggage and travel specialist, made a few imaginative perfumes around 1925–27. André Perugia, the shoe designer, joined the fashion houses in 1928, and even the glovemaker Gants Jouvin, which had sold L. T. Piver perfumes in its shops in the 19th century, introduced its own in 1927.

Some perfumes were first offered to clients of couturiers and of luxury goods companies, and sometimes received press coverage, but were only later trademarked and sold to the public, hence it is very difficult to place exact dates on the introduction of these early perfume presentations by couturiers. The exquisite Callot Sœurs fashion designs offered an eclectic range of styles, many of them inspired by China, and their perfume presentations reflected this stylistic variety (pl. 131). Thus, 'La Fille du Roi de Chine' ('The King of China's Daughter') not only had an unusual name, but also a most unusual bottle that looked either like an angular stylized shoe (perhaps an allusion to the Chinese tradition of binding the feet of girls) or like a folded paper design (in the shape of a *cocotte en papier* or 'paper chick' inspired by Origami art). In another case, 'Bel Oiseau Bleu' ('Beautiful Blue Bird') was presented in a simple bottle with an enamelled decoration depicting an empty cage on the front and a blue bird on the back. When the bottle was handled, the bird appeared to move around inside its cage. The Callot Sœurs perfume boxes were in the same shape as those used for the fashion house's clothes, and even the bottle of 'ChichiCallot' was similarly shaped.

Jeanne Lanvin clearly preferred the classic tradition. Around 1909, she had introduced mother-and-daughter collections, and her style was youthful, feminine, poetic, allowing freedom of movement. It was a style appropriate both for young girls and for mature women – a style to which the wearer would remain loyal for life. In 1922, Iribe created the Lanvin logo, depicting Jeanne Lanvin and her daughter Marie-Blanche facing each other, holding hands and both wearing elegant ball gowns and headdresses. The Lanvin style and fashion philosophy was clearly expressed in this drawing and in a rare gilded bronze sculpture (87) which, though seemingly static, was replete with tension and movement.

Another artist and interior designer, Armand Albert Rateau, who was in sole charge of decorating Jeanne Lanvin's home and shops, also created the spherical clear- or black-glass perfume bottle which was used for all Lanvin perfumes. This shape was ideal for displaying the gilded Lanvin logo. It is possible that Rateau may also have been involved in the design of the Lanvin logo. Special editions of this model were developed. Some bottles were gilded overall except for the Lanvin logo reversed out in black (88). In 1926, limited and numbered editions were introduced in Sèvres porcelain –

87 Gilded bronze of logo for Jeanne Lanvin, *c.* 1929, designed by Paul Iribe with possible involvement of Armand Albert Rateau. On front of base: 'Jeanne Lanvin et Sa Fille'; 'Bal Masqué'. On back: 'Fabrication Française'. H. 28.5 cm (11¼ in.).

88 Jeanne Lanvin: chrome sachet, c. 1929; black papier-mâché powder box, c. 1925; bottles (with logo by Paul Iribe) used for various perfumes c. 1925-34, designed by Rateau and made by Romesnil in clear and black glass (a rare example of black glass with gilding is shown fourth from the right in group); miniature with cap, 1940; boxes for 'My Sin' (blue trim), 'Rumeur' (burgundy trim). H. of largest bottle 16.5 cm (6½ in.); miniature 3.2 cm (1¼ in.).

the known colours being turquoise-blue, burgundy and cobalt-blue (pl. 165), but it seems most likely that these luxury Sèvres editions were offered as presents to special clients, rather than sold to the public.

Unlike Poiret, who opted for a dramatically different presentation for each perfume, Lanvin preferred a single standard model. Other fashion houses, Chanel in particular, shared Lanvin's preference for a distinctive 'house style' bottle. The Lanvin labels were merely discreet strips of paper placed, indeed almost concealed, on the underside of the bottle's base. No prominent label would ever be allowed to vie with the Lanvin logo for attention, and the same principle applied to the boxes, where the perfume name appeared on the inside. The boxes were generally covered in cream-coloured paper, with trimming in a different colour for each perfume: 'My Sin' in navy blue, 'Arpège' in black, 'Scandale' in red and 'Rumeur' in brown.

When Louise Boulanger founded her own fashion house in Paris, she combined her two names so as to create a more powerful identity. The Louiseboulanger salons at 3 rue de Berri were decorated by Jean Dunand, who also executed a portrait of her in lacquer. She established a unique fashion style, specializing in evening clothes, notably small-waisted ball gowns, often displaying an outburst of flowing panels in the back, and made from particularly rich fabrics. She was very fond of taffeta and of the colour apricot. She produced only one perfume, which she called 'Louberri', coined from her own first name and her street address. It was an extremely small production, possibly not sold anywhere outside her couture house. The shape of the bottle was reminiscent of a full skirt (pl. 161), and its colour a very unusual citrine yellow – a shade never previously used in association with perfume, nor since. When filled with the perfume, the bottle acquired a warm apricot tone – Louise Boulanger's favourite colour. The flat octagonal stopper was gilded with the couture house name, address and the Louiseboulanger logo, depicting her distinctive 'Pouf' evening dress. If a perfume presentation of a fashion designer could ever embody the design philosophy of its proprietor, then 'Louberri' achieved this to the maximum effect.

Martial et Armand was a leading Paris fashion house with important international clients and very close ties with the theatre, designing both

89 Martial et Armand, 'Un Rien', 1924, bottle designed and made by René Lalique featuring logo by Umberto Brunelleschi (U.B. initials visible on this rare large-size bottle). H. 19.3 cm (7⅝ in.).

90 Martial et Armand, 'Gardenia', c. 1924, bottle on base of open box. H. 6.5 cm (2½ in.).

on-stage and off-stage fashions for many famous actresses. Around 1923–24, the Italian artist Umberto Brunelleschi designed this fashion house's logo, which depicted a pair of 18th-century beauties wearing extravagant wigs that formed a heart-shaped motif. The initial 'M' of Martial and the final 'D' of Armand harmonized with and framed the heart shape. This logo was featured on the front of a Lalique bottle for the 1924 perfume, 'Un Rien' ('A Little Nothing') – and Brunelleschi's initials also appeared on the giant-sized model (89). The shape of the bottle was ideally suited to the logo, and the stopper featured the monogram 'MA' in relief. This elegant creation was certainly far more than 'a little nothing'. Other perfumes, such as 'Gardenia', were introduced in faceted bottles, but the decoration on their boxes – almost Gothic in shape and feeling – included the Martial et Armand logo (90). Brunelleschi lived in Paris and worked from c. 1900 as an illustrator for many prestigious publications, and designed costumes and sets for music-hall productions. While influenced by Bakst, he developed a distinctive style, combining French 18th-century gallantry and grace with Venetian, Florentine and Commedia dell'Arte subjects. His exaggerated period-style logo was perfectly attuned to the élitist atmosphere of the Martial et Armand salons.

The Premet fashion house, established in 1911, became very avant-garde under Mme Charlotte, its director in the 1920s. She had her hair cut short, *à la garçonne*, and coloured lilac. She introduced a short, simple, boyish dress which was named 'La Garçonne' and which became an instant worldwide success in an age of women's emancipation. The Premet perfume, 'Etrange Inconnu' ('Strange Stranger') of 1924 had an unconventional name and was presented in a simple modern design, the surface of the crystal bottle being moulded with a plaid-like pattern (91). This presentation's name and plaid pattern could have referred to Poiret's very unsuccessful 1924 Scottish collection. (While some felt that plaid would become a daytime fashion classic, it did not become one until much later.) Another modern perfume presentation was 'Le Secret de Premet' ('The Secret of Premet'), in which the bottle resembled a full evening skirt surmounted by a prominent smooth metal cover, symbolic of a belted waistline (91).

Only two perfume models are known to have been introduced by Madeleine Vionnet, one of the greatest fashion innovators of the 1920s, both of them in extremely small productions which probably were not sold outside the Vionnet couture house. In order to understand the nature of the Vionnet perfume creations, it is necessary to understand the fashion philosophy of the woman who claimed to have been the first to free women from corsets, even before Poiret – a claim which is quite plausible. She was known to have developed a unique style in her designs for clothes in which the fabric was cut on the bias, resulting in dresses that looked as if the fabric had been moulded directly onto the wearer's body, providing a sculptural effect and allowing elegant movements. The bias cut may have looked very simple and natural, but it was deceptively so, for in order to produce a perfect result, the most precise measurements and geometry had to be applied when cutting the fabric. Merely by looking at the flexible drape of the Vionnet dresses, it would be difficult to appreciate the rigorous technique required to produce this effect. Her favourite fabric, ideally suited to her bias cut, was crêpe-de-chine. Geometry was the essential foundation of the Vionnet fashion style, of her environment (both at her salons and her homes) and of her perfume creations. In 1919 she chose the Italian artist Ernesto Thayaht, a Symbolist and Futurist, to design the Madeleine Vionnet logo. This extraordinary logo was used for fashion advertising and was also printed on the Vionnet perfume boxes. Boris Lacroix, a talented designer who had been employed as a draughtsman for her couture house in 1924, soon extended his range, becoming Vionnet's interior designer and the creator of most of her furniture and home accessories, whilst at the salons he was equally influential through his introduction of design ideas that resulted in many fashion creations, including accessories.

'Temptation' (the English spelling perhaps a reminder of her youth spent in England) was most probably Madeleine Vionnet's first perfume, created in 1924. While this perfume may initially have been offered to her clients, it was available to the public only for a short while c. 1940. The overall shape of the very simple, tall square bottle was similar to that used for the Fioret perfume 'Jouir' in 1919. A gilded glass cover concealed the small inner stopper. Ivory-coloured paper was used for the label and for the covering of the box, both being trimmed in red. The label displayed a geometric motif inspired by the letter 'V' and also had very avant-garde lettering. Inserted into the top of the box was a square piece of ivory-coloured crêpe-de-chine, the fabric closely associated with the Vionnet bias cut. It is interesting to note that Lacroix (in collaboration with Jean Dunand) also designed a pair of armless chairs – resembling the 'Temptation' box – upholstered in ivory-coloured leather trimmed with red, and with red lacquered feet. It is particularly appropriate in this context to discuss the presentation for 'Crêpe de Chine', introduced by Millot in 1925, which was destined to become one of the best-selling perfumes ever, not only in France but worldwide. At first it may seem paradoxical that a stark geometric bottle was chosen for a perfume named 'Crêpe de Chine', the fabric associated with draped fashions. However, when this Millot bottle is seen next to that for 'Temptation' it becomes apparent that the Millot design was very possibly adopted in direct homage to the innovations of Madeleine Vionnet (pl. 162).

A design by Lacroix for a Vionnet perfume presentation was in fact used for four different perfumes called simply 'A', 'B', 'C' and 'D'. The concept of using letters of the alphabet as perfume names was an innovation in itself, though previously numbers had been used. This design consisted of a simple cube-shaped bottle with a cube-shaped metal cap (92). The corners of the four vertical sides were highlighted either in black on clear glass or gold on black glass, a striking detail reminiscent of a black-lacquer games table and

91 Premet, 'Etrange Inconnu', 1924; 'Le Secret de Premet', 1930. Bottles with boxes. H. 8.0 cm (3⅛ in.); 4.7 cm (1⅞ in.).

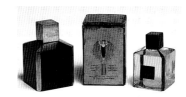

92 Madeleine Vionnet, unidentified perfume (gilded black glass), 'C' (enamelled clear-glass bottle and box), 1924, designs by Boris Lacroix, Dépinoix bottles. H. 6.3 cm (2½ in.); 5.3 cm (2⅛ in.).

93 Les Parfums de Rosine, 'Sakya Mouni', 1922, designed by Julien Viard. H. 12.5 cm (4⅞ in.).

four short matching chairs by Jean Dunand for Madeleine Vionnet *c.* 1930. When the chairs were pushed under the table, the entire unit became a cube. Rather than being a coincidence, this similarity was surely the result of the consistency of design philosophy on the part of Madeleine Vionnet and her circle of artist-friends.

By contrast, the long-established fashion house of Worth, which introduced its first perfume presentations in 1924, employed René Lalique to create classic models from the outset. The spherical bottle for 'Dans la Nuit' ('In the Night') was produced in frosted blue-stained glass with moulded surface decoration of glistening stars (pl. 164). The original 'Dans la Nuit' logo (crescent moon and stars) was featured on the stopper, but when this perfume was exported to the United States, there was a conflict with the existing Procter & Gamble logo, and the name 'Dans la Nuit' was substituted on the stopper. A reverse colour combination (blue enamelled stars on a background of frosted glass) was produced by Lalique for the special edition 'Dans la Nuit' powder box (pl. 164).

In 1925 Jean Patou introduced his 'Amour-Amour' ('Love-Love'), 'Que Sais-Je?' ('What Do I Know?') and 'Adieu Sagesse' ('Goodbye Wisdom'), all in Baccarat bottles designed by Louis Süe in his traditional Art Deco style. Perhaps their most distinctive feature was the gilded stopper in the shape of a pine-cone (pl. 163). Louis Süe and André Mare were entrusted with the decoration of the Patou couture salons, as well as the designer's Paris apartment and house in Biarritz, and eventually Louis Süe would even design Jean Patou's tomb.

In the post-war period, Paul Poiret's new perfume presentations had adopted more and more the simplicity of the modern style, while still retaining his originality and opulent perspective. 'Sakya Mouni' (derived from 'Sakyamuni' or 'Buddha'), a Rosine perfume introduced in 1922, signalled the direction in which Poiret's style would evolve. The bottle was a simple upright container, square in section, serving as a pedestal for the sculptural stopper, a large Chinese Fu dog in amethyst-coloured glass, rendered by Viard in the Poiret style (93). In 1923, the abstract design for 'Arlequinade' used modern geometric elements to preserve a Commedia dell'Arte character, and this was followed in 1924 by the fantasy presentation for 'Cœur en Folie' (see p. 12 and pl. 6). Perhaps as early as 1925, Poiret conceived the mysterious avant-garde creation 'Coup de Foudre' ('Flash of Lightning' or figuratively, 'Love at First Sight'). This Rosine presentation (pl. 166) may have been his homage to Jeanne Lanvin, whose fashions Poiret greatly admired (when he closed his own couture house during the war years he referred his clients to Lanvin). In *La Gazette du Bon Ton* (1924–25), a Lepape fashion plate entitled 'The Judgment of Paris' depicted three similar Lanvin evening dresses with curiously tiered, rigid skirts to which the 'Coup de Foudre' bottle bore a resemblance. Both the glass stopper and the box featured the characteristic shade of blue for which Lanvin was known. However, by this time

Poiret's financial condition was steadily worsening. His fashions were no longer in the mainstream; and after the 1925 exhibition, because of the great costs incurred in constructing and decorating his three barges, he lost financial control of Les Parfums de Rosine, though initially he still retained creative control over new Rosine perfumes. It is possible that 'Coup de Foudre' may not have been introduced to the public until the early 1930s, and then only briefly by the company which had taken over the Rosine perfume name. 'Coup de Foudre' was thus probably the last of the Rosine perfumes in which Poiret was creatively involved.

The American designer Hattie Carnegie visited Paris many times after 1919, seeking inspiration from the latest French fashions. To emulate French couturiers, she too introduced her own perfume around 1925, called simply 'Hattie Carnegie'. The influence of Japanese design was apparent in this somewhat representational bottle. The gilded stopper resembled a Far Eastern headdress, and the black bottle with gilded decoration resembled an inkwell (pl. 167). This bottle, possibly a Viard creation, was produced by Dépinoix, in a French-made box. Even the perfume was French in origin, having been produced for Hattie Carnegie by Rallet. Following the French couture house practice, it is likely that this perfume was presented to her New York clients, and later sold to the public.

Cadolle Frères, makers of *haute couture* lingerie, introduced their first perfume, 'Amour en Cage' ('Caged Love') in 1926 (pl. 115). This French expression, which had been in fashion since 1910, was derived from the title of a very successful play, *L'Amour en Cage*. Although Poiret stated that it was he who introduced the brassière, Cadolle also claimed to have been first, asserting that 'Amour en Cage' was used to describe a woman's bust when she was wearing a brassière.

Louis Vuitton, a firm specializing in travel goods, introduced its first perfumes *c*. 1925, even though the names were not trademarked before 1927. 'Heures d'Absence' ('Hours of Absence'; 94) and 'Je Tu, Il' (see p. 13 and pl. 4) were presented in very fragile bottles, housed in elegant gold and black boxes. The 'Heures d'Absence' name and the Vuitton outer boxes, with their drawings of ships and trains, referred, appropriately, to travel.

Fourrures Max were long-established fashion furriers, well known for their sumptuous and avant-garde creations. In 1925, Mme Andrée Leroy, the firm's proprietor, introduced 'Le Parfum Max' (pl. 134). The logo of Fourrures Max, designed *c*. 1923 by the fashion illustrator Benito, and reproduced in steel by the sculptor Edgar Brandt for the fur salon door, also appeared as enamelled decoration on a classic Baccarat bottle which was shown at the 1925 exhibition.

When the furriers Weil offered their own perfumes, advertised as 'perfumes for furs' in 1927, it was only natural that the names of the first three perfumes were associated with furs: 'Chinchilla Royal', 'Hermine' ('Ermine') and 'Zibeline' ('Sable'). The Weil label, used on most bottles and

94 Louis Vuitton, 'Heures d'Absence', 1927, outer box, box cover, and bottle in base of box. H. 8.0 cm (3⅛ in.).

95 Weil, 'Zibeline', 1927, smaller bottle and box; 'Chinchilla Royal', 1927, larger travel version and leather box (vaporizer attachment in box). Label design probably by Georges Barbier. H. 5.5 cm (2⅛ in.); 10.0 cm (4 in.).

96 E. Blondel, 'Le Sauvage', 1928, Baccarat bottle no. 655. H. 14.0 cm (5½ in.).

boxes, depicted an 18th-century winter scene with a fur-clad woman, seated in her sleigh, being pushed by a man on skates (95). This vignette was almost identical to a drawing by Georges Barbier called 'Skating' from *Les Fêtes Galantes*, a book of poems by Paul Verlaine illustrated by Barbier, issued in a limited edition in 1927. However, Weil had already presented perfume informally to clients. 'Padisha' ('Great King'), a title given to Ottoman sultans, was a Weil perfume of *c.* 1922 (pl. 102), predating the creation of Weil's own perfume company. This presentation depicted the luxury of a sultan's environment, and suggested the aura of luxury created by Weil furs.

A very exclusive furrier, E. Blondel, introduced 'Le Sauvage' ('The Savage') in a streamlined Baccarat crystal bottle with a startling design etched on the front (96). It portrayed an American Indian trapper with his recently killed fox slung over his shoulder, while rising behind them an elegant Parisian woman was shown wearing a superb fox stole. This image was stylish but it involved a direct and graphic juxtaposition of killing animals and fashion, which by today's standards would be considered to be objectionable.

André Perugia was one of the greatest shoe designers of the 20th century. While he produced very classic shoes, in response to demand from his private clients, his more extravagant styles were publicized in the fashion press. His advertising was headed 'Les Heures de Perugia' ('The Hours of Perugia'), and stated that Perugia offered different shoes for morning, afternoon and evening wear. He used the same name for his perfume company, established in 1927, but it seems that his perfumes existed before that date. The luxury edition for Perugia perfumes was a clear crystal bottle with silvered crystal cover (pl. 158). Flowers were hand-painted on the front of the bottle and the A.P. monogram and 'Les Heures de Perugia' discreetly silvered on the back. Perugia was a friend of Madeleine Vionnet and her second husband, also a shoe designer. Their friendship may explain why this Perugia presentation featured the same design concept as the Vionnet 'Temptation' bottle of 1924. Another model was a similar, shorter black bottle with gold lettering (pl. 160). The A.P. monogram and 'Les Heures de Perugia' appeared on its front, and the appropriate perfume name on its right side. 'Matin' ('Morning'), 'Après Midi' ('Afternoon') or 'Soir' ('Evening'). André Perugia evidently hoped to orchestrate for his clients their choice of shoes and perfumes to be worn throughout the day.

The decade had started with the aftermath of a political and human cataclysm, and was destined to end in an economic cataclysm. In the years between 1920 and 1929, life was to be lived to the hilt. In this tumultuous decade, a profusion of brilliant perfume creations was introduced, so numerous that they almost defy classification. It was a decade of supreme achievement, a time to be remembered and cherished. It may also have been a period which generated almost an excess of creativity, and sadly, we may never see such a period again.

92, 93 Silka, 'C'est?', *c.* 1920,
Lucien Gaillard design, Dépinoix
bottle. Front of bottle showing
perfume name and, question mark,
and back showing (much smaller)
the company name – the answer to
the riddle.
H. 10.2 cm (4 in.).

94 Honoré Payan, 'Bakanir', 1927.
Dépinoix bottle in open box.
H. 10.0 cm (4 in.).

95 Ciro, 'Le Chevalier de la Nuit', 1923, Julien Viard design, miniature, h. 6.0 cm (2⅜ in.); black bottle with box. h. 12.0 cm (4¾ in.). Eau de Toilette (with shield-shaped label) and frosted bottles in graduated sizes, with two boxes in background; h. of largest bottle 19.0 cm (7½ in.), smallest 8.2 cm (3¼ in.).

96 Variations on the mask theme: Colgate, 'Piquante' powder tin, *c*. 1926; d. 4.0 cm (1⅝ in.). L. T. Piver, 'Mascarade', 1927 (red glass); h. 9.5 cm (3¾ in.). Les Parfums de Rosine, 'Arlequinade', 1924, Julien Viard design; h. 15.3 cm (6 in.). Marcel Guerlain, 'Masque Rouge' boxes and bottles, powder boxes and rouge boxes; h. of bottle 8.5 cm (3⅜ in.). Cherigan, 'Mascarades', 1929, gilded black-glass bottle by Cristalleries de Nancy; h. 10.0 cm (4 in.). Ciro, 'Maskee', 1923, clown bottle; h. 9.0 cm (3½ in.). L. T. Piver, 'Mascarade', *c*. 1929, clear-glass bottle with box; h. 8.0 cm (3⅛ in.).

97 Lubin, 'Kismet', 1921.
Baccarat bottle no. 477.
H. 10.3 cm (4⅛ in.).

Far left
98 Lubin, 'Eva', 1920. Julien Viard
design.
H. 9.5 cm (3¾ in.).

Left
99 Rénaud, 'Ghedma', *c.* 1925.
Bottle by Cristalleries de Nancy in
two sizes, with boxes.
H. 7.0 cm (2¾ in.) and 9.0 cm
(3½ in.).

100 Forest, 'Ming Toy', 1923.
Baccarat bottle no. 512.
H. 11.0 cm (4⅜ in.).

Below left
101 Les Parfums du Lido, 1929.
Box, with bottle designed and made
by Maurice Dépinoix.
H. 9.0 cm (3½ in.).

Below right
102 Weil Furs, 'Padisha', c. 1922.
Box with bottle on base.
H. 9.0 cm (3½ in.).

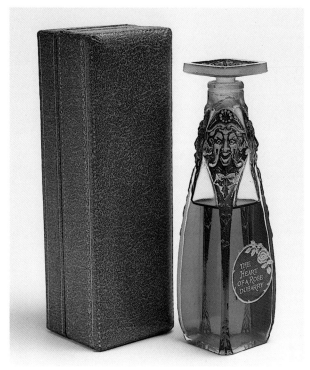

103 Lubin, 'Magda', 1921. Julien Viard design.
H. 12.7 cm (5 in.).

Above right
104 Biette, 'Narciris', 1927. Julien Viard design.
Dépinoix bottle.
H. 11.3 cm (4½ in.).

Right
105 Dubarry, 'The Heart of a Rose', *c*. 1920.
Julien Viard design, originally created for
'Arcadia'. Box and bottle.

106 Parfums de Paul, 'Nuit de Mariage', 1926. Box, bottle and label by B.T.C.I.C. H. 11.2 cm (4⅜ in.).

107 Isabey perfume bottles by Bobin Frères, 1924 (from left to right): 'Bleu de Chine' with black patina, and 'Mon Seul Ami' with beige patina (design by Henri Hamm c. 1914); 'Lys Noir', bottle and box, 'Route d'Eméraude' in background, 'Ambre de Carthage' and 'Chypre Celtic' (all Julien Viard designs). H. 8.7 cm (3⅜ in.), 14.5 cm (5¾ in.), 12.5 cm (4⅞ in.), 7.5 cm (3 in.), 11.8 cm (4⅝ in.).

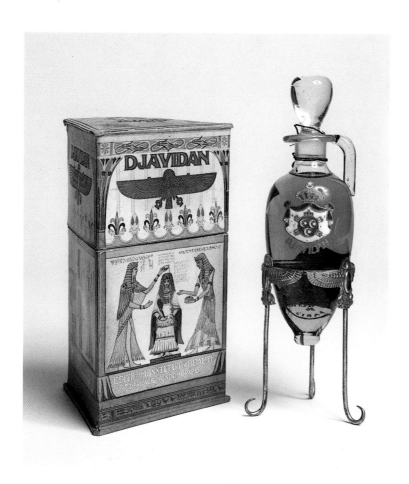

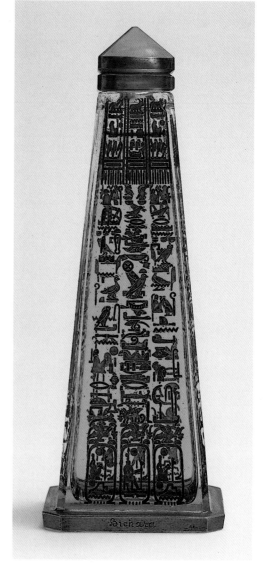

108 L'Institut de Beauté, 'Djavidan',
c. 1925. Box, with bottle by
Cristalleries de Nancy on stand.
H. 13.0 cm (5⅛ in.).

109 Bichara, 'Ramsès II', 1928.
Bottle by Cristalleries de Saint-Louis.
H. 20.5 cm (8⅛ in.).

Opposite above
110 Lubin, 'Enigma', 1921.
Julien Viard design.
H. 9.0 cm (3½ in.).

Opposite below
111 Colgate, 'Egypt', bottle and
box; h. 9.5 cm (3¾ in.). La Ducale,
'Egizia', powder box; d. 7.7 cm
(3 in.). Dralle, 'Sphinx'; h. 10.8 cm
(4¼ in.). All *c.* 1923.

128

Opposite above
112 Gabilla, 'Chin Li'. *c.* 1924. Green Dépinoix bottle in matching box, and orange-coloured box.
H. 6.7 cm (2⅝ in.).

Opposite below
113 Roger & Gallet, 'Le Jade', original line introduced 1923, with graphics designed by René Lalique (from left): soap in open box; clear-glass bottle with box; oval powder box. Also (centre left) moulded green-glass bottle, 1926, designed and made by Lalique, and its ornate box with tassel.
H. of green bottle 8.3 cm (3¼ in.), clear-glass bottle 6.2 cm (2½ in.).

Above
114 Gabilla, 'Jasmin', box and bottle; 'Lilas', bottle. Both designed and made by René Lalique, 1925.
H. 9.7 cm (3⅞ in.); 9.0 cm (3½ in.).

Above right
115 Cadolle, 'Amour en Cage', 1926. Bottle in open box.
H. 6.5 cm (2½ in.).

Right
116 De Morny, 'Narcisse Blanc et Noir', *c.* 1922. Box and bottle, André Jolivet design.
H. 6.0 cm (2⅜ in.).

117 Benoît, 'Lune de Miel', 1926.
Bottle designed and made by Maurice
Dépinoix.
H. 11.0 cm (4⅜ in.).

Below
118 Group of omnibus bottles and
boxes by Cristalleries de Nancy,
1920–1934. Companies represented:
d'Alamode, Bischoff, du Bois,
Bourbon, Burdin, de Burmann,
Chenier, Drialis, Marie Magdeleine,
Miga, Offenthal, Rénaud and Serey.
H. of largest green bottle 15.5 cm
(6⅛ in.), smallest purple bottle
5.3 cm (2⅛ in.).

Top
119 Two Demours powder boxes,
1927 (left), and Lionceau powder
box and brass rouge case, 1925
(right). Centre group: Lionceau
bottles by H. Saumont featuring two
types of stopper; 1925: green,
'Parfum pour Blondes'; red, 'Parfum
pour Brunes' (one with box); black,
'Fleuve Bleu'.
H. of large bottles 15.0 cm (5⅞ in.),
medium 10.0 cm (4 in.), small
8.0 cm (3⅛ in.), smallest 6.5 cm
(2½ in.).

Opposite centre
120 Richard Hudnut, 'Le Début',
1927. Perfume bottles in five sizes
and various colours, with boxes,
powder box (centre) and lotion
bottles (right).
H. (largest size to miniature): 13.0
cm (5⅛ in.); 6.5 cm (2½ in.); 5.5 cm
(2¼ in.); 4.3 cm (1¾ in.); 3.2 cm
(1¼ in.).

Opposite below
121 Rimmel, 'Art Moderne', 1925.
H. of larger bottle 14.5 cm (5¾ in.),
smaller bottle 12.0 cm (4¾ in.).

Top
122 Elizabeth Arden: Venetian powder box; 'Lilac' perfume bottle;
rouge box possibly designed by Georges Lepape. All *c.* 1922.
H. of bottle 15.7 cm (6⅛ in.). W. of rouge box 9.0 cm (4¼ in.).

Above
123 Lydès, 'Narcisse', *c.* 1922. Bottle in open box.
H. 4.8 cm (1⅞ in.).

Right
127 George Baring, 'Le Comble',
1929.
H. 9.5 cm (3¾ in.).

Below
125, 126 Guyla, 'Divin Narcisse',
1926. Bottle hand-painted by Atelier
Martine, upside-down (as
'champagne flute') and right side up
showing stopper.
H. 14.5 cm (5¾ in.).

Above
128 Houbigant, 'La Belle Saison',
1925. René Lalique bottle in box.
H. 10.3 cm (4 in.).

Left
124 Roger & Gallet, 'Pavots
d'Argent', 1927. René Lalique design
(including graphics). Lalique bottles
in two sizes, smaller with box, and
sample size in box. Powder boxes
(in background) in two sizes, and
presentation box (right) containing
perfume and powder.
H. of bottles 8.5 cm (3⅜ in.), 6.3 cm
(2½ in.), sample 5.5 cm (2⅛ in.).

135

Above left
133 De Vigny, 'Chick-Chick', 1923, designs by Michel de
Brunhoff: bottles in three sizes, with boxes.
H. 13.7 cm (5⅜ in.), 8.7 cm (3⅜ in.) and 7.2 cm (2⅞ in.).

Above right
134 Fourrures Max, 'Le Parfum Max', 1925. Baccarat bottle
no. 647 in three sizes, all with logo by Benito.
H. 23.5 cm (9¼ in.), 18.5 cm (7¼ in.) and 15.0 cm (5⅞ in.).

Right
135 Violet, 'Conte de Fées', *c*. 1922. Box and Dépinoix bottle.
H. 4.3 cm (1¾ in.).

Opposite above

136 Black bottles with colour or gilding, all Julien Viard designs (from left): Lemoine, various perfumes, *c.* 1922; A. Euzière, 'Source Bleue', *c.* 1924; Rallet, 'No. 1' (with green-glass stopper), *c.* 1923; Myrurgia, 'Suspiro de Granada', 1922, with Bakelite box (with pom poms) and outer box; Agnel, 'Fête de Nuit', 1920, with box; Drialis, 'Extracto Mariposa' (with butterfly stopper) in box. H. of largest bottle 13.5 cm (5¼ in.).

Opposite below

137 Black bottles with gilding (from left): Mury, 'Notturno', 1926, Baccarat bottle no. 367 in two sizes; Delyna, 'Sensation', *c.* 1927; de Musset, 'Poème', 1928, Dépinoix bottle; Delyna, 'Nuit Romantique', box and bottle, 1927; Lionceau, 'Pierre Précieuse', 1927, H. Saumont bottle; Cherigan, 'Fleur de Tabac' (with gold leaf), 1929; Fragonard, 'Xmas E', *c.* 1929, H. Saumont bottle; Gabilla, 'My Sin', *c.* 1927, Julien Viard design; Marcel Guerlain, 'Caravelle', 1924, Dépinoix bottle; d'Amboise, 'Mimosa', *c.* 1925, H. Saumont bottle. H. largest 12.5 cm (4⅞ in.); smallest 5.0 cm (2 in.).

Top left

138 L. T. Piver, 'Astris', 1927. Baccarat bottle no. 638. H. 17.0 cm (6¾ in.).

Top right

139 Delettrez, 'Silver Butterfly', 1927. Baccarat bottle no. 633. H. 10.0 cm (4 in.).

Centre

140 L. T. Piver, 'Fétiche', 1925. Perfumed card, powder tin, perfume bottle and box, and presentation box with perfume and rouge samples. H. of perfume bottle 8.5 cm (3⅜ in.); sample 5.0 cm (2 in.).

Left

141 Lenthéric, 'Le Miracle', 1924. Georges Dumoulin design. Dépinoix bottles, smaller size with box. H. 8.0 cm (3⅛ in.), 15.0 cm (5⅞ in.).

142 Benoît, 'Merry Christmas',
1927. Bottle designed and made by
Maurice Dépinoix, in box.
H. 12.0 cm (4¾ in.).

Below
143 Marcel Guerlain, 'Le Roy le
Veult', 1923. Bottle in box.
H. 8.0 cm (3⅛ in.).

Below right
144 Oviatt, 'Le Parfum des Anges',
1928. René Lalique design and
bottle, on base of open box.
H. 8.3 cm (3¼ in.).

Opposite top
145 Marcel Guerlain, 'Pavillon
Royal', 1924. Bottle in box.
H. 10.5 cm (4⅛ in.).

Opposite below left
146 Lérys, 'Le Présentoir', 1926.
Six individual bottles in box; all
bottles covered with gilded
Cellophane.
H. 9.0 cm (3½ in.).

Opposite below right
147 Parfums de Marcy, 'L'Orange',
c. 1925. Box and eight individual
bottles as 'orange segments'.
H. 6.5 cm (2½ in.).

Opposite top
148, 149 Ota, 'Lilas', single bottle
in box; and 'Violette', set of three
bottles in box. Both 1929.
H. 3.0 cm (1⅛ in.).

Opposite centre
150 Parfums de Marcy, 'Le Collier
Miraculeux', 1927. Box with pearl-
shaped bottles in graduated sizes
(with a simulated pearl at each end),
containing perfumes 'No. 7' (2),
'No. 5' (2), 'No. 3' (1), 'No. 1' (1),
'No. 3' (1), 'No. 5' (2), 'No. 7' (2).
H. of largest 4.3 cm (1¾ in.),
smallest 2.8 cm (1⅛ in.).

Opposite below
151 Volnay, bottles with pearlized
finish by André Jolivet, designed and
made by Nesle Normandeuse, all
c. 1929. From left: 'Rosée de Bois',
'Lilas'; 'Perlinette' (large sphere);
'Firefly' (smaller elliptical);
'Perlinette' (cylinder); 'Firefly' (rare
mercury glass cylinder); 'Perlinette'
(miniature).
H. of large spherical bottle 19.5 cm
(7⅝ in.), miniature 5.5 cm (2⅛ in.).

Right
152, 153 Parfums de Marcy,
'Le Bracelet Miraculeux', 1928.
Presentation box (front view with
inner section closed, and top view
with inner section open) with set of
five bottles containing 'No. 9', 'No. 2'
(3) and 'No. 9'.
H. 5.8 cm (2¼ in.).

Below right
154 Isabey, 'Le Collier d'Isabey' or
'Le Collier Parfumé', 1925. Set of six
bottles in presentation box.
H. 5.5 cm (2⅛ in.).

Opposite top
155, 156 Ybry, perfume bottles and vaporizers in carrying cases. Square Baccarat bottle no. 583, smaller case with René Lalique medallion, containing 'Femme de Paris' and 'Désir du Cœur' (both sets) plus 'Mon Ame' (set of three). H. 8.0 cm (3⅛ in.).

Opposite below
157 Ybry perfumes in Baccarat bottles of various sizes and colours, 1925-28. Perfumes include 'Femme de Paris' (clear and green), 'Désir du Cœur' (red), 'Devinez' (orange), 'Mon Ame' (purple) and 'Amour Sauvage' (black). H. of largest green bottle 19.5 cm (7⅞ in.), smallest sample bottle (not by Baccarat) 3.5 cm (1⅜ in.).

Top left and centre
158, 160 André Perugia, 'Les Heures de Perugia' (clear glass with painted decoration), and 'Soir' (black glass), both 1927. H. 21.5 cm (8½ in.) and 11.7 cm (4⅝ in.).

Top right
159 Guerlain, 'L'Heure Bleue', special presentation after the 1925 exhibition. Box and bottle (Baccarat model no. 598). H. 5.5 cm (2⅛ in.).

Centre left
161 Louiseboulanger, 'Louberri', 1923. Bottles in three sizes, smallest with stopper removed to show design. H. 12.8 cm (5 in.), 10.7 cm (4¼ in.) and 8.2 cm (3¼ in.).

Bottom left
162 F. Millot, 'Crêpe de Chine', 1925, and Madeleine Vionnet, 'Temptation', model of 1924. Open boxes with bottles. H. 12.0 cm (4¾ in.) and 12.5 cm (4⅞ in.).

163 Jean Patou perfumes and
(right) Bakelite powder box, 1925.
Designs by Louis Süe (from left):
three miniatures (with box)
containing 'Amour-Amour', 'Colony'
and 'Moment Suprême'; Baccarat
bottle no. 531 in four sizes, smallest
(shown with box) 'Que Sais-Je?',
medium 'Amour-Amour', two larger
sizes used for various perfumes.
H. of largest perfume bottle 26.0 cm
(10¼ in.), miniature 5.8 cm (2¼ in.)

164 Worth, 'Dans la Nuit', 1924.
Bottles in various sizes, all except
miniatures designed and made by
René Lalique, and rare reversed
colour glass powder box (in
foreground).
H. of largest bottle 24.0 cm (9½ in.),
smallest (in box) 8.0 cm (3⅛ in.);
powder box 13.0 cm (5¼ in.).

165 Jeanne Lanvin, Sèvres porcelain
bottles, 1926. Special limited
editions.
H. (blue bottle) 8.7 cm (3⅜ in.),
(burgundy bottle) 9.0 cm (3½ in.).

Bottom left
166 Les Parfums de Rosine, 'Coup
de Foudre', *c.* 1925. Brosse bottle on
base of open box.
H. 8.7 cm (3⅜ in.).

Bottom right
167 Hattie Carnegie, 'Hattie
Carnegie', *c.* 1925, possibly Julien
Viard design. Dépinoix bottle on base
of open box.
H. 7.5 cm (3 in.).

les allume-lèvres
de
PAQUIN

PARIS

Sergei Diaghilev died in Venice on 19 August 1929, and two months later, on 24 October, the New York Stock Exchange crashed. It could be claimed that in the arts and the world of finance the end of the 1920s had arrived prematurely. For most people, the hopeful and carefree years of the 1920s would be replaced by disappointment and general depression. The unemployment and panic of the early 1930s in the United States was to have a chilling effect on the fortunes of the French luxury trades. Until the latter part of the decade most of the industrialized world was, or felt, impoverished, though France was not as severely affected as other countries. There were still some affluent citizens in France, as well as some very rich clients and patrons, many of them from South America and Asia, who loved Paris and its luxurious creations. This patronage enabled most couture houses to stay in business by slashing prices, by using fabrics of reduced quality – but never by resorting to inferior standards of workmanship.

The major established French perfume houses – Lubin, Guerlain, Roger & Gallet, Bourjois, etc. – survived, but many newcomers to the perfume industry, especially those who specialized in luxury presentations, went bankrupt in the early 1930s. Simon Jaroslawski (the force behind Fioret, Ybry and Mÿon perfumes – all luxury productions) went into personal bankruptcy in 1932 and, although the brand names and original presentations would continue for a while, the Jaroslawski spirit was no longer present. The glass industry was equally affected by the general economic collapse, and among French glassworks specializing in perfume bottles Cristalleries de Nancy ceased production in 1934, as had Maugenest in 1933, though important companies, such as Baccarat, Brosse and Lalique, were able to continue.

For those who remained in the perfume business in France, the new realities introduced by the Great Depression had to be taken into account. A general desire for practicality and simplification finally allowed the Constructivist, De Stijl and Bauhaus philosophies to pervade the arts and decorative arts in France, their new ideas being absorbed and reinterpreted by French artists. Gone, however, were the skilled artisans whose craftsmanship had contributed to the individuality, but also to the cost, of perfume presentations. Gone were the flowered basket and the overflowing bowl so symbolic of Art Deco. Gone was the influence of the Orient and its elaborate

Facing page
168 Paquin, 'Les Allume-Lèvres', 1939. Lipstick in the form of a match-book.
H. 6.0 cm (2⅜ in.).

97 Molinelle, 'No 29', 1930, smaller bottle next to its box, larger size in open box. H. 10.5 cm (4⅛ in.); 15.0 cm (5⅞ in.).

98 Ciro, 'Réflexions', 1933, Baccarat bottle no. 746. H. 13.5 cm (5¼ in.).

ornamentations. Now, instead of turning east as a source of inspiration, artists turned west, adopting American ideas, even though many of them never actually crossed the Atlantic. Instead, movies and photographs provided ample visual information to stimulate new and strong modern French styles in perfume presentations. Practical, simplified, linear, mostly machine-produced, the new designs were nonetheless dramatic, elegant and harmonious. Such well-known figures as Poiret, Iribe, Lepape, Erté and Barbier, who directly or indirectly influenced the development of perfume presentations, would work at some time or other for Hollywood, Broadway theatres or for American fashion magazines.

As a result of these influences, a new group of perfume presentations emerged. Functional and streamlined shapes, simple and reflective surfaces, and the use of chrome finishes rather than gold would be the primary characteristics. Perfume no longer found its inspirations in nature, but in the dream of the urban metropolis (with its skyscrapers and its emphasis on machine-made products), as well in fantasies evoked by Hollywood movies. A flashy sense of luxury was added through the use of sleek and reflective materials. Gems, modernist architecture and interiors and, sometimes, faraway celestial bodies were favourite themes. There was a reaction against the visual distortion associated with such art movements as Cubism and Futurism. There was now a need for realism in art. The contrast provided by the trends towards realism and escapism gave rise to divergent tendencies towards both the real and the surreal in 1930s perfume presentations.

The Martial et Armand perfume 'Présence' of 1930 was the quintessential modernist creation, featuring the use of steel and Bakelite – a glorification of the machine age (see p. 14 and pl. 10). Its style represented a dramatic departure from the now totally out-of-date Martial et Armand logo. Also in 1930, Mÿon introduced a Baccarat crystal bottle in various colours (produced in the same manner as the earlier Ybry bottles), in the form of a flat square with a hinged metal cover on one corner concealing an inner stopper – an extravagant, yet abstract concept. 'Cœur de Femme' ('Woman's Heart') was in green crystal and 'Femme Moderne' ('Modern Woman') in red (pls. 175, 176). These were to be Jaroslawski's last superb creations.

Recently built New York skyscrapers such as the Chrysler Building and the Empire State Building provided the inspiration for the Worth presentation 'Je Reviens' ('I Return') of 1931. Lalique produced the tall, ribbed bottle in dark-blue glass (pl. 184), which bore an uncanny resemblance to a drawing by Mies van der Rohe, 'Project for a Glass Skyscraper' of 1921. Sky-blue was the colour chosen for the stopper. The plain reflective chrome surface of the box added to the serene and very modern aloofness of this presentation.

Another important trend, which had originated in the United States in the 1920s, was the rise of the interior decorator, who became a new arbiter of taste – the person who interpreted the client's wishes, or who might impose his own taste if the client had none. In the early 1930s, the work of a new group of English decorators had a wide impact on modern tastes and manners. They translated the Hollywood style into a new English chic, and a few of them became the new dictators of taste.

Some new English perfume presentations were in great demand in the United States and even in France. Molinelle, a newly founded London company, introduced 'Beau Geste' ('Gracious Gesture') in 1930 and thanks to its immediate success, most other Molinelle perfumes such as 'No. 29' (also of 1930) would be offered in the same presentation (97). A co-ordinated octagonal shape was used for bottle and stopper, echoed by the conforming box. An allegorical scene depicted on the stopper provided the meaning of the name 'Beau Geste' – a seated figure of Aphrodite, the goddess of love giving bubbles of love to Eros to deliver. A special and very unusual crystal edition for the Molinelle perfume 'Gardenia' (pls. 172–174) featured a gilded version of this scene, while the overall shape was transformed to resemble a brilliant-cut diamond. In its construction this bottle was unique: when viewed from above, it looked more like a powder box made of glass, but when the top cover was removed, it was possible to see that this bottle was very compressed. Three threaded crystal beads, attached to the stopper, served as a very unusual dauber.

Although all-white interior décor had already been seen in the work of Jean-Michel Frank, Oliver Messel and others, it was the English decorator Syrie Maugham who achieved considerable fame with her well-publicized Chelsea home in London. Her living room featured white walls, white fabrics, white-lacquered furniture, and an impressive mirrored folding screen to reflect the stark environment. Writing about her design philosophy, she said 'Elimination is one of the secrets of successful decoration.' (*The Studio*, 1933). This concept was already known to designers of perfume presentations, and consequently that same year two new presentations revealed the direct influence of the Maugham living room. The angular Baccarat crystal bottle for the Ciro perfume 'Réflexions' was presented on the mirrored base of a white-lacquered stepped pedestal, and had a white silk cover (98). The Lucien Lelong presentation for 'Mon Image' ('My Image') was stark and uncompromising, without colour, warmth or softness to the touch. This abstract object was made of crystal and mirror glass only. Thus the faces and immediate surroundings (whatever they might be) would be reflected by 'Mon Image' (99). This unique perfume concept was never repeated or emulated. Although these designs were unfeminine and 'cold', their geometry and materials ensured that the resulting presentations were highly dramatic.

Another striking creation was that for the Lucien Lelong perfume 'La Première' of 1934, sold in the United States as 'Opening Night'. The glittering pyramid-shaped bottle on its black Bakelite base was reminiscent of a film set, and the cover of the box was black with a white satin top and silver trimmings, the surface decoration consisting of white painted dots representing the Paris Opéra and the Eiffel Tower in outline (100). The overall effect

99 Lucien Lelong, 'Mon Image', 1933. Romesnil miniature and perfume bottle with its mirrored box. H. 4.0 cm (1⅝ in.); 9.3 cm (3⅝ in.).

100 Lucien Lelong, 'Opening Night', 1934, bottle and box. H. 7.5 cm (3 in.).

101 Lucien Lelong, 'Impromptu', 1937, in two sizes, larger with box. H. 14.5 cm (5¾ in.); 9.0 cm (3½ in.).

151

102 Dana, 'Tchad', black Bakelite lipsticks, *c.* 1938. H. 7.0 cm (2¾ in.).

103 Lubin, 'Ouvrez-moi', 1936. H. 7.7 cm (3 in.).

104 Varva, 'Suivez Moi', 1938, pearlized bottle, inverted in ring setting affixed to box base. H. 3.3 cm (1¼ in.).

was to suggest the American dream of a glorious opening night in the French capital. The name 'Vega', given to a Guerlain perfume of 1936, was adopted from one of the brightest stars visible in the northern hemisphere. The Baccarat crystal bottle suggested the trajectories of various planets around a central star – the stopper (pl. 182). Also featuring an octagonal Bakelite and leather-covered box, this presentation was a stylish rendering of the idea of a first magnitude star, given that in the 1930s – the age of cinema as a new type of mass entertainment – the word 'star' was acquiring a fascinating new meaning. Despite its name, the Lucien Lelong perfume 'Impromptu' of 1937 was anything but hasty or improvised. The presentation, which included a very unusually constructed bottle and its matching box, was a highly evolved visual concept (101). The sunburst motif used on the bottle, stopper and box might be seen as a graphic rendering of the name 'Impromptu'.

However, this decade also witnessed a strong reaction against abstraction in art, which in the context of perfume presentations was expressed through representational, neo-Romantic and Surrealist styles. Particularly sophisticated representations were seen both in perfume items and related cosmetics. A black Bakelite lipstick case, 'Tchad' ('Chad'), was inspired by African artefacts – in this case a carved standing figure – shown at the Colonial Exhibition in Paris in 1931. 'Tchad' (102) was produced by Dana, a company founded in 1932, which often chose names inspired by Africa or other exotic themes, e.g. 'Voodoo', 'Tabu', 'Totem', 'Aloha' and 'Tundra'. Another case of literal borrowing was the use of the distinctive hat – the *chapeau bras* – favoured by Napoleon as the dominant feature (the stopper) in two Molinard presentations (pl. 179), both with names evoking the Emperor's military campaigns: '1811' and 'Soir d'Italie' ('Evening in Italy').

In 1935 the launching of the luxury liner *Normandie* was a major event marked by the introduction of a prestigious new Patou perfume, appropriately named 'Normandie'. The leading French artists of the day had contributed to the ship's lavishly decorated interiors, and Louis Süe created a special limited edition perfume presentation for the ship's maiden voyage from Le Havre to New York, departing on 29 May. All first-class passengers received as a souvenir a model of the *Normandie* in metal with a simple removable crystal bottle concealed in a central container in the shape of a ship's funnel emblazoned with the name and the French flag (pl. 180).

For chic women, smoking in public had not only become accepted, but the habit also introduced a range of elegant gestures. The entire presentation of the Lubin perfume 'Fumée' ('Smoke') of 1934 was a simulation of familiar cigarette packaging. The moulded bottle and its white-paper label and cap were designed to resemble a row of five cigarettes when seen in the box (pl. 181). The five 'cigarettes' each bore one of the letters of 'Fumée' and 'Lubin', thus spelling out the two names. When the bottle was removed from its box, the back was seen as a mirror image of the five realistically modelled cigarettes, but without decoration. A somewhat outrageous name, 'Ouvrez-moi' ('Open Me'), given to another Lubin perfume was offset by its toy-like bottle in the form of a small black-glass replica of a lady's handbag (103).

On many occasions previously, realistic imitations of jewelry had been designed for perfume presentations, and in 1938 the New York company Varva introduced 'Suivez Moi' ('Follow Me'), presented as a large pearl ring. The simulated pearl bottle was placed upside-down into the bezel of a silver ring, the hoop of which was secured to the velvet-covered base of the box (104). A Russian *émigré*, Prince George Matchabelli, had introduced his first perfumes in New York in the 1920s. The names he chose emphasized royalty, e.g. 'Princess Norina', 'Queen of Georgia', 'Katherine the Great' and 'Duchess of York'. The nostalgic associations of these perfumes with royalty led to extraordinary commercial success worldwide, despite the fact that by the 1930s many royal houses in Europe no longer existed. The characteristic crown-shaped bottle was made in different sizes, colours and finishes, accompanied by an interesting variety of box designs (pls. 170, 171).

Realism in perfume presentations was everywhere, and even music found a literal rendering in 'Trois Notes' ('Three Notes'), a Ciro presentation for three different perfumes in which the box imitated a group of three quavers (105). Also a longing for the exotic and faraway places was sometimes graphically expressed, as in a modern glass version of a Chinese ginger jar, in a Chinese Imperial yellow box, for 'Shanghai' by Lenthéric (106), and a pineapple-shaped bottle in a straw box, both with a label decorated with a sailing ship on the high seas, for 'Colony' by Jean Patou (107).

The now very famous Hattie Carnegie of New York introduced quite a few perfumes and, like Bichara Malhamé twenty-five years before her, she had herself portrayed on the stoppers of gilded and clear-glass bottles (pl. 178) in a variety of sizes – identical except for 'Hypnotic', a perfume of 1939, where she was depicted staring with wide-open eyes.

In the 1930s, at a time when Europeans unable to cross the Atlantic had merely dreamt of the magic of New York skyscrapers, the presentation for 'Je Reviens' was an ideal design concept. Similarly, many Americans would have wished to visit Paris, but for the vast majority it would remain only a dream. Maybe this explains why 'Soir de Paris' ('Evening in Paris'), the romantic Bourjois line introduced in 1928, became a symbol of that dream and an all-time bestseller. A variety of further imaginative 'Evening in Paris' presentations were introduced during the 1930s, with individual bottles sometimes presented in star-shaped boxes, or a grouping of smaller items in a specially designed larger box such as a rare special-edition example in crescent-moon shape – relating to the 'evening' theme (pl. 169). Because this Bourjois line was popular-priced, the less expensive packaging materials, such as Bakelite and screw-top bottles, were made to appear more special by evoking the ideas of romance and fun associated with the French capital (108).

In the United States it was the time of *Gone with the Wind*, and flowing crinolines were back in style. In 1938 a Chicago fashion house, Eisenberg,

105 Ciro, 'Trois Notes' presentation, 1936, box lid removed showing three perfumes on base: 'Gardenia Sauvage'; 'Surrender'; 'Doux Jasmin'. H. of each bottle 6.3 cm (2½ in.).

106 Lenthéric, 'Shanghai', 1934, bottle on base of open box. H. 5.0 cm (2 in.).

107 Jean Patou, 'Colony', 1937, two bottles, smaller with gilded stopper, both with boxes. H. 13.0 cm (5⅛ in.); 10.0 cm (4 in.).

108 Bourjois, 'Soir de Paris', 1930s to 1950s, Bakelite novelties: (in background) champagne bucket; Easter egg; owl; hotel door; grandfather clock; Eiffel tower; (in foreground) clam; horseshoe; slipper; turtle; match box. H. (clock) 11.0 cm (4⅜ in.); (bucket) 9.5 cm (3¾ in.); (match box) 4.2 cm (1⅝ in.).

109 Eisenberg, '847-A' (smaller); '847-B' (larger), both 1938. H. 8.5 cm (3⅜ in.); 12.5 cm (4⅞ in.).

introduced two perfumes, '847-A' and '847-B', in superb frosted glass bottles moulded to resemble an elegant lady in an evening gown (109). Meanwhile, in Paris, the new romantic movement was closely tied to Surrealism, and the fashions and perfumes it inspired were of a very different nature. The couturier Lucien Lelong introduced some of the most beautifully romantic presentations of his day. 'Indiscret' ('Indiscreet') of 1935 featured partially drawn draped curtains (pl. 183) – a theme borrowed from the Surrealist movement, which used the drapery motif in art, as well as in theatre and movie sets. However, 'Indiscret' represented something more – the Lelong couture salons. The main salon was classic and streamlined, with ivory-coloured walls and furnishings. An entire wall covered in white vertical drapery had, slightly off-centre, an opening in the shape and size of a doorway, created by the drapery being drawn to one side. The mannequins modelling Lelong fashions would emerge from this opening. A short distance behind this opening was more drapery, with the result that no other decorative feature would distract the viewer's eye as the mannequins appeared.

The 'Indiscret' line included a talcum-powder holder made of plaster-of-Paris, a material for home accessories, lamps and decorations used by Alberto and Diego Giacometti, who created such objects for many interior design schemes by Jean-Michel Frank. Moulded wall-plaster draperies were also used in many areas of the Lelong salons. An unusual box for 'Indiscret' was called 'Ensemble' (110). It contained a matching pair of metal cases, one for powder, one for cigarettes, and a glass ashtray with the Lucien Lelong logo was also available (111). Smoking accessories and matching cosmetics were common. The name of another Lelong perfume of 1939, 'Jabot', revealed the source of its inspiration, the draped bow design of this bottle and its stopper being adapted and continued on the lid of its box (112).

As a versatile accessory, whether in the context of hair style, clothing or interior decor, the bow was also used in another perfume presentation. A bow-shaped, blue Baccarat bottle almost entirely covered in a 'shell' of gilding was used by Guerlain for 'Coque d'Or', the literal translation of which – 'Golden Shell' – would usually be associated with eggshell. The cover of the accompanying box, made of wood, was decorated with a metal trellis to create an appearance resembling that of basket-weave egg-boxes (pl. 177).

'Cyclamen', a Baccarat bottle for Elizabeth Arden, depicted another familiar fashion accessory having possible romantic associations – the fan (pl. 185). This presentation offered, as a bonus, a detachable floral pin which could be worn as a piece of costume jewelry. Another Baccarat bottle design for Elizabeth Arden was an almost exact replica of a well-known Victorian bud vase, the body of which was held by an applied moulded hand. This intriguing bottle, for a perfume called 'It's You', was produced in a variety of colour combinations and finishes (pl. 190). Some of these bottles were placed inside glass globes, creating an appearance similar to that of preserved bridal bouquets.

A further fashion item used as a source of inspiration was the hat. Suzy, a successful French milliner, took one of her own hats placed on a dummy as the model for a Baccarat bottle and its stopper. This was used for two of her perfumes. 'Ecarlate' ('Scarlet'), of 1939, decorated with red enamel, and 'Golden Laughter' of 1941, decorated with green enamel (pl. 186). These bottles were placed on a dressing-table base with oval mirror, and the entire Suzy presentation was a witty and very Parisian concept.

Since her arrival in Paris in 1922, the couturière Elsa Schiaparelli had been befriended by Dada artists and writers. She also met Paul Poiret, who eventually became her mentor. Although her fashion style was very different from Poiret's, they both loved colour, fantasy and extravagance, and were good friends until Poiret's death in 1944, even though the latter's business had collapsed many years earlier. The colour most associated with Schiaparelli – 'shocking pink' – was, incidentally, used first by Poiret at the height of his success. He, however, had called it *rose ignoble* (in fashion slang, 'dreadful pink'). Schiaparelli had introduced her first perfume in 1928; known simply as 'S', it was sold on a limited basis in a standard bottle and box. The year 1933 saw new Schiaparelli perfumes called 'Schiap', 'Shsh', 'Stunt', 'Syncopate', 'Salut' and 'Soucis' being contemplated, but in the following year only 'Schiap', 'Salut' and 'Soucis' were introduced to the public. The simple trapezoidal bottle for 'Salut' and the distinctive letter S on labels and boxes for these three new perfumes of 1934 were probably designed by Jean-Michel Frank.

In 1936, Schiaparelli introduced her own logo, which would thereafter appear frequently, printed on labels, boxes and packaging papers used for her perfumes, cosmetics and toiletries. It depicted a stylized figure of Schiaparelli, as a juggler with heart-shaped torso – probably an allusion to her seemingly inexhaustible vitality. The figure, energetically moving from left to right, was shown with the right foot raised and arms outstretched; on her right foot and on each hand was balanced a 'Salut' bottle. The style of the logo clearly reflected Schiaparelli's fascination with the circus, which would be the theme for one of her most successful fashion collections – aptly called the Circus Collection – shown in February 1938.

The years 1936 to 1938 were Schiaparelli's most creative period, when her circle of friends included the great Surrealist and neo-Romantic artists Jean Cocteau, Salvador Dali and Christian Bérard. The 'Shocking' and 'Sleeping' perfumes were closely related to Schiaparelli fashions. The 'Shocking' presentation – conceived by the painter Leonor Fini – featured shocking pink. Its bottle, shaped like a dressmaker's dummy (a Surrealist symbol), was inspired by the ample figure of Mae West, one of Schiaparelli's clients. Schiaparelli used the heart motif on her paper graphics, and even as soaps, all in the shade of pink identified with the 'Shocking' perfume (pl. 189). In *Harper's Bazaar* in 1938, a pink heart pinned on a dressmaker's dummy appeared in an advertisement for the perfume. By contrast,

110, 111 Lucien Lelong, 'Ensemble'. *c*. 1935. Presentation box. w. 22.5 cm (8⅞ in.). Ashtray with Lucien Lelong logo, and open box containing compact and cigarette box; w. 7.1 cm (2¾ in.); 7.0 cm (2¾ in.); 11.8 cm (4⅝ in.).

112 Lucien Lelong, 'Jabot', 1939, bottles in four sizes, two with boxes. H. large 9.0 cm (3½ in.); medium 6.5 cm (2½ in.); small 5.5 cm (2⅛ in.); miniature with Lucite screw top, 4.5 cm (1¾ in.).

113 Schiaparelli, 'Snuff', 1940, pipe-shaped bottle with 'cigar' box. H. 14.0 cm (5½ in.).

'Sleeping' was associated with pale blue, a cool colour. The 'candlestick' bottle in Baccarat crystal was presented in a snuffer-shaped box, the red stopper imitating a flame protruding at the top. The 'Sleeping' presentation was a fantasy object, evoking dreams and the surreal (pl. 191).

In an exceptionally rare special edition, the two very different themes, 'Shocking' and 'Sleeping', were combined in a Surrealist metaphor. This idea was unique, since perfume companies did not combine contrasting perfume themes in a presentation for only one of the perfumes. A heart-shaped box covered with blue satin displayed two 'Shocking' mannequins with blue 'Sleeping' labels side-by-side as if sleeping on a bed of paper shreds (pl. 188) – the same type of paper shreds as would be used for the 'Snuff' presentation. The covering of the box, without identifying labels, was hand-sewn to the same standard of workmanship as would be expected of Schiaparelli evening wear (pl. 187). This very special presentation might have been offered as a gift to a favoured client. 'Snuff', a perfume for men, was introduced in 1940. The bottle was realistically modelled in imitation of a tobacco pipe, presented lying on paper shreds inside a wooden cigar-box – a presentation which was realistic to the point of being surreal (113).

The Schiaparelli perfume presentations were romantic and stylish and, even though they were associated with Surrealism, did not feature the kind of disturbing displacements which was at the core of Surrealist art. A realistic and deceptive cosmetic object by the house of Paquin might have created such disorientation. Though associated with the beginnings of *haute couture*, and with the advent of the 'New Woman' (so prominently featured at the 1900 exhibition), Paquin was among the last long-established Paris couture houses to have its own perfumes. Only in 1939 was the decision to introduce perfumes and cosmetics taken by Ana de Pombo (who became Paquin's director after World War II). 'Les Allume-Lèvres' ('The Lip-Lighters') were real wood match-sticks with lipstick tips, presented as realistic matches (*allumettes*) and intended to be carried in a lady's handbag (pl. 168). This Surrealist object must have been the work of an excellent artist, since the association of flames and lips could be interpreted through the name and the image as either frightening or erotic.

The emphasis on realism in the 1930s brought about by drastically altered economic conditions, together with the ideas of the Surrealists, provided a dramatic contrast to the creativity and the opulence which had characterized the 1920s. Perfume presentations of the 1930s could almost be classified in two broad categories: those that still used the luxury approach, even though the form and subject-matter might have changed; and those that stressed humorous associations and novelty, coupled with the use of cheaper materials and mass-production techniques to help make them more competitive in a wider market. Just as economic recovery was beginning to take hold, the threat of war loomed larger. This decade, which began in the aftermath of the stock-market crash, would end with the outbreak of World War II.

169 Bourjois, 'Soir de Paris',
c. 1935, rare luxury edition box in
the form of a crescent moon
(containing lipstick, compact,
powder box and perfume bottle), and
two star-shaped boxes (each
containing a perfume bottle).
H. of crescent-moon box 25.7 cm
(10⅛ in.).

Right

170 Prince Matchabelli, grouping of miniature presentations, 1950s. Miniature bottles in two sizes.
H. 4.0 cm (1⅝ in.), 3.3 cm (1¼ in.).

Below

171 Prince Matchabelli, grouping of perfumes, lipstick and brooches, 1930s to 1950s. Perfumes: 'Ave Maria' (black opaline); 'Duchess of York' (blue opaline); 'Queen of Georgia' and 'Princess Norina' (red opaline); 'Katherine the Great' (white opaline); 'Beloved' (blue enamel); 'Wind Song' (green enamel); 'Added Attraction' (red enamel); 'Princess of Wales' (clear in brown box); 'Stradivari' (largest clear).
H. largest 16.0 cm (6¼ in.).
'Infanta', different crown shape in open box, right foreground, h. 4.0 cm (1⅝ in.).

172–174 Molinelle, 'Gardenia', special edition, 1930. Bottle seen from above, with top removed, and with stopper removed showing glass beads as dauber.
H. 4.7 cm (1⁷⁄₈ in.).

Centre below
175, 176 Mÿon, 'Femme Moderne' (red) and 'Cœur de Femme' (green). 1930. Baccarat bottle no. 719.
H. 7.8 cm (3⅛ in.).

Bottom
177 Guerlain, 'Coque d'Or', 1938. Baccarat bottle no. 770 in three sizes; medium size in open box with brass lattice work on lid.
H. 8.7 cm (3⅜ in.), 7.7 cm (3 in.) and 5.7 cm (2¼ in.).

Opposite above
180 Jean Patou, 'Normandie', 1935.
Design by Louis Süe.
H. 7.3 cm (2⅞ in.).

Opposite below
181 Lubin, 'Fumée', 1934. Box and
back view of bottle with top
removed, and front view of bottle in
open box.
H. 7.5 cm (3 in.).

178 Hattie Carnegie perfumes, all
c. 1938. 'Perfume No. 7' in clear-
glass bottle on base of open box; h.
6.0 cm (2⅜ in.). Gilded bottles in
various sizes containing (from left)
'Carte Blanche', 'Hypnotic' (with
eyes shown open), 'Perfume 49', and
'Perfume Carnegie II' with box.
H. of largest bottle 10.7 cm (4¼ in.),
smallest 4.8 cm (1⅞ in.).

Right
179 Molinard, '1811', 1938, and
'Soir d'Italie', *c.* 1938.
H. 10.0 cm (4 in.) and 8.2 cm
(3¼ in.).

Bottom left
183 Lucien Lelong. 'Indiscret',
1935. Purse flacon and plaster
talcum-powder holder.
H. of flacon 7.0 cm (2¾ in.), powder
holder 14.5 cm (5¾ in.).

Bottom right
184 Worth. 'Je Reviens', 1931. René
Lalique design and bottle, shown on
base of open box.
H. 13.5 cm (5¼ in.).

Below
182 Guerlain, 'Vega', 1936.
Baccarat bottle no. 759 on base
of open box.
H. 8.5 cm (3⅜ in.).

Right
185 Elizabeth Arden, 'Cyclamen',
1938. Baccarat bottle no. 776.
H. 13.0 cm (5⅛ in.), 16.0 cm (6¼ in.).

Centre
186 Suzy, 'Golden Laughter', 1941, on
presentation stand; 'Ecarlate', 1939,
miniature and full-size bottle. Both full-
size bottles Baccarat no. 782.
H. 11.0 cm (4⅜ in.).

Far right
187, 188 Schiaparelli, 'Sleeping',
c. 1938. Satin-covered heart-shaped
box closed and open, with two
miniature bottles.
H. 4.7 cm (1⅞ in.).

Below
189 Schiaparelli, 'Shocking', 1936.
Bottles, boxes, pouch, soaps, solid-
perfume pendant, and gilded Christmas
edition bottle, 1951.
H. of largest bottle 11.0 cm (4⅜ in.),
miniature (with lace) 4.3 cm (1¾ in.).

Opposite
190 Elizabeth Arden, 'It's You', 1939.
Baccarat bottle no. 781 in five versions,
one on stand with glass globe.
H. 16.0 cm (6¼ in.).

191 Schiaparelli, 'Sleeping', 1938.
Bottles in the form of candlesticks,
larger sizes with snuffer-shaped covers,
and white Bakelite lipstick.
H. of largest bottle (Baccarat no. 778)
21.0 cm (8¼ in.), smallest (on base)
12.0 cm (4¾ in.).

Although the first half of this decade was overshadowed by the effects of wartime destruction and austerity in Europe, the spirit of hope endured. Motivated by a strong sense of euphoria following the Allied victory, an outburst of post-war creativity was soon evident in art, fashion and other luxury trades. However, not all activities associated with perfume had ceased during the war years. Several new presentations appeared in France, most of them around 1940-41, and the couturier Marcel Rochas introduced his 'Femme' ('Woman') for Christmas 1944. During the war years many existing pre-war French perfumes were manufactured and bottled in the United States to meet the demands of the American domestic market, as well as for export. During this period, most perfumes originating in the United States also displayed a strong nostalgia for France, often reflected in French-sounding names and the use of design elements associated with French style. More and more Americans were becoming familiar with common French words – both from returning servicemen, and from frequent use in the American media. Because of lack of funds, however, as well as a dearth of qualified artisans and acute shortages of materials, many perfume presentations introduced in the 1940s displayed an unavoidable decline in quality. Not only were high standards difficult to attain, but such an aim was also somewhat undesirable, since perfume prices had to be kept within the means of a less affluent public.

One very specific area of perfume presentations which was not new to the 1940s, but which developed rapidly after World War II, was the small-size category containing only a small amount of perfume. For obvious economic reasons, the small-size presentations became very popular, and would remain so. Traditional ground-glass stoppers were usually replaced with metal or plastic screw-tops, and the appearance of luxury gave way to an industrial machine-made look. Often boxes were designed differently, in order to provide better visual support for the simpler, smaller bottles. Many small-size presentations were for portable 'purse bottles', while some extremely small presentations – miniatures – were given away as perfume samples. In France such samples were marked '*échantillon*' ('sample'), '*offert par . . .*' ('presented by . . .') or were described as 'not for sale'. This category would gain in importance with the developement of large-scale tourism and the expansion of international trade.

Facing page
192 Lilly Daché, 'Dashing', 1941.
Bottle on base of open box.
H. (including base) 19.5 cm (7⅝ in.).

114 Lucien Lelong, 'Clips', 1939, set of two bottles with brass tops and clips, in presentation box; 'Les Plumes', 1938, set of three purse bottles on base. H. 5.7 cm (2¼ in.).

115 Richard Hudnut, 'RSVP', c. 1945, box and bottle. H. 8.0 cm (3⅛ in.).

It was difficult, however, though not impossible, to introduce real quality in the small-size category. Wit often replaced luxury – a good idea, since many small sizes were purchased by young women. Some small-size examples displayed whimsical features that were not present in the corresponding larger presentations, and miniatures created for special occasions, such as the Christmas season, were particularly humorous and attractive in appearance. Therefore, the choosing of clever names became much more desirable in the marketing of perfumes. This decade also witnessed a new kind of 'chic', a concept which had been introduced by French Surrealist fashion designers, often making use of aesthetically unpleasing images, foreign to the field of fashion, incorporating them into a design characterized by beauty and elegance. The result could be 'unbeautiful' as long as it was 'chic'.

Looking back on many of the perfume presentations of the 1940s, it is important when trying to evaluate them to take into account the innocence and exuberant temperament of this decade, otherwise some of them may be simply dismissed as less expensive novelties, or regarded as just too sweet by current standards of taste. One such perfume was 'Dashing', introduced by Lilly Daché in 1941. This French-born, French-trained milliner achieved considerable success in the United States, where she lived and worked, becoming a member of New York society. Apart from the obvious aural allusion to her own name, the name 'Dashing' could be thought of as meaning dressy or spirited, both of which ideas were expressed by the bottle in the shape of a pampered French poodle sitting up, holding a letter and eager to please its owner (pl. 192). Also in 1941, Lilly Daché introduced 'Drifting', one of the great Surrealist perfume presentations. While 'Dashing' presented a humorous and somewhat absurd image, 'Drifting' was enigmatic (see p. 15 and pl. 2). Its feather motif recalled a favourite Surrealist theme familiar from avant-garde stage and movie sets. Christian Bérard loved using feathers, as did the milliners and fashion designers who came under the influence of the Surrealist vocabulary.

In 1938, Lucien Lelong had been the first to introduce this feather theme to perfume, with 'Les Plumes' ('The Feathers'), a set of three identical feather-shaped purse bottles. Then, in 1939, he introduced 'Clips', two identical feather models, now mounted on metal clips and intended to be worn as brooches (114). Various Lelong perfumes were presented in bottles of this type. Continuing this trend of associations between fashion and perfume presentations, the Dorothy Gray perfume 'Lady in the Dark', of 1941, was introduced in a bottle of unusual proportions, with an oversized stopper that resembled a feathered headdress (pl. 197). The topical connection lay in the fact that the perfume name was derived from the title of a musical by Kurt Weill, in which the leading lady was the editor of a fashion magazine.

In a different use of the feather theme, two presentations featured inkwell and quill pen. The first, 'RSVP', a Richard Hudnut perfume of 1935, received a new presentation c. 1945 (115). It was a dreamy object, with a pale silvery quality. The second, 'My Love' by Elizabeth Arden, introduced in 1948, featured a box that opened to reveal a stage set with a bottle of almost classic shape at the centre (pl. 198). This presentation was possibly inspired by Jean Cocteau, who designed the advertising for this perfume.

Yet another use of a feather was seen in 'Gala Performance', a dramatic presentation introduced by Helena Rubinstein in 1940. The obvious association with the theatre was conveyed by the use of a figural bottle, embellished with a feather, in the form of an actress acknowledging the applause of the audience, the label was threaded on to a gold cord which served as a belt and the bottle was appropriately placed in an open-fronted box resembling a stage backdrop.

A light-hearted, witty, yet superior design was used in 1949 for 'Griffonnage' ('Scribble'), a perfume by Jacques Griffe, a Paris fashion designer with a penchant for elaborate and extremely well-made clothes. The French word *griffe* means 'claw', as well as the 'signature', 'stamp' or 'clothes label' that a fashion designer would apply to his creations. The name 'Griffonnage' was conceived as a verbal and visual pun on the designer's name, and the presentation was an excellent example of a perfume name being represented by a co-ordinated theme incorporating its bottle, stopper and box: a book that opened to reveal scribbled notes, and an imitation ink-well and quill pen, sitting on a miniature replica of a desk blotter (pl. 206).

In an entirely different 'Griffonnage' presentation, a box in the shape of a wooden bobbin contained a simple spherical bottle. In this case, rather than express the meaning of the word *griffonnage*, the realistic bobbin of sewing-thread related to Jacques Griffe's role as a fashion designer (117, 118).

Two humorous approaches using French-style cliché elements were those adopted for the Renoir perfume 'Chi-Chi' and for 'Savoir Faire' ('Know-How') by Dorothy Gray. The 'Chi-Chi' bottle displayed a heart pierced by an arrow, lacy ruffles and a music-hall figure on its box (119), while the 'Savoir Faire' bottle was strangely bulbous, and decorated with a mask (120). Another humorous, but very daring idea for a perfume was 'Zut' (then a rude expletive in French, but now considered mild and acceptable). Introduced in 1948, this was one of the very few Schiaparelli perfume names not starting with the letter S. Schiaparelli's couture house had been closed during the war, when she was in the United States. After her return to Paris in 1945 it seemed as if the Schiaparelli fashion magic had evaporated. The new styles she introduced – the Talleyrand look, the Gibson Girl look, the Mummy look and the Broken Egg look – were all failures, and the fashion critics' verdicts had been unkind. 'Zut' may have been her answer to them. The 'Zut' bottle depicted a woman's figure from the waist down. Her star-studded skirt has fallen around her ankles, leaving her wearing only under-wear and a taffeta ribbon belt (121). The ribbon and box both featured the same unusual shade of dark green, which afterwards came to be known as *vert zut*. Although the perfume name and presentation were very popular in

116 Helena Rubinstein, 'Gala Performance', 1940, bottle, white ostrich feather, on presentation base. H. 14.5 cm (5¾ in.).

117, 118 Jacques Griffe, 'Griffonnage', 1949, bobbin-shaped box closed, and with cover removed showing inverted bottle attached to Bakelite and wood base. H. of bottle 5.0 cm (2 in.).

119 Renoir, 'Chi-Chi', 1942, box and bottle. H. 10.0 cm (4 in.).

120 Dorothy Gray, 'Savoir Faire', c. 1947. H. 10.0 cm (4 in.).

121 Schiaparelli, 'Zut', 1948, in four sizes, one with box. H. 14.5 cm (5¾ in.); 12.5 cm (4⅞ in.); 5.7 cm (2¼ in.); 4.5 cm (1¾ in.).

the American market, the very idea was considered too extreme in France, where 'Zut' was much less successful.

Perfume creations in the bold Hollywood style had begun to gain favour among Europeans in the 1930s, and this trend continued to grow in the 1940s. One such presentation was 'Cap à la Vie' (see p. 15 and pl. 3), in which the nautical associations of a distinctive and unusual bottle and box worked together to produce a stylish and original result. Unfortunately for this Mury perfume, wartime conditions meant that it was not fully distributed and that its success was limited. As hostilities in Europe came to an end in 1945, 'Insidia' (p. 16 and pl. 5), a beautiful, but oddly disturbing perfume presentation, was introduced by the Italian company GI. VI. Emme. The intriguing combination of a 'dagger' and a red velvet casket was a concept that seemed to hark back to the spirit of the 1920s, here reinterpreted in a cinematographic 1940s style.

Another startling creation, dating from 1947, was 'His' men's cologne and after-shave, together with the elegant 'Mondain' special edition, from The House for Men, Inc., based in Chicago. The bottle was in the form of a torso, and a modernist head made of Bakelite served as the stopper (pl. 204). While unusual artistic designs were rarely attempted for men's fragrances and toiletries, the 'His' élite series were impressive objects worth keeping, the suggestion of worldliness or high society implicit in the name being inspired by the popular idols of the time, the suave heroes of the silver screen.

Although the theme of gossip might seem a most unusual choice for a perfume presentation, in 1944 'On Dit' ('They Say') by Elizabeth Arden conveyed this association of ideas through an imaginative scene of women gossiping. This was elegantly moulded as decoration on a frosted-glass bottle of classic proportions (122).

The couture house of Lanvin, the style of whose elegant perfume presentations had not changed since the 1920s, now introduced charming ceramic figurines (actually bottles) as perfume displays (pl. 200). The 'Sandwich-board Man' carried advertising for Lanvin products, perfumes on the front and powders on the back. On one arm the 'Snowman' held a black Lanvin bottle with a minute paper label with gilded Lanvin logo for 'Prétexte' (introduced in 1937) – an amazing detail. The replica of a 'Colonne Morris', a familiar feature of streets in Paris on which posters are pasted, actually served as a means of publicizing the names of Lanvin perfumes. These figures were based on the witty Lanvin advertising created by Guillaume Gilet.

A most unconventional presentation, 'Anonyme', was introduced by Legrain in 1945, featuring a 17-line letter opening with 'Chérie' ('Darling'), a total of 69 words about perfume, love, absence and memories (pl. 194). The words were enamelled on the gently waisted bottle and printed on the conforming box, both of which simulated a parchment scroll and displayed a gilded spiral motif. To prevent the 'scroll' from opening, a lilac ribbon was tied around the bottle, its colour matching that of the enamelled words.

Marquay perfumes were founded after the war. In 1948, and for the next few years, many museums and galleries celebrated the centenary of the birth of Paul Gauguin with special exhibitions. The first of these was a major retrospective at the Orangerie in the Jardin des Tuileries in Paris. One of the last commemorative exhibitions took place at Pont Aven in 1953, the 50th anniversary of the artist's death. Gauguin's works were now being rediscovered in depth. His love for the exotic world of the South Sea islands found echoes in a widely felt contemporary desire for escape from post-war difficulties in Europe. Although by that time Gauguin's paintings were well known, a more esoteric side of his art – the sculptures – was only then becoming known to many viewers for the first time. Among those exotic sculptures were wood-carvings, including the rare cylinders carved in-the-round depicting two or three Polynesian figures. One of the first Marquay perfumes, 'Douka', was directly inspired by this renewed interest in Gauguin and the Polynesian style (pl. 201).

The moulded bottle for the special edition of 'Douka' – a tall, relatively simple model of square section – had three circular indentations on each of its sides, and matching scalloped corners (pl. 201). The bottle resembled a length of sawn timber with carved decoration, and the figural stopper depicted a stylized head, somewhat reminiscent of the colossal carved stone heads on Easter Island. The face was indicated by a depressed oval area, without eyes or mouth, but with a prominent geometric nose, and an additional striking touch was provided by a pair of gilded loop earrings and a gold paper label around the narrow neck of the bottle. The design of the magnificent box for the 'Douka' special edition was inspired by Gauguin sculptures of the 1890s in the form of wooden cylinders. It was carved with three standing figures and marked *acajou massif sculpté* ('sculpted solid mahogany') on a label placed on the underside. This box may possibly have originated in one of the French colonies. Wood-carvings were very rarely used in French perfume presentations; in fact the de Vigny 'Guili-Guili' head and foot of 1926 may have been the only instance before 'Douka'. This 'Douka' presentation was quite unlike any other. Powerful, visually unbeautiful or unconventionally beautiful, this was a very avant-garde perfume concept. Possibly because it could not hope to attract a wide audience, and on account of the skill, time and cost required to make each individual carved box, 'Douka' was only a minimal production.

By contrast, small-sized bottles provided opportunities for particularly playful fantasies, and the results were very appealing when displayed in sets. The American perfumer Mary Chess introduced her 'Chess Pieces' in the late 1930s, but they were distributed mainly after 1941, when they became very popular. Both the perfume name and the bottles modelled on standard chess pieces were an obvious play on her surname. Schiaparelli may have been the first perfumer to introduce this type of perfume name, to be followed by Mary Chess, Lilly Daché, Jacques Griffe and Christian Dior. Chess even had

122 Elizabeth Arden, 'On Dit', 1944. H. 10.5 cm (4⅛ in.).

a perfume named 'Yram' (Mary spelled backwards). Sets of 'Chess Pieces' – king, queen, bishop, rook, knight and sometimes pawns – were displayed together in various presentation boxes, and the use of a rotary stand – a small lazy Susan – was particularly novel (pl. 202). Elizabeth Arden and Elsa Schiaparelli both made excellent use of miniature replica bottles, their samples being high-style fantasies (pls. 199, 203).

Although the majority of perfume companies adapted their presentations to the new realities of the market place – less luxury, lower prices – a few French companies, primarily couturiers, dared to take the opposite direction and met with success. Marcel Rochas led the way with 'Femme', introduced during the war as a luxury limited edition. The curvaceous Marc Lalique bottle, presented in a box covered with black lace, was based on an original idea of Leonor Fini. Miniature purse bottles, oval shaped and made in white, pink or yellow opaline glass, were entirely covered in delicate black lace (pl. 196). This was only the second time that a perfume bottle had been tightly covered in lace – the first had been 'Le Minaret', a Poiret creation for Rosine in 1913. Since Rochas was an admirer of Poiret's designs, this use of a lace-covered bottle may have been an act of homage, although it also symbolized the femininity of a black-lace *guêpière* ('waspie'), a new short corset that only cinched the waist, designed by Rochas in 1942. In 1946, Rochas presented an exhibition in his own salons called 'Les Parfums à Travers la Mode' ('Perfumes as Seen through Fashion'), possibly the first of its kind.

Immediately after the war, many new perfumes were introduced. To celebrate the Allied victory, Salvador Dali designed 'Le Roy Soleil' ('The Sun King') for Schiaparelli (see p. 16 and pl. 1), a striking surreal image which must count as one of the greatest ever perfume presentations. Another commemorative object, this time created for Jean Patou by Louis Süe, was 'L'Heure Attendue' ('The Awaited Hour'). This romantic presentation of 1945 also depicted the sun, here seen rising over the horizon to herald the hour of Liberation (pl. 195).

In the 1940s, two leading fashion designers, Christian Dior and Nina Ricci, reintroduced the great French tradition in their perfume presentations. Christian Dior was a young, but experienced, fashion designer when he opened his own couture house in 1946. As a very young man, he had an art gallery in Paris, where works by important artists such as Giorgio de Chirico, Picasso and Fernand Léger were exhibited. Later, he sold his fashion sketches to various established fashion designers, and was employed by Lucien Lelong, for whom he created many successful styles. He had also designed costumes for French film productions, and had made many friends among artists in all fields.

The first Dior collection was shown on 12 February 1947. The original, romantic and elegant fashions became known as 'The New Look', a phrase coined by Carmel Snow, then editor-in-chief of *Harper's Bazaar*. The first Dior perfume, 'Miss Dior', also introduced that year, was presented in an elegant amphora-shaped bottle in clear crystal (pl. 208). This Baccarat bottle expressed the 'New Look' of the Dior fashions very well – rounded shoulders, emphasis on bust and hips, and a very narrow waist. The first 'Miss Dior' bottle was immediately followed by a sumptuous overlay model in which an outer layer of coloured crystal was partially cut away to reveal areas of clear crystal, the resulting stylish effect being emphasized by gilded details. The wave of patriotism seen after the war inspired the choice of colours – blue, white and red – adopted from the French tricolor (pls. 209-211). This 'Miss Dior' model was also used later for 'Diorama' (1948).

The amphora-style Dior bottles and their luxurious classic boxes were also in keeping with the grey-and-white décor of the salons, designed by Victor Grandpierre in Louis XVI style. The elegance of the Dior style, a consistent feature of all his fashions and surroundings, was also synthesized in his perfume presentations.

The couture house of Nina Ricci, founded in 1932, became known for its feminine and romantic creations. During the war, four new perfumes were created: 'Cœur Joie' ('Joyful Heart') and 'Barbaresque', both in 1943; and 'L'Air du Temps' ('The Air of the Times') and 'Douce' ('Sweet'), both in 1944. However, 'Barbaresque' was not sold to the public. To celebrate the Allied victory, the first major Nina Ricci perfume, 'Cœur Joie' was introduced in 1946 (pl. 205). The bottle had been designed by Marc Lalique during the war, but its production was delayed. From then until after 1960 Marc Lalique would design all Ricci perfume bottles. The ideal Ricci woman, as conceived by Christian Bérard, was represented on the box-lid, wearing a heart-shaped hat. 'Cœur Joie' was remarkably original, very feminine and sweet, and thus perfectly suited to the Nina Ricci romantic fashions.

The second major Ricci perfume, introduced in 1948, was 'L'Air du Temps', the first edition of which was sold in a sunburst-shaped bottle. The sunburst motif was still associated with the outcome of the war, and the button stopper was decorated with a dove – symbolic of peace and love (123). The lid of the extraordinary box, moulded in white paper and lined with white silk, depicted a woman and a flying dove in low relief. The effect resembled that of neo-romantic plaster wall-decorations used in interiors and in stage and movie sets by such artists as Alberto and Diego Giacometti, Emilio Terry, Jean Cocteau and Christian Bérard. This lid design, by Bérard, was similar to a plaster medallion designed by Alberto Giacometti for Baron Roland de l'Espée's ballroom in 1936. In 1951, a limited edition of 'L'Air du Temps' was introduced in a bottle different in shape from the original. Here, the stopper featured two doves in flight. The display box, covered in yellow pleated silk (pl. 207), was in the shape of a domed bird-cage and could be illuminated (an electric battery was supplied in a matching yellow pouch). The yellow outer box had Bérard-style drawings printed on the outside.

Christian Bérard set the tone for all the advertising and paper graphics associated with Ricci perfumes. After his premature death in 1949, his style

123 Nina Ricci, 'L'Air du Temps' (sunburst edition), 1948, bottles designed and made by Marc Lalique, in three sizes, medium size with box. H. 7.7 cm (3 in.); 10.0 cm (4 in.); 4.7 cm (1⅞ in.).

was continued by other artists working for Ricci perfumes. Originally, Bérard studied with Vuillard, and both artists were strongly influenced by Japanese art. Later, he worked for many fashion magazines and fashion designers, but he preferred to work in the field of the theatre and ballet, designing sets and costumes of exquisite sensitivity. His spontaneous and poetic style was never simply accurate, and was always evocative. From the early 1930s until his death, the Bérard influence was generally felt in the arts, fashions and lifestyles of France. The enduring Nina Ricci images are among his most outstanding achievements.

The prestigious Revillon company, the successor to possibly the oldest fur-designing house in France (dating back to 1723), introduced its first perfumes in 1935. 'Cantilène', a new perfume of 1948, was named after a type of French song which is deeply tender and sentimental. The limited edition bottle created for the 'Cantilène' introduction was an abstract design by Fernand Léger. The artist had spent the war years in the United States, where the 'American intensity', as he called it, had a profound effect on the evolution of his art. It was in New York that Léger became seriously interested in sculpture, and after his return to France he produced over fifty ceramic sculptures and plaques, and even several bronzes. Léger had always been concerned with bringing art to the people, and more precisely, with bringing poetry to the streets. Many poets were drawn to Léger's art, and in turn, Léger illustrated some of their poetry, thus creating 'Object-Poems' to be introduced into the humdrum routines of daily life. It was in New York, during the war, that Léger illustrated a short anthology of poems, 'Chansons de France' ('Songs of France') by Ivan Goll, published in *Poet's Messages*.

The overall biomorphic shape of the 'Cantilène' bottle was familiar to Léger, who had used such anti-geometric shapes many times in his paintings. A triptych painted by Léger in 1941, *Les Plongeurs sur fond jaune* ('Divers on a Yellow Background'), depicted in the left hand panel a shape very similar to that of the 'Cantilène' bottle. The abstract composition can be interpreted as the surface of the water seen from above immediately after the divers have disappeared below it; nothing remains except the sunny ripple effects and the play of light and shadows. The 'Cantilène' bottle was in effect a three-dimensional rendering of that portion of the painting, while the stopper may be seen as a rendering of the map of north-western France as it had been poetically sketched by Léger for the cover of 'Chansons de France' (pl. 193). The three-dimensional poetry achieved by Fernand Léger in 'Cantilène' was an integral part of his work. The design fulfilled his wish to reach people through poetry – in this case that of a perfume presentation.

The 1940s, particularly the years 1945 to 1949, provided a period of transition both from the styles expressed during the 1930s and from the depressing reality of World War II. It was a period during which ideas associated with both 'beautiful' and 'chic' were redefined, and it set the stage for the more romantic and fun-loving decade of the 1950s.

193 Revillon, 'Cantilène', 1948.
Fernand Léger design.
H. 13.5 cm (5¼ in.).

194 Legrain, 'Anonyme', 1945.
Open box with bottle on stand.
H. 13.5 cm (5¼ in.).

Below
195 Jean Patou, 'L'Heure Attendue',
1945. Design by Louis Süe. Bottle in
open box.
H. 7.5 cm (3 in.).

Below right
196 Marcel Rochas, 'Femme', 1944.
Marc Lalique design and bottle,
shown in open box; (background)
luxury Baccarat edition; 'La Rose',
1948, miniature; 'Mouche', 'Femme',
'La Rose', Christmas edition purse
bottles and pouches, 1948.
H. of Baccarat bottle 10.2 cm (4 in.);
purse bottles 6.8 cm (2⅝ in.).

Opposite, above left
197 Dorothy Gray, 'Lady in the
Dark', 1941.
H. 7.5 cm (3 in.).

Opposite, above right
198 Elizabeth Arden, 'My Love',
1948. Three bottles in different sizes
and miniature.
H. of largest bottle 10.0 cm (4 in.),
miniature 5.5 cm (2⅛ in.).

Opposite below
199 Elizabeth Arden, 'My Love'
and 'Blue Grass' miniatures, 1940s
to 1950s.
H. largest 7.7 cm (3 in.), smallest
4.0 cm (1⅝ in.).

Opposite above
200 Lanvin, ceramic display bottles, 1940–45:
H. 26.0 cm (10¼ in.) to 27.0 cm (10⅝ in.).

Opposite, below left
201 Marquay, 'Douka' special limited edition,
1948. Bottle on base of sculpted mahogany box.
H. 14.0 cm (5½ in.).

Opposite, below right
202 Mary Chess, 'Chess Pieces', *c.* 1942. Open box
with stand and set of bottles containing 'Strategy',
'Yram', 'White Lilac', 'Tapestry' and 'Carnation'.
H. of tallest bottle 8.0 cm (3⅛ in.).

Right
203 Schiaparelli miniatures, 1930s to 1950s:
'Shocking' with box; 'Sleeping' candle bottle;
'Sleeping', 'Shocking', 'Zut' samples; 'Zut' (with
ribbon); 'Salut (with Bakelite top); rouge box.
H. of candle bottle 8.0 cm (3⅛ in.).

204 The House for Men grouping, 1947 (from left):
'Mondain' after-shave lotion; 'His' gold élite series
(after-shave, cologne); 'His' burgundy series (after-
shave, talcum).
H. 16.5 cm (6½ in.).

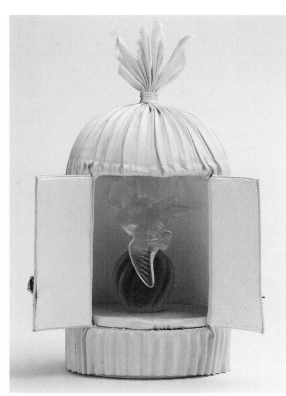

Opposite above
205 Nina Ricci, 'Cœur Joie', 1946. Marc Lalique designs and bottles. Graphics by Christian Bérard. Bottles and boxes, with purse flacon in foreground.
H. 12.0 cm (4³⁄₄ in.), 10.0 cm (4 in.), 6.5 cm (2¹⁄₂ in.); flacon 9.7 cm (3⁷⁄₈ in.).

Opposite, below left
206 Jacques Griffe, 'Griffonnage', 1949. Open box with 'writing set' presentation.
H. of bottle (without quill) 5.5 cm (2¹⁄₈ in.).

Opposite, below right
207 Nina Ricci, 'L'Air du Temps' special limited edition, 1951. Marc Lalique design and bottle, shown in 'birdcage' presentation box.
H. 10.5 cm (4¹⁄₈ in.).

Below
208 Christian Dior, 'Miss Dior', 1947. Baccarat bottle no. 814. Presentation box with clear-crystal bottle.
H. 17.7 cm (7 in.).

Right
209-211 Christian Dior, 'Miss Dior', 1947. Baccarat bottle no. 814. Open presentation boxes with blue, white and red overlay crystal bottles.
H. 17.7 cm (7 in.).

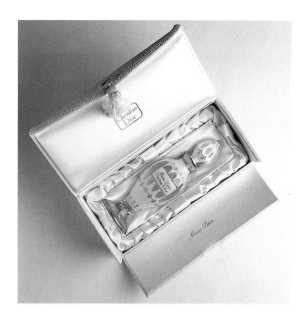

1950 to 1959

The End of Innocence

Chapter 7

E ven if the conditions of post-war austerity were in many respects still present in Europe in the 1950s, the decade was on the whole a light-hearted period as expressed in stage plays and the cinema. There was a breath of fresh air both in the arts and in fashion, and the mood was one of innocent gaiety. It was a time for romance. Paris and perfumes together, more than ever, provided inspiration for artists and ordinary people, while the continually evolving presentations of perfumes gave rise to romantic objects with joyful associations.

One such object - 'Succès Fou' ('Raving Success'), the Schiaparelli perfume of 1953 - was inspired by the French artist Peynet whose work appeared constantly in the Paris press during this decade, depicting a pair of innocent young lovers who came to be known as 'Les Amoureux de Peynet' ('Peynet's Lovers'). They were constantly together, usually shown sitting on a park bench surrounded by flying leaves and a few doves, while words or feelings were sometimes indicated through small heart shapes, which were often incorporated into the drawings. The romantic and whimsical innocence of these young lovers became a byword for the 1950s in France, and during those years the artist could be said to have enjoyed a *succès fou* in Paris. Peynet recalls being approached by Michel de Brunhoff, then editor-in-chief of French *Vogue*, and being asked by him on behalf of Elsa Schiaparelli to design the advertising for the perfume 'Succès Fou', the presentation for which incorporated the two basic Peynet motifs – the leaf (as the green-glass bottle) and the heart (as the shape of the heart-shaped pink and green box). This presentation was designed jointly by Elsa Schiaparelli and Michel de Brunhoff. Elsa Schiaparelli had captured the spirit of the 1930s through her fashions and perfumes, and although her fashions were no longer attuned to the new age of the 1950s, her 'Succès Fou' perfume (pl. 214) did reflect the spirit of this prosperous period of innocence.

In the early 1950s, Marquay introduced its 'Monsieur Marquay' cologne for men, which was sold in a bottle designed by Salvador Dali. Like the 'His' élite series of the 1940s, it featured an elegant man, this one a top-hatted dandy wearing a silk bow tie. Incorporated into this asymmetrical abstract bottle was a hint of body movement not unlike a Fred Astaire pose, and printed on the simple white box was Dali's familiar moustache and his

Facing page
212 Lancôme, 'Les Danseurs', limited edition presentation, 1954, Georges Delhomme design, with 'Magie' and 'Trésor' bottles fused together, and box.
H. 11.5 cm (4½ in.).

124 Marquay, 'Monsieur Marquay', c. 1953, bottle designed by Salvador Dali in front of its box. H. 19.0 cm (7 in.).

125 Nina Ricci, 'Fille d'Eve', 1952, bottle designed and made by Marc Lalique in open straw-basket presentation. H. 6.5 cm (2½ in.).

126 Nina Ricci, grouping of miniature bottles: 'L'Air du Temps', 'Cœur Joie', 'Fille d'Eve', 1940s–1950s. Bottles designed and made by Marc Lalique. H. of largest 5.7 cm (2¼ in.); smallest 3.2 cm (1¼ in.).

signature. Thus, 'Monsieur Marquay' was one of the rare perfume presentations intended specifically for men which revealed a design that was at once original and witty (124). Another whimsical presentation was developed for 'Si' ('Yes'), a Schiaparelli perfume of 1957 (pl. 215). Its gilded and enamelled bottle for the de luxe presentation was in the shape of a Chianti wine bottle – suggesting the Italian associations of the name. The miniature version was a charming replica in the same spirit as the full-size bottle, while on the box of a more modest presentation musical notes were printed as a punning reference to the seventh note of the musical scale, *si* (*ti* in English).

In the course of this decade Venice experienced a renaissance as an international centre of culture, with artists and patrons of all nationalities travelling to or living in the city, and tourism became a very important aspect of its everyday life. Two ceramic perfume presentations included bottles in imitation of famous Venetian sights: the granite column surmounted by the lion of St Mark in the Piazzetta was reproduced for a Vidal perfume, and 'Notte di Venezia' ('Venetian Night') by Linetti was sold in a gondola-shaped presentation (pl. 217).

The image of romantic luxury, initially created by Christian Bérard, was continued by Nina Ricci with 'Fille d'Eve' ('Eve's Daughter'), introduced in 1952. In its introductory presentation the appropriately apple-shaped frosted bottle by Marc Lalique was placed inside a silk-lined woven basket (125). Miniatures and samples were more successful than ever, and several perfumes were often presented as a set in one box. 'Cœur Joie' and 'L'Air du Temps', two successful existing perfumes, together with the new 'Fille d'Eve' were presented in a box which was designed to be in keeping with the Christian Bérard style (126). Romantic luxury was also the theme for 'Mémoire Chérie' ('Cherished Memory'), a new perfume from Elizabeth Arden in 1953. In a nostalgic spirit this bottle depicted a woman with arms folded, as if contemplating her own personal memories (127).

In 1956, Christian Dior introduced 'Diorissimo', the special edition of which featured a superb Baccarat crystal bottle in the form of an amphora – actually an inverted amphora shape – and a stopper topped by a magnificent flower bouquet in gilded bronze (pl. 216). This presentation was reminiscent of a classic Louis XVI crystal and bronze perfume burner. The bronzework for 'Diorissimo' was designed and executed by the artist Chrystiane Charles. Although metal had often been used previously in association with glass and crystal to create a feeling of luxury in perfume bottles, rarely, if ever, had a bronze sculpture of such singular beauty been created for this purpose. Perhaps even more remarkable was the fact that it was created in 1956, when superb design and workmanship were already becoming very scarce.

Lancôme, a company founded in 1935, was a dominant force during the 1950s, creating some of the most enduring romantic perfume images. Georges Delhomme, the artistic director, was the moving spirit behind the Lancôme concepts and style. In 1950 the company introduced 'Magie'

('Magic'), in a Baccarat bottle that was meant to depict a rectangular block of crystal, reminiscent of the modernist rectangular shapes of the 1920s, but now twisted, as if by magic (pl. 219). The box covered in ivory-coloured leather or satin suggested the magic of a firework display through the glittering reflections of a multitude of coloured sequins. Every year, from 1951 to 1960, a special edition of 'Magie' in a spherical bottle with stars in relief, was made available for the Christmas season. In 1952, when a new Lancôme perfume called 'Trésor' ('Treasure') was introduced in a diamond-shaped bottle, 'Magie' was already a bestseller worldwide. To transfer the image of success from 'Magie' to 'Trésor' two different presentations were offered, each with two bottles – one for 'Magie', the other for 'Trésor' – individually labelled.

These combined Lancôme presentations really amounted to a single object, a brilliant promotional and artistic innovation by Delhomme. The first of these introduced in 1952 was called 'Jumelles', which can mean either twin sisters or binoculars, both meanings being equally appropriate. The 'twin' perfumes were joined together, and the fused bottles, in their colourful box, resembled a pair of binoculars in its case (pl. 218). The second presentation, introduced in 1954, was called 'Les Danseurs' ('The Dancers'). In this masterpiece of abstract movement the two fused bottles – each with its own label – seemed to be intertwined, suggesting the closeness of an amorous couple. The image presented by the frosted surface was a swirling shape, a waltzing movement, and was in turn emphasized by the long thin decorative ribbons which gave added life to the whole presentation (pl. 212).

In 1954, another special edition was introduced for use with various Lancôme perfumes, each example bearing a label on which the specific perfume was identified. The presentation, called 'Mélisande', featured a pink crystal bottle in the form of a draped female figure (pl. 213) which reflected the Lancôme ideal of expressing the beautiful, mystical, elegant and romantic associations of its products.

With the advent of the space age in 1957, when the first satellite, Sputnik I, was launched on 4 October by the U.S.S.R., to be followed soon after by the American Explorer I on 31 January 1958, Lancôme entered into the spirit of the new era with two limited editions. One was a small round full-moon purse bottle with a smiling face, made of blue-tinted opalescent glass (128); the other was in the form of a giant smiling crescent-moon bottle, of blue-tinted opalescent glass, attached to a cobalt-blue glass base (pl. 220). Both models were used as containers for various Lancôme perfumes, each identified with a specific label. Whereas the crescent moon was issued in a limited edition of only 100 examples, both Lancôme bottles can be considered poetic sculptures in glass and masterpieces of imaginative design.

By 1950, although some small perfume companies were still producing perfumes under their original name, many had been acquired by large holding companies and were therefore no longer independent. This new trend temporarily affected the development of perfume presentations, since the

127 Elizabeth Arden, 'Mémoire Chérie', 1953, bottles in three sizes. H. 7.7 cm (3 in.); 18.0 cm (7⅛ in.); 13.0 cm (5⅛ in.).

128 Lancôme, 'Spoutnik' limited edition presentation, 1959, designed by Georges Delhomme: box containing 'Magie'. Presentation also used for other perfumes. H. 6.7 cm (2⅝ in.).

large companies made every effort to make production more centralized and hence more efficient. The lack of skilled artisans and the rising cost of hand-made products reinforced the need to produce perfume presentations exclusively by mechanical means. Industrialization made it possible to reduce production costs, and practical realities limited the scope for individuality and luxuriousness in perfume presentations. Some companies even became interested in developing a somewhat industrial and uniform look. While artistic creations were still being conceived and produced at considerable cost, many of the superior presentations of the decade were so expensive that they were issued only as limited editions.

Soon new techniques and materials entered into the production process. For instance, instead of ground-glass stoppers, plastic caps were introduced to provide tight and secure closures. As a result, during the 1960s and the early part of the 1970s there was a temporary lull in the production of inventive and original presentations. However, since the 1980s there have been signs of a renaissance in the development of new designs that will be a source of pleasure for decades to come.

France took the lead in promoting the perfume industry and has also played a special role in inventing and nurturing the art of presenting this luxury product. At first imprinted with the French style, the French perspective and even the French culture, perfume presentations now have an international dimension, with new designs being produced in many countries. However, in order to retain a sufficiently detached and historical perspective, the coverage of this book stops as the decade of the 1960s begins. With the passage of time, it will become easier to recognize and to analyze more recent trends in society's cross-currents when they are viewed from a necessary distance. While the art of presenting perfume will continue to reflect the events and the spirit of the times as society evolves, the allure of perfume will remain constant.

213 Lancôme, 'Mélisande' limited
edition presentation, 1954, Georges
Delhomme design. Box containing
'Trésor'. Presentation also used for
other perfumes.
H. 15.0 cm (5⅞ in.).

214 Schiaparelli, 'Succès Fou', 1953. Design by Elsa Schiaparelli and Michel de Brunhoff. Heart-shaped box with small bottle, and large bottle; limited edition brooch containing perfume bottle in heart-shaped box.
H. of large bottle 9.3 cm (3⅝ in.), small bottle 6.5 cm (2½ in.); brooch 6.0 cm (2⅜ in.).

215 Schiaparelli, 'Si', 1957. Chianti-shaped miniature (in celluloid case) with box; gilded and enamelled luxury edition bottle (Chianti shape); and Baccarat bottle no. 788 on base of open box.
H. 4.0 cm (1⅝ in.), 12 cm (4¾ in.) and 9.3 cm (3⅝ in.).

216 Christian Dior, 'Diorissimo', 1956. Limited edition Baccarat bottle no. 819 with gilded bronze ornamentation by Chrystiane Charles.
H. overall 22.3 cm (8¾ in.).

Below
217 Vidal, bottle in the form of column with the lion of St Mark in the Piazzetta, Venice, *c.* 1958; and Linetti, 'Notte di Venezia', gondola-shaped presentation, 1948. Limited ceramic editions.
H. of column 30.0 cm (11¾ in.), gondola 6.0 cm (2⅜ in.).

Bottom left
218 Lancôme, 'Jumelles' limited edition presentation, 1952, Georges Delhomme design. Box in the form of a case for binoculars, 'Magie' and 'Trésor' twin bottles fused together as 'binoculars'.
H. 8.0 cm (3⅛ in.).

Bottom right
219 Lancôme, 'Magie', 1950. Georges Delhomme designs. Powder box, spherical bottle, Baccarat bottle no. 805 with open box, and small sample bottle.
H. of large bottle 11.5 cm (4½ in.), sphere 4.0 cm (1⅝ in.), sample 5.0 cm (2 in.).

MAGIE DE LANCÔME

PARIS   FRANCE

An A–Z of Perfume

A wide range of sources has been consulted in the course of preparing this extensive listing of over 500 individuals and companies involved in the history and evolution of perfume presentations. In the case of most perfumers and fashion designers, business addresses – past or present – are provided, but information about some leading designers and companies connected with the art of perfume is scarce; hence the relative length of entries should not be taken as a reflection of the importance of, or the creative contribution made by, individuals or commercial organizations. An asterisk indicates a cross-reference to another entry. Unless otherwise stated, all prizes referred to were awarded at international exhibitions in Paris.

A

Académie Scientifique de Beauté
376 rue Saint-Honoré, Paris
Beauty salon est. by Lamotte family, mid-19th c. Perfumes, cosmetics, toiletries known as 'Produits Lamotte'. Georges Gay proprietor in 1920s.

Adrian
Beverly Hills, California
Fashion house est. by Gilbert Adrian (b. Adrian Adolph Greenburg; 1903–59). Dressed many Hollywood stars, on and off the screen, particularly Joan Crawford, whose dress style with padded shoulders resembled an Ionic column. 'Saint' and 'Sinner' perfumes used identical 'Ionic column' bottles, 1944.

Agnel
16 avenue de l'Opéra, Paris
Perfumes, cosmetics, toiletries. Alexandre Agnel opened small shop in 1858. Participated in 1878, 1889, 1900 and 1925 exhibitions; gold medals 1900, 1925. Lamb on Agnel logo derived from *agneau* ('lamb'). 'Dolly' named after famous Dolly Sisters, 1913. Closed 1958.

Albessard, Joseph
Graphics, labels, boxes. In 1920s employed: Front, Wuitz, Emile Gaudissard, Paule Richard and Bernard Naudin (who also worked for *Poiret). Participated in 1925 exhibition. Bankrupt 1932.

Albret, Jean d'
53 avenue George V, Paris
Perfumes, cosmetics, toiletries. Est. 1946 by Guillaume, Michel and Hubert d'Ornano. 'Jean d'Albret' an invented name.

Alexandrine
10 rue Aubert, Paris
Gloves. Company est. in 19th c. Perfumes *c.* 1925. *Baccarat was a supplier; a notable bottle was engraved with raised gloved hand, inside shield (emblem of glove makers-perfumers).

Amboise, d'
15 place de la Nation, Paris
Perfumes. Est. by G. Brunet, F. Friry et Cie *c.* 1900. Interesting 1920s presentations.

Amiel et Cie, C.
Paris
Perfumes. Late 19th-c. luxury presentations.

Amiot et Cie, A.
68 rue de Rivoli, Paris
Perfumes, cosmetics, toiletries. Est. 1862. Some luxury presentations.

Antoine de Paris
5 rue Cambon, Paris
Hairdressing salon – perfumes, cosmetics, toiletries. Est. *c.* 1920 by Antoine Cierplikowski. Introduced fashionable 'La Garçonne' (urchin cut) style for women. Salons featured streamlined, avant-garde white interiors. Most successful products: skin pastes called 'Blanc Mystérieux' ('Mysterious White'), 'Blanc de Fée' ('Fairy White'). Logo of 1926 depicted female nude with urchin cut.

Applications du Verre, Les
Glassworks. Active 1920s. Speciality: double, triple, quadruple crystal overlays.

Arden, Elizabeth
673 Fifth Avenue, New York
Beauty salons – perfumes, cosmetics, toiletries. Florence Nightingale Graham (1878–1966), born in Canada, arrived in New York 1908. Opened first salon 1910 and adopted business name Elizabeth Arden 1915. First cosmetic line 'Venetian' 1915. Paris and London salons. Bestselling perfume 'Blue Grass', 1934, featured blue horse motif for state of Kentucky, where she bred racehorses.

Arly
15 rue Royale, Paris
Perfumes, cosmetics, toiletries. Franco-American company est. by *Vivaudou, 1914 (both affiliated to *Delettrez). Best-selling line 'La Bohème'.

Arnoux, Guy (?–1951)
Draughtsman, illustrator worked for *Maquet in 1920s. Designed paper fans for perfumes, perfume advertising.

Arts du Papier, Les
Labels. Speciality: luxury embossed paper labels simulating bronze, ivory.

Arys
3 rue de la Paix, Paris
Perfumes, cosmetics, toiletries. Est. 1916 by Dr Lucien Graux, who had already produced perfumes with Arys name. Perfumer to Royal House of Spain. *Lepape style seen in early Arys graphics. Graux played major role in 1925 exhibition.

Atkinson Ltd, J. & E.
24 Old Bond Street, London
Perfumes, cosmetics, toiletries. Est. 1799. Luxury presentations, 1910s-20s, used *Dépinoix and *Viard bottles.

Au Carnaval de Venise
3 boulevard de la Madeleine, Paris
Shop est. in 19th c. by G. Clasens, originally specializing in *articles anglais*. Interesting 1920s perfume presentations.

Augustabernard
3 rue du Faubourg-Saint-Honoré, Paris
Couture house est. 1919 by Augusta Bernard. Sober fashions, contrasting colours reflected in 1920s classic perfume presentations. Closed 1934.

Avenel
24 rue du Rocher, Paris
Perfumes. Est. by Louis Avenel 1900. Major exports to Great Britain. Some superb *Viard creations.

Avon
New York
Perfumes, cosmetics, toiletries. Est. 1886 by David Hall McConnell as California Perfume Company at 126 Chambers Street, New York. Pioneered door-to-door home selling, employing women as agents. Known as Avon since 1929. Low-priced humorous presentations appealed to middle-class Americans.

Ayer, Harriet Hubbard
321–323 East 34th Street, New York
Perfumes, cosmetics, toiletries. Harriet Hubbard, b. 1850 in Chicago, est. company in 1886; famous HHA logo created 1894. Became *New York World* beauty columnist 1896. Perfumes introduced 1922. Successful worldwide, opened Paris shop.

B

Babani
93, 98 and 98bis, boulevard Haussmann, Paris
Importers of oriental wares, couture house, perfumes. Obscure beginnings *c.* 1890. V. Babani acquired existing shop in Boulevard Haussmann specializing in goods imported from China and Japan; opened other shops. V. Babani diversified *c.* 1900 with fashions and Liberty fabrics; then in 1906 created a style inspired by Far East, 'Le Niu-Tsé'. Influenced by Ballets Russes, V. Babani produced oriental and Arabian fashions, ornate patterning, gold embroidery. Introduced 'Sphinxia' sewing machine (for gold chain-stitch embroidery), 1920. S. Babani was also a prestigious importer of oriental wares. In 1919 Maurice Babani became the second Paris couturier to introduce perfumes. Sumptuous presentations, gold and black bottles expressed fashion spirit very well. Perfumes distributed by Elizabeth *Arden in USA, acknowledged in choice of perfume name 'Mon Amie Elizabeth' of 1926. (129)

129 Babani, 'Jasmin de Corée', 1919, bottle and box; box, stamped with Babani signature, features pattern almost identical to Rosine, 'Nuit de Chine'. H. 5.5 cm (2⅛ in.).

Babcock
New York
Perfumes, cosmetics, toiletries. Active in 19th c. and 20th c. Also produced for other companies, e.g. 'We Moderns' for Saks Fifth Avenue.

Baccarat, Cristalleries de
Glassworks. Est. in Lorraine under the patronage of Louis XV in 1764 to stem Bohemian glass imports, and reduce unemployment in eastern region. Has produced crystal since 1816. In 19th c. produced classic models for *Houbigant, *Lubin, *Pinaud, *Violet and other leading companies. After 1911 Baccarat style changed, influenced by *Lalique and *Viard. In 1930s and 1940s many Baccarat models inspired by Surrealist movement. Important artists (*Chevalier, *Süe, *Viard, *Dali, etc.) designed bottles produced by Baccarat. From inception crystal production was of superior quality (30% lead oxide content). Prior to 1936, some Baccarat bottles displayed small circular paper labels with Baccarat logo, others were stamped. After 1936, all models stamped with logo. Most perfume companies were clients.

Baher, Maxime
Cosmetics cases. Speciality: figural lipstick cases.

Facing page
220 Lancôme, Crescent Moon presentation, 1959, designed by Georges Delhomme (limited edition of 100). Bottle containing 'Magie', also used for other perfumes.
H. 25.0 cm (9⅞ in.).

Bakst, Léon (1866–1924)
Russian painter, graphic artist, costume and set designer who came to Paris 1909 with *Diaghilev; worked for Ballets Russes. His dynamic style, a mixture of popular Russian art and French modern art, influenced performing arts, decorative arts, fashion. After 1910 many perfume names and presentations reflected his oriental, erotic style.

Balenciaga
10 avenue George V, Paris
Couture house est. 1937 by Cristobal Balenciaga (1895–1972). Perfumes introduced 1947. Closed 1968.

Ballet, André-Victor (1885–?)
Painter, engraver, bookbinder, home accessories designer. Designer of enamelled bottles produced by *Baccarat after 1920, but few identified.

Balmain
44 rue François I er, Paris
Couture House est. in 1945 by Pierre Balmain (1914–82) with own perfumes. Advertisements designed by *Gruau.

Barbier, Georges (1882–1932)
Draughtsman, illustrator, costume and set designer. Worked for Folies Bergère. Important book illustrator – designed pochoir reproductions for *Romance of Perfume* (1928, limited edition published by *Hudnut). Very influential on perfume presentations; he probably designed some labels or graphics.

Bardin et Cie
35 boulevard des Capucines, Paris
Druggists. Introduced toiletries, cosmetics c. 1900. 'Perles Fines' powder of 1909 was bestseller. Afterward est. perfume company called La Perle. Perfumers to Belgian Court.

Baring, George
56 rue du Faubourg-Saint-Honoré, Paris
With Austrian partners, opened luxury gift shop (accessories and perfumes) 1929, bankrupt 1930 but continued producing perfumes into 1950s.

Baumann, Fernand
Engraver. Produced luxury metallic labels for *Weil, *Bourjois ('Soir de Paris', 'Fiancée'), etc.

Beardsley, Aubrey (1872–98)
English artist and illustrator, whose distinctive style influenced early 20th-c. fashion illustrators and designers of perfume presentations.

Benda, G. K.
French painter, illustrator. Designed 1920s posters for Mistinguett, music-hall star. Designed and sometimes signed *Bryenne 'Chu Chin Chow', 1918.

Bendel, Henri
10 West 57th Street, New York
Luxury fashions, perfumes, cosmetics, toiletries. Henri Bendel (1858–1939) from Louisiana opened first New York shop in 1896, and luxury store at above address 1912. Introduced distinctive brown-and-white striped pattern for packaging. Bendel's own designs supplemented by imported exclusive French fashions and accessories. Among many prestigious clients was the opera singer Geraldine Farrar, who had a private dressing room at the store. In 1915 introduced perfumes, cosmetics. First American fashion house to introduce perfume. In 1920s opened Paris shop at 15 rue Royale. 'Cinque, Triple Cinque' ('Five, Triple Five') of 1928 referred to Paris street number, and '10 West' of 1943 referred to New York address.

Benito, Edouard Garcia (1892–?)
Spanish-born painter, engraver, fashion illustrator, active in Paris. Painted important portrait of Denise and Paul *Poiret. Designed Fourrures *Max logo and advertisments.

Benoît
10 boulevard Bonne Nouvelle, Paris
Perfumes. Est. 1926 by Marco Barouh (Barouh & Hermanos) whose brother Venturero was an important exporter; affiliated with *Brécher. Original, luxurious presentations with unusual names: 'Chamelle' ('Female Camel'), 'Un Soir de Folie' ('An Evening of Madness').

Bérard, Christian (1902–49)
Painter, illustrator, costume and set designer. Worked extensively for theatre, fashion designers and perfumers, notably Nina *Ricci.

Bergeron, René
Manufacturer of superior-quality perfume boxes. Est. 1890.

Berlan, Lederlin et Cie
Manufacturer of metal accessories. Est. 1867. Produced artistic soap and powder boxes in aluminium (then called *métal anglais*) with antique silver patina; also a large variety of brass covers for perfume bottles.

Bertelli, A.
26 Via Paolo Frisi, Milan
Pharmaceuticals, perfumes. Luxurious French-produced presentations.

Berthon, Paul (*c.* 1848–1909)
Artist, illustrator. Inspired by nature, women and Middle Ages. Influenced perfume graphics at turn of century. Style similar to that of *Grasset.

Best & Co.
Fifth Avenue at Thirty-Fifth Street, New York
Department store est. 1879 as the Lilliputian Bazaar. Perfumes in 1920s. Closed 1960s.

Bichara
10 rue de la Chaussée-d'Antin, Paris
Perfumes, cosmetics, toiletries. Est. 1896 by Bichara Malhamé (from Beirut), who styled himself 'The Syrian Perfumer'. First located in Rouen and Dieppe. The hair dye 'Extrait de Henné Bichara' of 1899 was so successful that it financed introduction of luxury perfumes. Maintained luxury image through shop, constant exposure in French press. Advertised 'Allah est grand et Bichara est son parfumeur' ('Allah is great and Bichara is his perfumer'). Clients included Edmond Rostand, Gabriel Fauré, Gabriele d'Annunzio, Edouard de Max and Sarah Bernhardt (who publicly endorsed perfumes). Supplied Royal Egyptian Court. In 1920s opened luxury London fashion shop, introducing 'couture made perfumes'. Exported worldwide. Early labels depicted Bichara seizing Fortune by the hair; redesigned in 1920s by F.-L. *Schmied in Art Deco style. Bichara Malhamé died c. 1930, was succeeded by daughter Rose; quality of presentations declined, and character of company changed, exemplified by 'Handle with Care' 1945. Continued until 1950s.

Bienaimé
396 rue Saint-Honoré, Paris
Perfumes. Est. 1935 by Robert Bienaimé, previously with *Houbigant.

Biette
Rue Beauséjour, Nantes, France
Soaps, perfumes. Est. 1892 by Alexis Biette. Branches in major cities in Europe, Africa and USA. Spectacular soap sets, often humorous. Introduced superb perfume presentations 1920s

Blondeau & Cie Ltd
Lever House, Victoria Embankment, Blackfriars, London
British-French soap company, active c. 1880-1930. Some beautiful perfume presentations.

Blondel, E.
11 place de la Madeleine, Paris
Furrier. Participated in 1925 exhibition. Perfumes 1928. Occupied same building as *Mÿon perfumes.

Blondy, E.
Manufacturer of metal articles for use with perfumes, cosmetics.

Bobin Frères
Glassworks. Specialized in high-quality, artistic bottles. Executed designs by *Hamm, *Viard and others. *Isabey was most important client.

Boissard, Felix
38 Chandos Street, London
Perfumes, cosmetics. British-French company est. by John-Ernest Jewel c. 1900 (probable predecessor in France was Pennès Fils et Boissard, est. 19th c.). Affiliated to and represented by Heppells Ltd.

Boldoot, J. C.
Singel 92, Amsterdam
Perfumes. Est. 1798.

Borsari
8 via Cavour, Parma, Italy
Perfumes, cosmetics, toiletries. Est. 1870 by Ludovico Borsari. Bestseller 'Violetta di Parma'. Gold medal 1925. (130)

130 Borsari, 'Violetta di Parma', 1925, rare clear-and frosted-glass bottle with silver mounts, made for the 1925 exhibition. H. 17.0 cm (6¾ in.).

Boué Sœurs
9 rue de la Paix, Paris
Couture house. Est. 1899 by sisters, Sylvie Boué Montégut and Jeanne Boué d'Etreillis. The perfume 'Quand les Fleurs Rêvent' ('When Flowers Dream'), in crinoline-shaped bottle with tall stopper, surrounded by ribbons and flowers, was totally representative of Boué fashions; this was possibly the only Boué perfume. Closed 1932.

Bourjois
28 place Vendôme, Paris
Perfumes, cosmetics, toiletries. Toiletries shop est. 1860 by M. Ponsin was purchased in 1869 by Alexandre Napoléon Bourjois. Emile Orosdi became co-proprietor c. 1880. Business acquired by Ernest Wertheimer c. 1900. After 1920s 'Evening in Paris' became most successful line.

Bouvet, F., et F. Gaud
Boxes. Est. 1893 as Maison A. Coste et Cie. Luxury *Bourjois boxes.

Brajan
17 rue Saint-Florentin, Paris
Perfumes. Est. 1926 by Ernest Weil and Georges Lévy-Say. 'Amour Suprême' ('Supreme Love') of 1927 very successful.

Brécher, Parfumerie
10 boulevard Bonne Nouvelle, Paris
Perfumes, cosmetics. Est. 1900 by Paul Brécher in Pontoise. Jacques-Ernest Mazurier proprietor after 1918. From humble quality to superb Lucien *Gaillard creations. Affiliated with *Benoît.

Breidenbach & Cie
48 Greek Street, London
Soaps, perfumes. Est. c. 1900 by Reginald Blackwell Breidenbach. Used *Dépinoix bottles 1920s.

Brissac, La Parfumerie
1958 calle Chile, Buenos Aires
Perfumes. Est. 1918 by L. Aubert y Cio. French-produced presentations.

Brissaud, Pierre (1885–1949)
Painter, engraver, illustrator. Worked for *Poiret, *La Gazette du Bon Ton*. Perfume advertising (*Vibert).

Brisson
65–67 avenue des Champs-Elysées, Paris
Perfumes. Est. 1945; first perfume called 'Tobogan'. *Camin designs.

Brocard
15 Mouitnaïa, Moscow
8 rue du Cardinal Mercier, Paris
Perfumes. French company est. 1864 in Moscow. After 1918 moved to Paris. Noted for use of spectacular labels. (131)

131 Brocard, 'Unforgettable' eau-de-cologne label, *c.* 1913. H. 12.7 cm (5 in.).

Brosse, Verreries
Glassworks. L. Caut, small glass trading company already specializing in perfume bottles, purchased 1854 by E. Thirion, and renamed Caut-Thirion. Also produced chemistry-pharmacy containers. After Berthe Thirion, the owner's daughter, married Luc-Léon Brosse, *c.* 1880, the firm became known as Brosse. Emile Barré (1893–1985) joined 1911, assumed ownership 1919. After WW1, became glass manufacturer, producing perfume bottles. Acquired and rented many Vallée de la Bresle factories (Saint Germer, Eu, Offranville, *Feuquières, *Rétonval, *Vieux-Rouen and Montenon). First French fully automatic glassworks est. by Barré at Sucy-en-Brie 1924. Partnership in various projects with Saint-Gobain until 1961. Glass artist *Schwander joined 1933. Superior-quality products, supplied to major perfume companies, including Elizabeth *Arden, *Bourjois, *Caron, *Chanel, *Lanvin and Nina *Ricci.

Brunelleschi, Umberto (1879–1949)
Italian painter, illustrator, costume and set designer. Worked in Paris after 1900, first as caricaturist (pseudonym Aroun-al-Raxid). Worked for *Maquet. Designed *Martial et Armand logo *c.* 1923.

Brunhoff, de (family)
Maurice de Brunhoff (1861–1937) est. *Comœdia Illustré*, 1908, theatrical, artistic and literary Parisian journal with photographs of famous actresses wearing latest fashions, *Bakst drawings, perfume advertising – notably designed by *Iribe. Started publishing Ballets Russes programmes 1912. During WW1, Brunhoff was spelled 'Brunoff'. Cosette (1886–1954), Maurice's daughter, married Lucien Vogel, participated in *La Gazette du Bon Ton* and *Jardin des Modes*. Jacques (1888–1973), Maurice's son, edited *Comœdia Illustré*, published Ballets Russes and Folies Bergère programmes. Est. *Le Décor d'Aujourd'hui* and *Arts Ménagers*. Conceived *Rosine 'Cœur en Folie'. Michel (1892–1958), Maurice's son, worked with brother-in-law, Lucien Vogel, and sister Cosette. Editor, *La Gazette du Bon Ton*, *Jardin des Modes*, French *Vogue*. Created de *Vigny 'Golliwogg', 'Chick-Chick', 'Guili-Guili', 'Be Lucky'; and later, with Elsa *Schiaparelli, 'Succès Fou'. Jean (1899–1937), Maurice's son, was author of children's *Babar* books; series continued by son Laurent. Lucien Vogel (1886–1954) est. *La Gazette du Bon Ton*, *Jardin des Modes*, French *Vogue*, also *Vu* and *Lu*, and collaborated in *Arts et Métiers Graphiques*. Est. de *Vigny, supervised early perfume presentations and advertising. Friend of *Poiret, *Iribe, *Lepape, *Domèrgue, *Marty, Charles *Martin, etc. Major influence in propagating Art Deco style, and on contemporary fashions, fashion magazines and journalism in general.

Bruyère
22 place Vendôme, Paris
Couture house. Est. 1924 by Marie-Louise Bruyère (apprentice to *Callot and *Lanvin). 'Caractère' ('Character'), 'Tendance' ('Tendency') related to *Les Caractères* of La Bruyère (1645–96). Favourite colour (grey) and draped, simple fashions inspired label and box designs. Elegant gilded couture salons inspired bottles of 1945.

Bryenne
17 rue de la Paix, Paris
Perfumes. Est. 1911 by Jacques Brach, financed by Botot (well-known mouthwash since the 18th c.), then owned by Mme Waldeck Rousseau, widow of famous French politician. Named after Monsieur de Bryenne, 17th-c. character noted for exaggerated elegance, good manners; his stilted phrases quoted in advertising.

B.T.C.I.C. (also known as Bétcic)
Glassworks, labels, boxes, papers. Active after WW1. One of the very few glass trading companies qualified to design and produce total perfume presentations.

Burmann, de
4 rue de la Verrerie, Paris
Perfumes. Est. 1934, with shop on Champs-Elysées. Name derived from those of joint founders – Stéphane *Bur*din and André Bau*mann*. Modest presentations using omnibus bottles from *Nancy. Most important perfume 'La Sirène' (*c.* 1935) presented in bottle designed *c.* 1912 by *Lalique, possibly intended for sale as a decorative perfume bottle.

Burval, Parfumerie
6 rue de Madrid, Paris
Perfumes. Est. 1922 by Jean-Luc Valli. Luxury presentations with bottles by *Jolivet. Bankrupt 1931, but mediocre Burval products continued.

C

Cadolle Frères
14 rue Cambon, Paris
Lingerie designers, perfumes. Herminie Cadolle est. corset shop in Buenos Aires 1889; designed *corselet-gorge*, first brassière. Opened Paris shop 1910, as a family business, with fashionable clientèle. Perfumes introduced 1926.

Calber
4 Misericordia, San Sebastian, Spain
Perfumes, cosmetics. Active 1920s. Superb labels, packaging papers created by *Sennet.

Calixte
277 rue Saint-Honoré, Paris
Couture house. Est. by Marguerite Setz early 1940s. 'Givre' ('Hoar Frost') 1945 was superb perfume presentation related to winter fashions.

Callisté
139 rue de France, Nice
Essential oils, perfumes. Est. *c.* 1918 by Charles de Coppet. Perfumes introduced 1926. Name derived from Greek *Kallistos*, 'most beautiful' or 'best'.

Callot Sœurs
9–10 avenue Matignon, Paris
Couture house. Est. 1895 by three sisters, Marie Callot Gerber (designer), Marthe Callot Bertrand, Régine Callot Chantrelle. Became leading fashion house, producing daytime clothes, Oriental and period at-home and evening gowns, featuring the use of luxurious fabrics, embroideries, spectacular fashion details. Perfumes introduced 1923, available until 1950s.

Camin, Pierre (1908–)
Perfume presentation designer. Worked for *Coty 1930-39. Designs include 'A Suma' (1932), 'Vertige' (1936), 'Muse' (1939). After WW2, became independent, designed for various perfume companies: *Brisson 'Tobogan', *Callot 'Jeep', *Rouff 'Secret' (all 1946).

Canarina
Possibly the name of a company, or a perfume name, or both. One known *Lalique perfume presentation, 1928.

Caravaglios, Isabelle
2 rue de la Paix, Paris
Millinery and fashions, beauty salon, perfumes, cosmetics, toiletries. Originally Italian, est. in Paris *c.* 1910. Beauty products advertised as 'made according to formulas of Dr Caravaglios, Rome'. Luxury production.

Carège
13 rue d'Hauteville, Paris
Perfumes. Est. 1929 by Robert-Laurent Lévy. Some interesting presentations.

Carnegie, Hattie
42–46 East 49th Street, New York
Fashion house. In 1909 Henrietta Kanengeiser (1889–1956), born Austrian, opened hat shop under new name; custom dressmaking shop from 1915. After her first Paris trip in 1919, she returned four times yearly, bringing latest Paris fashions back to USA. 'Hattie Carnegie' perfume introduced 1925. From 1938, a sculptural self-portrait bottle was used for all perfumes.

Caron
10 rue de la Paix, Paris
Perfumes, cosmetics. Est. by Ernest Daltroff 1903. Purchased small factory, Parfumerie Emilia, and small haberdashery and perfume shop, Parfumerie Caron – to acquire use of name, which he considered simple, elegant and very French. Opened shop at above address 1904. By 1924, Caron was among the most important French perfume companies, exporting worldwide. Daltroff and Félicie Vanpouille were joint proprietors until Daltroff's death in 1941. Vanpouille, as sole proprietor, sold firm in 1962. Original 'Royal Emilia' perfume renamed 'Royal Caron' 1904; 'Radiant' first new Caron perfume. From 1906, with 'Chantecler' (named after a play by Rostand), until last Caron perfume in 1950s, Vanpouille created or supervised all names and presentations.

Carrère
45 rue Pierre-Charron, Paris
Perfumes. Est. 1945 by Maurice Bertrand Carrère. Short-lived.

Cartier
9 rue Garnier, Neuilly (Seine)
Perfumes. Est. *c.* 1900 by Marius Cartier as Parfums d'Art, Grand Luxe. *Baccarat was a supplier. Affiliated to *Salomé.

Carven
Rond Point des Champs-Elysées, Paris
Couture house est. by Mlle Carven 1944. First perfume 'Ma Griffe' ('My Signature') introduced 1945.

Cassard, G.
Boxes, paper. Est. 1893. Specialized in cylindrical boxes.

Caubère
Printer. Speciality: vivid coloured papers.

Cavalieri, Lina
78 boulevard Victor Hugo, Neuilly (Seine)
Perfumes. Est. by Lina Cavalieri and Lucien Muratore (famous opera singers) 1924. Short-lived.

CEDIB (Institut de Beauté des Champs-Elysées)
39 avenue des Champs-Elysées, Paris
Beauty salon, toiletries, cosmetics. Est. 1924 by Henriette Valentin Font, who also est. Université de Beauté, at 24 place Malesherbes. She was related to Elise-Marie Valentin Le Brun, proprietor of *L'Institut de Beauté.

Cellophane, La
Superb gilded Cellophane labels and coverings simulating silk – *Lérys, 'Le Présentoir', 'Lucidité', 'Amour de Rose'.

Chalon, Louis (1866–?)
Painter, illustrator, sculptor, costume designer, jeweller. Awarded prizes 1889, 1900. Designed *Roger & Gallet 'Bouquet Nouveau'.

Chanel
31 rue Cambon, Paris
Couture house. Gabrielle Chanel (1883–1971) first designed hats 1908 and est. business as milliner

1910. Fashions introduced shortly afterwards. Moved to above address 1918. Simple, relaxed, well-constructed, elegant style was huge success. Introduced perfumes 1921. Sober presentations, avant-garde for their time; basic design still in use. Pierre Wertheimer became Chanel's perfume partner 1924, and in late 1950s the Wertheimers (also owners of *Bourjois) became sole proprietors of the Chanel name.

Charbert
21 West 52nd Street, New York
Perfumes, cosmetics. Est. 1933.

Charles, Chrystiane
Sculptor. Designed and produced 'Diorissimo' bronze ornamentation for Christian *Dior. Proprietor of Charles Bronze d'Art Gallery and foundry in Paris.

Charles of the Ritz
New York
Perfumes, cosmetics, toiletries. Charles Jundt opened beauty salon in Ritz-Carlton Hotel 1916. Became major international company. Perfumes introduced 1927.

Chénier, André
Paris
Perfumes. Franco-American, 1920s. Affiliated to Marques de *Elorza.

Cheramy
19 rue Cambon, Paris
Perfumes, cosmetics. Raymond Couin created 'Cappi' perfume 1921. Business sold to *Houbigant 1922; became division producing lower-priced products, primarily for US market. Received prize 1925.

Cherigan
120 avenue des Champs-Elysées, Paris
Perfumes. Est. 1929 by Ota Polacek. 'Chance' was first perfume.

Chéruit
21 place Vendôme, Paris
Couture house. Est. by Madeleine Chéruit. Perfumes introduced 1925.

Chess, Mary
334 Park Avenue, New York
Perfumes. Humble beginnings. Est. 1932 by Grace Mary Chess Robinson; small shop opened 1933. Became very important perfumer after 'Chess Pieces' introduced 1938.

Chevalier, Georges (1894–1987)
Painter, architect, interior designer, costume and set designer, glass artist. Worked on interior designs for Maurice Dufrêne, 1918–24. Collaborated with *Bakst for Ballets Russes. From 1916 designed for *Baccarat; also worked for *Pochet and *Romesnil. Most designs are unidentified.

Chimène
74 boulevard de la Saussaye, Neuilly (Seine)
Perfumes, cosmetics. Est. c. 1905 by Lafontaine and Seedorf; later purchased by Francisco de Matarazzo Fils. Luxury presentations 1920s.

Chiris, Antoine
Place Neuve, Grasse
Essential oils, perfumes. Est. 1768 by Antoine Chiris who was succeeded by sons and descendants. Became major supplier to perfumers, including some in Russia. First prize at 1855 exhibition. Purchased *Rallet 1898. Still in existence.

Choisy-le-Roy et de Lyon-Houdaille et Triquet, Cristalleries de
Glassworks. Major producer of crystal perfume bottles, especially 1910–1930.

Choquet, Alice
9 boulevard Malesherbes, Paris
Luxury fashions, dresses, coats, suits, furs. Est. 19th c. as family business. Acquired similar shop, Scotland, c. 1910; business became known as Choquet-Scotland at 9 rue Auber. Became Alice Choquet c. 1920. Perfumes introduced c. 1926. 'Le Double Cinq' used in domino format, gilded on black-glass bottles. Acquired by *Gilot 1946. (132)

132 Alice Choquet, 'Le Double Cinq', 1926, gilded black-glass bottles, with matching box for smaller size. H. 6.0 cm (2⅜ in.);.7.7 cm (3 in.).

Ciro
20 rue de la Paix, Paris
Perfumes, cosmetics, toiletries. Est. 1923 by La Société Gladstone et Cie (originally a British company, est. 1869), major exporter of luxury goods. Became important Franco-American company under Guy T. Gibson. *Gabilla created first Ciro perfumes and presentations. Name adopted from famous night-club. French affiliated company known as Substancia.

Claire
44 rue des Petites-Ecuries, Paris
Luxury fashions, perfumes. Elegant Paris shop called Claire est. 1924 by Rodney Wanamaker (a member of the founding family of John Wanamaker department stores in USA).

Clamy
Arcade des Champs-Elysées, Paris
Perfumes. Est. 1913 by Philippe de Back as Les Parfums de Clamy, Créations d'Art. Luxury *Gaillard presentations. Acquired by *Grenoville 1943.

Clio et Claire
15 rue de La Tour-d'Auvergne, Paris
Perfumes, cosmetics. Franco-American, active in 1920s.

Cocteau, Jean (1889–1963)
Poet, novelist, playwright, film maker, painter, illustrator, costume and set designer, ceramist. Versatile artist, influenced *Diaghilev and designed first Ballets Russes poster. Also worked in fashion and advertising.

Colette (Sidonie Gabrielle) (1873–1954)
French writer. Friendly with, and inspired several perfumers. In 1932 she opened her own cosmetics shop.

Colgate
105 Hudson Street, Jersey City, New Jersey
Household products, perfumes. William Colgate est. starch, soap and candle business 1806. First toothpaste 1873. Merged with Palmolive-Peet 1928. Introduced toilet waters and handkerchief extracts c. 1900. Introduced French-made perfume presentations 1920s.

Colin, Atelier
Est. by *Poiret 1911. Produced papier-mâché dolls, also packaging materials for Poiret's fashion house and *Rosine perfumes.

Colmy
348 rue Saint-Honoré, Paris
Perfumes. Est. 1924 by Edouard Colmant, proprietor of *Coudray, to produce extremely luxurious presentations.

Comptoir Niçois de Verrerie
Glassworks. Speciality: colourful striped cylindrical sample bottles (e.g. for those produced for *Rosine perfumes).

Corday
15 rue de la Paix, Paris
Perfumes, cosmetics. Est. 1924 by Blanche Arvoy, one year after *Jovoy. Named after Charlotte Corday, Marat's assassin. Arvoy created early perfume concepts and presentations. After her involvement, Corday remained very important Franco-American company.

Cortiglioni, René
Labels. Luxury production (*Bourjois, *Brécher, etc.)

Coryse
64 rue de la Chaussée-d'Antin, Paris
Perfumes, cosmetics, toiletries. Est. 1919 by Maurice Blanchet. Purchased *Salomé 1929, thereafter known as Coryse-Salomé.

Cotigny, Maison
Boxes. Luxury production, many intricate models. Participated in 1925 exhibition.

Cottan
40 rue de Chateaudun, Paris
Perfumes, cosmetics, toiletries. Est. by Dr Cottan 1832; named La Parfumerie de la Societé Hygiènique du Docteur Cottan 1840. Unusual, luxurious presentations in 1920s.

Coty
23 place Vendôme, Paris
Perfumes, cosmetics, toiletries. François Spoturno (1874–1934) born Ajaccio, Corsica, adopted Coty, mother's maiden name. Moved to Paris 1900, opened first shop selling his own perfumes. By 1907 Coty perfumes were sold in department stores and exclusive perfume shops. New shop opened 1908 in Place Vendôme, near *Lalique premises. Soon Lalique designed Coty labels and bottles. Branches opened throughout France, also in North Africa, Germany, Italy, Spain, Great Britain, Russia. 1912, luxurious New York shop, 714 Fifth Avenue, decorated by Lalique. Stock-market crash of 1929 almost ruined Coty. Financial difficulties affected health. Production of Coty perfumes continued after Coty's death. Coty introduced colour coding and innovative presentations, with Lalique and others.

Coty, Ernest
8 bis, rue Martel, Paris
Perfumes, cosmetics. Est. 1917 by M. de Bertalot, Ernest Coty and his wife, with financing from perfume exporters Orosdi-Back managed by Léon Orosdi. Intentionally traded on similarity of name with extremely successful *Coty. Perfume names, graphics and advertising resembled Coty's, de-emphasizing 'Ernest'. Products sold internationally. Later in 1917, François Coty sued company and principals in France and USA. US courts ruled quickly, allowing Ernest Coty to trade under own name, but requiring printed disclaimers on all packages and advertising that products were not original Coty items. After 9 years, French courts ordered Ernest Coty and de Bertalot to pay damages of 100,000 francs, and to pay for advertisements admitting guilt in 20 publications selected by François Coty. De Bertalot went to prison. Léon Orosdi died during trial. This affair ruined *Ramsès (also est. by de Bertalot and Orosdi-Back). Although the original Ernest Coty company was dissolved, Ernest Coty produced perfumes and cosmetics under his own name until 1930s.

Coudray, Parfumerie E.
348 rue Saint-Honoré, Paris
Perfumes, cosmetics. Small shop, Maugenet & Coudray, est. c. 1810. Became major exporter during 19th c. Family business until 1908, when Edouard Colmant acquired an interest. Many luxury presentations.

Court, Bruno
Grasse
Essential oils, perfumes. Est. by a father and son named Court in 1812. Bruno Court was a later proprietor. Major supplier to other perfumers. Own perfumes introduced in 1920s.

Crown Perfumery Co., The
177 New Bond Street, London
Perfumes. Major exporter est. 19th c. *Baccarat was a supplier ('Parfum Adorable', 1910).

Cussons, Sons & Co. Ltd
Manchester
Toilet and laundry soaps, perfumes. Some luxury French presentations.

Cyber, Maison
4 place de l'Opéra, Paris
Couture house. Introduced perfumes 1925.

D

Daché, Lilly
78 East 56th Street, New York
Milliner. Lilly Daché (1893–1990). French-born and trained, est. first hat shop 1925. Speciality: draped turban and half-hats. Clients included Sonja Heine, Marlene Dietrich, Carole Lombard, Loretta Young. In 1931, married Jean Despres (1903–88), a senior *Coty executive and first president of the Fragrance Foundation, perfume trade organization in the USA.

Daillet
Glass artist. Designed important glass pieces and perfume bottles, some signed (e.g. *Nesly).

Dali, Salvador (1904–90)
Spanish-born Surrealist painter. Worked extensively for fashion houses and magazines. Perfume presentations for *Marquay, *Schiaparelli.

Dalon
Paris
Perfumes. Est. 1924, affiliated to *Pléville. Short-lived.

Dana
9 rue de la Paix, Paris
Perfumes, cosmetics. Est. 1932 by Javier Serra, formerly director of *Myrurgia. Named after Danaë, Greek mythological character, noted for beauty. Logo a beautiful head of a woman (from model by Mariano Andreu).

Debar & Cie, H.
Printers. High-quality perfume papers.

Delaunay, Sonia (*née* Terk; 1885–1979)
Painter, illustrator, costume, set, fashion and fabric designer. Russian-born; active in France from 1906. In 1910 she married the painter Robert Delaunay, whose 'Simultaneous Contrasts' inspired her 'Simultanés' (brilliant geometric fabric patterns). Participated in 1925 exhibition with Jacques *Heim, for whom she designed fox-head logo, used on 'Alambic' stopper.

Delettrez
15 rue Royale, Paris
Perfumes, cosmetics, toiletries. Est. 1835. From 1853 subtitled Parfumerie du Monde Elégant. Created early luxury presentations. Awarded two gold medals 1900. Major exporter.

Delhomme, Georges (1904–89)
Painter. Exhibited at Salon d'Automne. Artistic director of *Coty 1931–35, of *Lancôme 1935–65.

Delyna
21 rue de la Brèche-aux-Loups, Paris
Perfumes. Est. 1925 by Maxime Patraud. Acquired 1945 by Cuban perfumer Bienvenido Fernández.

Demours
110 rue Demours, Paris
Perfumes, cosmetics. Est. 1927 by Michel Schasseur (also founder of *Lionceau).

Dépinoix & Fils, C.
7 rue de la Perle, Paris
Glassworks, glass trading company. Est. 1846 by Théophile Coenon (1815–88). Constant Dépinoix (1854–1936), son-in-law, became proprietor 1888; company renamed C. Dépinoix. Early involvement in perfume-bottle production: did 'finishing work' on bottles produced by others. Innovative crescent-moon stopper for *Monpelas 'Triple Extrait d'Odeurs' *c.* 1875. Maurice Dépinoix (1884–1961), son of Constant, was leading designer. Company renamed C. Dépinoix & Fils. Greatly expanded by association with London-based International Bottle Company. In 1920s Dépinoix created many new models, averaging 300 per year. Villejuif factory purchased 1929. Maurice created many avant-garde models, which evolved from nature-based designs to abstract forms; always elegant and sophisticated. Worked with *Viard, *Gaillard. Greatly respected. Maurice was sometimes commissioned to create and/or produce models carrying the name of another glassworks or artist. Although the company and Maurice Dépinoix were not well-known to the public, the trade press and others in the field considered him one of most important artists. Some bottles were marked 'Made in France' inside a circle; some bore round paper labels with drawing of bottle, 'TC', and 'Paris'. Supplied leading perfumers, including: *Arys, *Caron, *Corday, *Coty, *Gabilla, *Gueldy, *Lanvin, *Lelong, *Lenthéric, *Lubin, *Patou, *Rigaud, *Roger & Gallet, *Sauzé, *Schiaparelli, *Tokalon.

Deroc
72 rue Pierre-Charon, Paris
Perfumes. Est. 1925 by Louis de Roquefeuil, who also est. Dorfeuil perfumes 1924. Company names derived from elements of founder's name. Both short-lived.

Desjonquères (Saint-Gobain Desjonquères)
Glassworks. Est. 1896 by Henri Desjonquères. Produced all types of glass objects, including perfume bottles. From 1924 new factory expanded bottle production massively. Merged 1972 with Saint-Gobain (leading glassworks, est. 1665). Clients included *Dana, *Dior, *Guerlain, *Rubinstein, *Roger & Gallet, *Weil.

Deslys
40 rue d'Enghien, Paris
Perfumes. Est. 1913 by Dufour et Cie.

Deslys, Gaby
Music-hall star, 1910s. Introduced Jazz Age to Paris. Inspired perfume presentations.

Desprez, Jean
17 rue de la Paix, Paris
Perfumes. Est. 1938 by Jean Desprez (1898–1973), great-grandson of Mme Félix Millot. Worked for *Millot. Created 'Crêpe de Chine' 1925.

Dessés, Jean
37 avenue George I, Paris
Couture house. Est. 1937 by Jean Dessés (1904–70). Draping, pleating and gathering of fabrics were favourite techniques, reproduced on 'Celui' ('The One') presentation.

Diaghilev, Sergei (1872–1929)
Russian theatrical producer. Brought Ballets Russes to Paris 1908. Strong artistic vision expressed in stage productions was major factor in Art Deco development. Influenced contemporary arts and decorative artists.

Diamant Bleu
156 rue du Faubourg-Saint-Honoré, Paris
Perfumes, dental products. Est. 1907 by F. Bagot & Cie. Acquired 1912 by *Groupement International des Grands Coiffeurs. Purchased 1926 by Maurice Chalom and Elie Devaux du Gourd de Brunière. Rare 'Nuit Etoilée de Bagdad' presentation. Acquired by *Cottan 1937.

Diaphane, La
4 rue Edith-Cavell, Courbevoie (Seine)
Perfumes, cosmetics. Est. in 19th c. by G. Mazuyer et Cie. 'Sarah Bernhardt' powder 1892. Luxury presentations. Affiliated to *Ysiane.

Dior, Christian
26–32 avenue Montaigne, Paris
Couture house. Est. 1946 by Christian Dior (1905–57). Perfumes introduced 1947. Major trendsetter. *Gruau created superb advertising for all Dior perfumes.

Dœuillet-Doucet
21–23 rue de la Paix, Paris
Couture house. Formed by merger of Dœuillet and Doucet 1929. Dœuillet, est. 1900 by Georges Dœuillet, introduced the 'cocktail dress'. Doucet family business est. *c.* 1820; Jacques Doucet had great reputation. Perfumes introduced 1929. Closed 1932.

Domergue, Jean-Gabriel (1889–1962)
Painter. Executed remarkable portrait of Andrée Leroy, proprietor of Fourrures *Max. 1920s. Well known for repetitive female nudes, e.g. as reproduced on cover of box for *Rigaud 'Féerie' 1938.

Dorilly
4 rue de la Paix, Paris
Perfumes. Est. 1920 by M. Pommez. Successful luxury presentations 1920s. Later est. *Marquay.

Dorin
27 rue du Grenier-Saint-Lazare, Paris
Cosmetics. Est. 1780 as small cosmetics shop, specializing in theatrical make-up, reputedly by famous, yet unsuccessful actress, Mademoiselle Montansier (*née* Marguerite Brunet; 1730–1820), friend of many well-connected men. Marie-Antoinette and revolutionary leaders. She had been director of Royal Theatre as well as proprietor of Théâtre du Palais-Royal. Company purchased by several people, including J. M. Dorin *c.* 1817. World-wide exports. Gold medal 1900.

Draeger Frères
Printers, graphic designers. Est. 1886 by Charles Draeger. Succeeded by sons (Georges, Maurice, Robert). Georges adapted *Lalique glass powder-puff design for *Coty paper powder boxes *c.* 1914. Graphic creations for Coty: 'Emeraude', 'L'Aimant' and (with *Camin) 'Vertige'. Redesigned *Houbigant's 18th-c. 'flowered-basket' logo in 1920s style. Created black and gold *Guerlain powder-box design (in 17th-c. metalwork style).

Dralle
11–17 Großer Burstah, Hamburg
Perfumes. Est. by Georg Dralle. Sold many French-created luxury presentations.

Drecoll
130 avenue des Champs-Elysées, Paris
Couture house. In late 19th c. M. and Mme Besançon de Wagner purchased existing Viennese business, Christof Drecoll & Kolmarch, and est. Paris branch 1902. Daughter, Maggy de Wagner, merged Drecoll with *Rouff 1929, changed name of couture house to Maggy Rouff. Drecoll perfumes introduced *c.* 1927; from 1929 sold under Maggy Rouff name. Interesting names: 'Tais-toi mon cœur' ('Be quiet, my heart'). Marcel *Guerlain purchased Drecoll perfumes 1944.

Drialis
Perfumes. Cuban company.

Drian, Etienne (*c.* 1890–*c.* 1965)
Painter, illustrator, costume and set designer (Casino de Paris). Worked for *La Gazette du Bon Ton*. Created *Lérys advertising, showing elegant Parisian women.

Dubarry et Cie
81 Brompton Road, London
Perfumes, cosmetics, toiletries. Est. 1916 with French name and style as perfume division of The Standard Tablet & Pill Company Ltd. Goldstone Chemical Works. Standard presentations produced since 19th c.. Dubarry luxury presentations used superb *Viard bottles, boxes resembling jewel caskets, French poetic and exotic names. Over 70 perfumes trademarked 1916–19, limited luxury productions. Subsequently, more industrial presentations, until closure in 1960s.

Ducale, La
Piazzale Staziano 8, Parma, Italy
Perfumes, cosmetics. Est. by Mario Negri, Laura Negri Tresoldi, Enrico Spaggiari 1923. Luxury to low-priced presentations.

Dufy, Raoul (1877–1953)
Painter, engraver. 1906–09 Fauve artist. Influenced by Wiener Werkstätte. Created fabric designs with animal and floral themes for *Poiret, some for *Rosine graphics 1911. Poiret's barge *Orgues* at 1925 exhibition was decorated with 14 paintings executed on fabric by Dufy. He made no distinction between decorative and fine art.

Dumoulin, Georges (1882–1959)
Painter, ceramist, glass artist. Trained as jeweller and goldsmith. Spent eight years at Sèvres porcelain

factory. Interested in experimental glass techniques. Glass pieces exhibited in 1928 received rave reviews. Designed bottles for *Lenthéric, possibly *Rosine and others – mostly unidentified.

Dune, Pierre
49 rue de Prony, Paris
Perfumes. Est. 1939 by Edmond Rosens. First five perfumes presented as potted plants in cart.

Dunhill, Mary
30 Duke Street, St James's, London
Perfumes. Est. 1934 by Mary Dunhill (related to Alfred Dunhill).

E

Edouardo
20 Broad Street, New York
Perfumes. Est. *c.* 1918 by Edward Tatum in Larchmont, NY. In 1926 'Bag-Dabs' (solid wax-based perfumes made in France by *Fragonard) were presented in tiny, colourful painted Bakelite containers.

Eisenberg
Chicago, Illinois
Fashion house, custom jewelry. Est. 1880 by Jonas Eisenberg. Perfumes introduced 1938 as 'Eisenberg Originals'.

Elesbé
20 rue Dagobert, Clichy (Seine)
Perfumes. Est. 1922 by Robert-Laurent Lévy, Roger de Soria, Pierre Bord with name based on initials LSB. Affiliated with *Lionceau.

Elorza, Marques de
73 avenue des Champs-Elysées, Paris
Perfumes. Est. 1926 by Ávran Moscovici. Affiliated companies: *Chénier and de *Paul. Early presentations interesting, luxurious. After 1930, lesser-quality.

Emme, GI. VI.
Via Monte-Napoleone, Milan
Perfumes, cosmetics, toiletries. Est. 1921 by Count Giuseppe Visconti di Modrone, co-proprietor of Carlo Erba which had sold perfumes since 1910. Company used acronym (Gi Vi M) derived from the founder's name. Some luxurious, unusual presentations.

Erasmic Co. Ltd
117 Oxford Street, London
Soaps, perfumes. Erasmic was successful soap name introduced by J. Crossfield & Sons 1889. Separate Erasmic company est. later for perfumes and wide range of products. René *Lalique designed bottle for the 1925 perfume 'De Lui' ('From Him'). Business acquired later by Lever Brothers.

Erizma
4–6 rue d'Hauteville, Paris
Perfumes, cosmetics. Est 1885. in Bordeaux by J. Bijon. Rare luxury presentations. Exporters to the Far East.

Erté (Romain de Tirtoff) (1892–1991)
Draughtsman, fashion designer, stage and film costume and set designer. Name Erté derived from his initials RT (as pronounced in French). Russian-born, worked in France and USA. Fashion draughtsman for *Poiret 1913. Designed costume for Mata Hari (then known as 'The Red Dancer') in *Le Minaret*. Designed costumes for major Paris music halls, Broadway shows and movies. Involved with many perfume personalities. His extravagant, elegant style greatly influenced 1920s perfume industry. 'Erté' was used for perfumes created by Emile Gutcheon, 1925–27, though it remains unclear if Erté was involved.

Esmé of Paris
Paris, New York
Perfumes. Est. *c.* 1929. Active until 1940s.

Euzière, A.
Grasse
Perfumes. Est. 1887 as Société Euzière et Seytre. Became Henri Euzière et Cie 1920. Superb *Viard presentations.

F

Fath, Jacques
39 avenue Pierre I er de Serbie, Paris
Couture house. Est. in 1937 by Jacques Fath (1912–54) Introduced perfumes 1945. Closed 1957.

Favolys
1 rue Pierre-Joigneaux, Asnières (Seine)
Perfumes. Est. 1925 by René Desseignes who also est. Parfumerie Francis (1924) and Rendès (1924). All short-lived.

Faÿ, Charles
9 rue de la Paix, Paris
Perfumes, cosmetics, toiletries. Known as Maison Faÿ when est. 1850 by Charles Faÿ. Following great success of powder 'Veloutine', company became known as Parfumerie Veloutine. Gold medal 1900.

Feuquières
Glassworks est. *c.* 1900 by Amédée Scobart in Vallée de la Bresle. Speciality: perfume bottles. Absorbed by *Brosse 1929.

Figène
Grasse
Perfumes. Est. 1931 by Eugène Miquelis.

Fini, Léonor (1908–)
Painter, engraver, illustrator, designer of stage and film costumes and sets. Born in Argentina, of Italian ancestry. Worked in France in Surrealist style (feminine, erotic, but anguished). Conceived *Schiaparelli 'Shocking' and *Rochas 'Femme'.

Fioret/Les Parfums des Jardins de Fioret
4–6 rue Ybry, Neuilly (Seine)
Perfumes, cosmetics. Est. 1919 by Simon Jaroslawski (also creator of *Ybry and *Mÿon). Initially, numerous avant-garde, luxurious presentations, all abstract-geometric. After 1930, marked decrease in quality of designs, although sales continued in USA until 1940s.

Flament & Devallon
Boxes. Many complex geometric models. Participated in 1925 exhibition.

Fontanis
38 boulevard de la Saussaye, Neuilly (Seine)
Perfumes, cosmetics. Est. 1919 by Daniel Jacquet, also founder of Madhva 1923. Luxurious presentations. Gold medal 1925. Fontanis vignette designed by *Heymann reproduced on labels, metal plaques.

Forest
48 rue de Richelieu, Paris
Perfumes. Est. *c.* 1910 by Léon Cohn, subtitled Parfumerie Moderne. Luxury presentations. Cohn est. Les Parfums Léon in 1924 for medium-priced perfumes, using 'Lucky Scents' in advertising.

Fornells, Eduard (1887–1942)
Glass, metal, plastics artist. From Andorra. Moved to Paris 1909. Met *Lalique 1911, and started working with him. Opened own workshops 1913. Many perfumers became clients, but working relationship with Lalique continued. Trained in engraving, chasing, tooling. Mould specialist, he transformed drawings into moulds for production of three-dimensional objects, using his own designs and those of others. For Lalique he designed many glass pieces, bottles, aluminium powder boxes (one in 1922 decorated with parrots for a *Roger & Gallet powder) from which 'Le Jade' graphics were derived. Designed and produced Lalique's wonderful Bakelite boxes. Became specialist in use of plastic materials, working as if it were bronze – even applying patinas – producing Bakelite perfume boxes for presentations, but not marked with perfume names.

Forvil
1 rue de Castiglione, Paris
Perfumes, cosmetics, toiletries. Est. 1922 by Leo Fink as Forval, with 'La Perle Noire' and 'Le Corrail Rouge', both designed by *Lalique. Sold 1923 to La Société Anonyme les Dentifrices du Docteur Pierre (dental hygiene company est. 1837 by Dr Pierre Mussot), and renamed Forvil. Lalique created black glass bottles only for *d'Orsay and Forvil, the two companies founded by Leo Fink.

Fracy
Paris
Perfumes, cosmetics. Est. 1922. Novelties and some *Viard luxury presentations.

Fragonard
20 boulevard Fragonard, Grasse
Essential oils, perfumes. Est. 1782 and known as P. Mottet et Cie and Cresp, Martinenq. Bankrupt 1914. Acquired by Eugène Fuchs. Interesting presentations 1920s–40s.

Fredericks, John
New York
Milliner. Introduced perfumes 1935.

Fuller, Les Parfums Loïe
52 rue des Saint-Pères, Paris
Perfumes. Loïe Fuller (1862–1928), dancer immortalized by artists (Toulouse-Lautrec, Cheret, etc.), est. perfume company 1925. Her death curtailed company development.

G

Gabilla
29 avenue Marigny, Paris
Perfumes, cosmetics. Est. 1910 by Henriette Gabilla, Syrian perfumer, friend of *Colette. Major company exported luxury to lower-priced presentations worldwide. Created perfumes and presentations for others (e.g. *Ciro). Prix d'honneur 1925.

Gaillard, Lucien (1861–c. 1930)
Jeweller, goldsmith, sculptor, glass artist. Became proprietor of father's important jewelry shop 1892. Master of gilding and metal patinating. Admired Japanese art. Imported Japanese artisans to work for him. Created numerous Art Nouveau *objets d'art*, fashion accessories. Gold medal 1889. Grand Prix 1900. Based at 107 rue La Boëtie, Paris. Encouraged by *Lalique, his friend, to concentrate on jewelry. Created jewelry and fashion accessories using similar materials and in same style as Lalique. After Lalique started working for *Coty, Gaillard worked for some select companies – *Brécher, *Clamy, *Silka, *Violet. Trademarked many perfume names, some subsequently sold to perfume companies. There are four very similar designs depicting a winged female nude, two by Gaillard and two by Lalique. Gaillard designed *Clamy 'Femmes Ailées' ('Winged Women') in 1913 and *Violet 'L'Heure Jolie' ('The Pretty Hour') c. 1922; and Lalique designed *d'Héraud 'Phalène' c. 1919 and executed four drawings for similar vases, all entitled 'Deux Figures Femmes Ailées', in 1922. Most Gaillard designs produced by *Brosse and *Dépinoix and signed 'LG'. (133)

133 Lucien Gaillard, bottles in clear and frosted glass designed by Gaillard and made by Brosse: Clamy, 'Femmes Ailées', 1913, with frosted stopper and brown patina on bottle and stopper, h. 6.5 cm (2½ in.); Violet, 'L'Heure Jolie', c. 1921, with ivory patina on female figure and brown patina on perfume name and stopper, h. 9.0 cm (3½ in.).

Gal
10 Paseo de San Bernardino, Madrid
Perfumes, cosmetics. Est. *c.* 1900. Many luxury presentations.

Galeries Lafayette
Department stores. Introduced own perfumes and presentations created by *Coty. (134)

134 Galeries Lafayette, 'La Feuillaison' ('Coming into Leaf'), c. 1922, possibly designed and made by René Lalique: bottle in clear and frosted glass with silvered front, clear-glass stopper and gilded label. H. 8.0 cm (3⅛ in.).

Galion, Le
11 bis, rue Amélie, Paris
Perfumes. Existing company, est. by Prince Murat and associates, acquired by Paul Vacher 1937. 'Sortilège' ('Witchcraft') bestseller.

Gellé Frères
6 avenue de l'Opéra, Paris
Perfumes, cosmetics, toiletries. Est. 1826 by the brothers Augustin and Jean-Baptiste Gellé after purchase of formulas and shop which previously belonged to Fargeon Jeune, descendant of perfumer to Louis XV. Émile Lecaron succeeded Augustin Gellé (his father-in-law). Became major company. Elegant presentations. Exports worldwide. Many prizes, gold medal 1925.

Germain & Cie, Evette
Printed paper. Produced most packaging papers for *Rosine. Participated in 1925 exhibition.

Gilot
68 rue du Faubourg-Saint-Martin, Paris
Soap, cosmetics, perfumes. Est. c. 1900, acquired important 19th-c. company, C. P. Blaize. Perfume posters featured Réjane, noted actress. Quality soaps, superb paper packaging. Trademarked perfume-cosmetics line 'Soir de Paris' in 1925, prior to *Bourjois.

Girard et Cie Ltd, Mme
182 Regent Street, London
Perfumes. Est. 19th c. Small, prestigious company.

Giraud Fils, Jean
Grasse and Paris
Perfumes. Est. 1853 as Giraud Frères. Later known as Jean Giraud Fils, acquired by various essential oils producers in Grasse, e.g. Honoré-Joseph Sozio c. 1900. Large exports to South America.

Givenchy
3 avenue George V, Paris
Couture house. Est. 1952 by Hubert de Givenchy. Perfumes introduced 1958.

Godet
37 rue Saint-Lazare, Paris
Perfumes, cosmetics. Est. 1908 by Julien-Joseph Godet. 'Ma Poudre' ('My Powder') was avant-garde representation of 1911. Major international company by 1913, when Godet died. He was succeeded by his widow Louise and director, Abel Ravaud. Gold medal 1925. Magnificent labels.

Gourde du Poète, La
36 avenue de Wagram, Paris
Perfumes. Est. c. 1914 by Rosalie Leforestier as Parfumerie de l'Etoile. Charming, high-quality novelties. Affiliated with *Rochambeau.

Gouvernet
Luxury boxes for *Godet, *Corday, *Mury and for *Fioret (with *Lalique glass medallions).

Grande Maison de Blanc, La
6 boulevard des Capucines, Paris
Linens, bridal trousseaus, fashions, millinery stores. Introduced own perfumes 1926, using *Gabilla creations.

Grands Parfums de France, Les
Grasse
Perfumes. Est. 1925 by Joseph Charrier.

Grasset, Eugène (1841–1917)
Architect, interior designer, painter. Originally Swiss, active in Paris. Numerous designs including posters ('Eau de Lubin', 1897). Many perfume labels and graphics produced 1890–1910 very close to his Art Nouveau motifs; but not known if Grasset was directly involved.

Gravier, A.
6 rue Casimir-Pinel, Neuilly (Seine)
Perfumes, cosmetics, toiletries. Alphonse Gravier est. small shop c. 1880. Became important after introducing 'Dr Peterson' products (toothpaste, soap, perfume). Magnificent presentations in 1920s. Silver medal 1925.

Gray, Dorothy
683 Fifth Avenue, New York
Beauty salons, perfumes, cosmetics, toiletries. Est. 1916. Acquired own Fifth Avenue building 1929. Interesting presentations in 1930s–40s.(135)

135 Dorothy Gray, unidentified perfumes, c. 1943, in bottles by Pochet et du Courval. Clear-glass bottle with gilded base and stopper; clear-glass sample bottle with Lucite cap over inner stopper. H. 14.5 cm (5¾ in.); 5.3 cm (2⅛ in.).

Grenoville
20 rue Royale, Paris
Perfumes, cosmetics, toiletries. Est. 1879 by Paul Grenoville (who changed family name from *grenouille*, meaning 'frog'). Succeeded by widow, Marie-Marthe Richard, after 1900. Major international exports. Range of luxury to low-priced presentations. Affiliated to *Parfise after 1923. Silver medal 1925.

Grès
1 rue de la Paix, Paris
Couture house. Workshop est. c. 1930 by Germaine Barton merged 1934 with Maison Alix becoming Alix Barton Couture. Renamed Alix Grès Couture 1942. First perfume, 'Cabochard', introduced 1959.

Griffe, Jacques
5 rue Royale, Paris
Couture house. Est. 1946 by Jacques Griffe (b. 1910) a protégé of *Vionnet. Perfumes introduced 1949. Took over *Molyneux salons when they closed 1950. Woman-cat image created by *Gruau for 'Mistigri'.

Grossmith & Son Ltd, John
29 Newgate Street, London
Perfumes, cosmetics, toiletries. Est. in 19th c. After 1900 John Lipscomb Grossmith introduced oriental-inspired perfume lines ('Hasu-no-hana', 'Phul-nana', 'Shem-el-Nessim', 'Tsang-Ihang', 'Wana-Ranee') which became very successful.

Groult, André (1884–1967)
Designer of interiors, furniture, home accessories. Considered Art Deco master. Elegant traditional French design adapted to modern style. Married *Poiret's sister Nicole. Collaborated on interior design of *Baccarat Pavilion for 1925 exhibition. Designed decorative perfume bottles for sale in his own shop. Possibly created perfume presentations.

Groult, Nicole
29 rue d'Anjou, Paris
Couture house. Est. 1912 by Nicole Groult (1887–1967), *Poiret's sister, wife of André *Groult. Introduced two perfumes, c. 1924: 'Le Bleu de Nicole Groult' ('Nicole Groult's Blue') and 'Le Rose de Nicole Groult' ('Nicole Groult's Pink').

Groupement International des Grands Coiffeurs
16 rue Saulnier, Paris
Perfumes, cosmetics, toiletries. Est. c. 1900 to provide luxury perfumes, beauty products for sale at hairdressing salons. Acquired *Diamant Bleu perfume company 1912.

Gruau, René (1910–)
Illustrator. His fashion and perfume advertising dominated the French press after WW2. Worked for many prestigious couture houses and perfumes. Powerful, whimsical, erotic, ultra-chic style. His 'Rouge Baiser' lipstick illustration became a 1950s icon.

Gueldy
370 rue du Faubourg-Saint-Honoré, Paris
Perfumes, cosmetics. Est. 1905 by Lelaurin and A. Sergent. Later acquired by P. Thibaud et Cie, major toilet-articles company affiliated to Gibbs (English toiletries and toothpaste company, est. 1712). Sergent also est. *Sergy (lower-priced perfumes, cosmetics). Gueldy became major company, large exports. Gold medal 1925. Later acquired by Lever Brothers.

Guerlain
15 rue de la Paix, Paris
Perfumes, cosmetics, toiletries. Pierre-François-Paschal Guerlain opened small perfume shop in 1828 at 42 rue de Rivoli; moved to above address 1840. 'Eau de Cologne Impériale' created for Empress Eugénie 1853. Founder's son Aimé (1834–1910) joined company 1861; created 'Jicky' 1889. After founder's death in 1864, Aimé's brother Gabriel (1841–1933) joined company. Gabriel's sons Pierre (1872–1961) and Jacques (1874–1963) joined company c. 1900. Jacques introduced 'Voilà pourquoi j'aimais Rosine' 1900. Second shop opened at 68 avenue des Champs-Elysées in 1914. Later Marcel (1909–91), son of Jacques, joined company. Shop moved to 2 place Vendôme 1935. Guerlain considered a most prestigious perfumer. More than 200 perfumes introduced. Many luxury presentation and worldwide bestsellers. Owing to existence of rival Marcel *Guerlain company, advertising in France in 1930 used slogan 'Nous n'avons pas de prénom' ('We have no first name').

Guerlain, Marcel
86 rue du Faubourg-Saint-Honoré, Paris
Perfumes, cosmetics. Est. 1923 by Marcel Guerlain; large capitalization of 7 million francs in 1926. Guerlain also formed other perfume companies: Hughes Guerlain, Hélène Gys (using HG initials), Gys, La Société des Parfumeurs Parisiens, Les Parfums d'Agnès and Marlaine (which distributed Marcel Guerlain products in USA). Splendid shop at above address. First perfume 'Le Roy Le Veult'. Many other superb, elegant presentations in 1920s. Trademarked very interesting names: 'Pour Mon Cousin' ('For My Cousin'), 'Morsure d'Amour' ('Love Bite'), 'Né d'Hier' ('Born Yesterday') and 'Harakiri'. Marcel Guerlain had same name as *Guerlain heir. Advertised in USA: 'no connection with any firm of similar name'.

Guermantes
24 rue de la Paix, Paris
Perfumes. Est. 1935 by Claude Caron, whose pharmacy was situated at same address.

Gui, Le
34 rue de la Clef, Paris
Perfumes. Est. by Marie-Hippolyte Salle 1911. Interesting presentations 1920s.

Guimard, Hector (1867–1942)
Architect, sculptor, interior designer. Considered Art Nouveau master, best known for his design of Paris Métro station entrances. Designed *Millot perfume presentations.

Guyla
40 rue de Paris, Epinay-sur-Seine
Perfumes. Est. 1926. Exceptionally original, rare perfume presentations.

H

Hamm, Henri (1871–1961)
Sculptor, designer of furniture, home and fashion accessories, perfume bottles. Friend of Apollinaire, Picasso, Max Jacob. Cézanne and Gauguin inspired his Cubist sculptures. Designed many Art Nouveau accessories. By 1918 he had designed nearly 400 perfume bottles, produced by *Bobin, but all unsigned and few identified. *Isabey purchased some of his models 1924. Participated in 1925 exhibition in perfume section.

Heim, Jacques
15 avenue Matignon, Paris
Couture house. Isidore and Jeanne Heim est. fur business 1898. Their son Jacques (1899–1967) introduced day and evening wear 1920s, incorporating fur ornamentation. Close associate *Delaunay created fabric designs, 'Cubist' clothes, accessories. Participated together in 1925 exhibition. Delaunay created Heim fox-head logo. Perfumes existed *c.* 1930, introduced to public 1947. (136)

136 Jacques Heim, 'Alambic', possibly introduced before 1930, clear-glass bottle, stopper in cobalt-blue glass featuring frosted intaglio fox-head logo designed by Sonia Delaunay, and silvered and blue label. H. 8.5 cm (3⅜ in.).

Helleu, Jean (1894–)
Painter and illustrator. Son of Paul Helleu (1859–1927), known as Belle Epoque portrait painter. Jean's style as painter totally unlike father's. As perfume and cosmetics advertising artist, reproduced father's style almost identically. *Coty advisor. *Bourjois artistic designer.

Hennessy
1457 Broadway, New York
Perfumes. Est. by Frank Reilly 1932. Short-lived.

Héra
81–83 rue de Chérzy, Neuilly (Seine)
Perfumes, cosmetics, toiletries. Est. by Marthe-Jeanne Thibault 1910. Important producer of 'Dentifrices Bleus'. Luxury presentations.

Héraud, d'
3 rue de la Sablière, Courbevoie (Seine)
Perfumes, cosmetics, toiletries. Est. 1920 by Delphin Héraud; produced perfumes earlier. Luxury presentations by *Gaillard, *Lalique.

Hérouard, Mathilde (*c.* 1880–?)
Painter, illustrator. Known for sensitive pastel portraits. As illustrator, designed charming scenes, elaborate backgrounds – mostly for *Dorin.

Herpin, L. H.
Glassworks. Sometimes produced bottles of unusual shape.

Heymann, Georges
Printer, publisher, designer. Produced labels, metal plaques. Designed and produced *Fontanis vignette. Worked for *Brajan. (137)

137 Georges Heymann, brass display sign for Fontanis, 1919. H. 8.5 cm (3⅜ in.).

Hoffmann, Josef (1870–1956)
Austrian draughtsman, illustrator, architect, interior designer. Joint founder of Wiener Werkstätte 1903. Directly and indirectly influenced fashion and perfume artists, particularly *Poiret.

Hortys, d'
100 avenue du Roule, Neuilly (Seine)
Perfumes, cosmetics. Est. 1917 by Max Heidelberg. Luxury, delicate presentations. Acquired by Maurice Blanchet of *Coryse-Salomé, 1937.

Houbigant
19 rue du Faubourg-Saint-Honoré, Paris
Perfumes, cosmetics, toiletries. Business, named 'A la Corbeille de Fleurs', est. at the above address by Jean-François Houbigant 1774. Succeeded by son. Following three proprietors were perfumers: Chardin, Magny, Gabillot. Acquired by Javal and Parquet 1881. During 19th c. supplier to French, British and Russian courts. Became major company, exported worldwide. Participated in all important exhibitions. In early 20th c. Robert *Bienaimé was director and co-proprietor. Presentations ranged from luxury to low-priced. Bottles in classic shapes with gilded motifs or labels depicted 18th-c. figures, landscape scenes (in style of Watteau, Fragonard), reminiscent of firm's 18th-c. origins.

House for Men
Chicago, New York, Los Angeles
Men's toiletries. Bold presentations.

Hoyt, Peggy
16 East 55th Street, New York
Millinery, fashions, perfumes. Possibly est. *c.* 1900. Advertised as 'Milliners and dressmakers to the American aristocracy', with drawing of hats growing on tree branches. Perfumes introduced 1916, making Hoyt second US fashion house with own perfumes, one year after *Bendel.

Hudnut, Richard
20 rue de la Paix, Paris
Perfumes, cosmetics, toiletries. Small druggist shop est. 1880 in New York. Richard Hudnut, son of proprietor, first American selling luxury perfume presentations (some created in France) in elegant shop, a practice typical of all major French, European perfumers. Company sold 1916 and thereafter Hudnut not involved. In 1920s company expanded into Europe, acquired French style. Prestigious Paris shop opened 1927 with 'Le Début' in very French luxury presentation. Other luxury presentations. Quality of new designs gradually declined 1930s–50s.

Hujarvis
175 boulevard Malesherbes, Paris
Perfumes. Est. by René Eyben 1920. Elegant presentations.

Hygiènof
13 rue de Londres, Paris
Soaps, cosmetics, perfumes. Est. 1915 by Mlle S. Bergeron. Speciality: delicate laundry soaps. Adopted Pierrot in spotless white coat as symbol,

used in presentation of 'Pierrot Vainqueur' 1918. Introduced 'Pierrot Eternel' 1943.

I

Institut de Beauté, L'
26 place Vendôme, Paris
Beauty salon, toiletries, cosmetics, perfumes. Est. 1895 by Victor François Merle with Elise-Marie Valentin Le Brun. All products known as Klytia (as was affiliated US company). Some superb presentations produced in limited editions – perhaps available only at Paris salon.

Iribe, Paul (1883–1935)
Artist, illustrator, cartoonist, interior designer. Pioneer of Art Deco. Worked for press, theatre, films, fashion and perfumes; designed furniture, home accessories. Advertisement for *Lubin 'Enigma' in *Le Témoin* 1906. Designed 'La Rose Iribe' 1908. Then advertisement for *Rigaud 'Près de Vous' ('Close to You'), L. T. *Piver 'Ilka', *Bichara cosmetics. Created *Lanvin logo 1922.

Isabey
20 rue de la Paix, Paris
Perfumes, cosmetics. Est. in 1924 by Maurice Loewe (with financing from Rothschild family) as Société Parisienne d'Essences Rares et de Parfums, known to public as Les Parfums d'Isabey – company named after painter Isabey (1767–1855). Conveyed image of long-established, refined French artistry. Well-financed, only best-quality perfumes, most luxury presentations, splendid shop. Participated in 1925 exhibition, and although barely one year old was awarded gold medal. Considerable exports to USA. Acquired by Marcel *Guerlain 1941.

J

Janey
5 rue Saint-Antoine, Cannes
Perfumes. Est. 1928 by Jean Romano. Charming names, presentations. Short-lived.

Jaspy
75 rue du Cardinal Lemoine, Paris
Perfumes. Est. *c.* 1910, subtitled 'Parfums Modernes et Originaux'. Small luxury production.

Jay-Thorpe
57th Street, West, New York
Luxury fashions. 'Jaytho' perfumes, cosmetics introduced 1921. *Lalique models. Best name 'Méchant, mais Charmant!' ('Wicked, but Charming!').

Jeanbin, Gaston
Boxes, labels. Est. 1840. Luxury production. Participated in 1925 exhibition.

Jean de Parys
7 rue Saint-Lazare, Paris
Perfumes, cosmetics, toiletries. Est. *c.* 1914 by Jean Cousin in Nanterre (Seine). Luxury presentations. Bottles designed by *Jolivet, some produced by *Lalique.

Jeurelle-Seventeen
551 Fifth Avenue, New York
Perfumes, cosmetics. Est. 1933 as division of *Colgate-Palmolive-Peet. Name 'Seventeen' derived from 17th-floor location. Extraordinary miniatures.

Jolivet, André
Glassworks, glass artist. Est. in Eu for cold finishing work. Designed and produced unusual, high-quality bottles. Developed new pearlized finish. Important clients: de *Morny, *Jean de Parys, de *Raymond, *Volnay.

Jones, Thomas
25 rue La Boëtie, Paris
Perfumes, cosmetics. British company est. in Paris 1856. Silver medal 1878, 1889. Always introduced avant-garde presentations.

Jouvin, Gants
1 bis, rue Auber, Paris
Gloves. Est. by Xavier Jouvin 1834. Succeeded by Rey-Jouvin Frères. Considered most prestigious 19th-c. French glove designers, with many branches

in France. L. T. *Piver perfumes often sold in Jouvin shops. Own perfumes introduced 1927.

Jovoy
127 rue de Longchamp, Paris
Perfumes, cosmetics. Est. 1923 by Blanche Arvoy (*née* Réneaux) who also est. *Corday. Personally awarded silver medal 1925 for Jovoy creations. High-quality representations. Perfume names interesting, often humorous, sometimes outlandish, reflecting founder's personality: 'Blanchette' (her nickname), 'Toujours Moi' ('Always Me'), 'Gardez-moi' ('Keep Me').

Jussy St James
Halle-aux-Vins, Paris
Perfumes, cosmetics. Est. 1890. Known first as 'James Ducellier'. Luxury presentations up to 1930.

K

Katorza, Mouna (Rahmouna)
Place Beauvau, Paris
Luxury fashions. Introduced perfumes *c.* 1925 'Les Parfums de ma Moune'. Presentations inspired by ancient Egypt.

Kerkoff
4 place de l'Opéra, Paris
Perfumes, cosmetics, toiletries. Est. 1908 by M. Darthiailh. 'Djerkiss' bestseller. Became major company.

Klimt, Gustav (1862–1918)
Austrian painter. Co-founder of Vienna Secession. Worked for Wiener Werkstätte. Inspired *Poiret, *Erté.

L

Laboureur, Jean-Emile (1877–1943)
Painter, engraver, illustrator. Worked for *Rosine.

Lacloche
8 place Vendôme, Paris
Jewellers. Jacques Lacloche introduced 'No. 1' perfume 1954.

Lacroix, Boris
Designer of fashion, home accessories. Avant-garde style. Active from 1920s on; designed one *Vionnet presentation.

Lalanne
104 rue du Faubourg-Saint-Honoré, Paris
Perfumes, cosmetics, toiletries. Est. *c.* 1910 by Charles Lalanne, possibly as beauty salon. Luxury presentations. *Dépinoix was a supplier. Acquired by *Académie Scientifique de Beauté 1933.

Lalique, Marc (1900–77)
Glass artist. Son of René *Lalique. Joined company 1922; succeeded father 1945. Created beautiful bottles for *Molinard, Morabito, *Raphaël, *Ricci, *Rochas, *Worth.

Lalique, René (1860–1945)
Jeweller, sculptor, glass artist. Trained with jeweller Louis Aucoc; Ecole des Arts Décoratifs, Paris; Sydenham College, London (jewelry design). Studied sculpture, drawing and engraving. Became independent jeweller, selling to Aucoc, Cartier, Destapes, Vever. First company, Lalique et Varenne, formed 1884. Unsigned Lalique models (produced by various jewellers) successful at 1889 exhibition. Experimented with many techniques, materials. Designed original, imaginative jewelry for Sarah Bernhardt. Started experimentation with glass – for small, unconventionally coloured and shaped elements for his poetic designs. Broad recognition 1895 during Salon des Champs-Elysées – overnight celebrity. Designed 145 pieces of jewelry and *objets d'art* for Calouste Gulbenkian collection. Yearly exhibitions, culminated at 1900 exhibition. Received international acclaim. Major museums purchased work. After 1900 built Cours Albert Ier as private residence, also used as headquarters. Est. Clairefontaine glassworks for glass research, production. Queen Alexandra purchased jewelry 1902. Exhibited in London (Grafton Galleries, T. Agnew

and Son Gallery) and at St Louis World's Fair 1904. Designed embroidered collars, some encrusted with extravagant Art Nouveau glass motifs. Opened shop at 24 place Vendôme 1905. New Combs-la-Ville factory opened 1909 for glass production. After 1912, Lalique concentrated on glass design. First exhibition devoted exclusively to glass pieces at Place Vendôme shop. Artistic glass production ceased with WW1, but resumed in 1918 with very advanced techniques permitting production of complex models. Numerous and varied perfume presentations in 1920s-30s (bottle, powder boxes, paper graphics, metal and Bakelite pieces). René Lalique's genius in Art Nouveau design greatly influenced other perfume artists. His powerful, sensitive, distinctive creations were often blatantly copied.

Lalo
Paris
Leather goods. Introduced perfumes 1919, all with names by *Gaillard. *Lalique luxury presentations.

Lancôme
29 rue du Faubourg-Saint-Honoré, Paris
Perfumes, cosmetics. Est. 1935 by Armand Petitjean, previously managing director of *Coty. First five perfumes introduced at 1935 Brussels exhibition. Firm awarded prize and became major company. *Delhomme, Coty artistic director, became first Lancôme artistic director; as creator of almost all presentations throughout 1950s, he was true source of Lancôme spirit.

Lancy
57 rue Sainte-Anne, Paris
Perfumes, cosmetics. Est. *c.* 1919 by Mme G. Piltan. Sober presentations.

Lanselle
5 rue Jean-Mermoz, Paris
Perfumes. Est. *c.* 1930 by René Lanselle and François de Perthuis. Names of first perfumes used card-game terminology.

Lanvin, Jeanne/Lanvin
22 rue du Faubourg-Saint-Honoré, Paris
Couture house. Jeanne Lanvin (1867–1946) was apprenticed in 1885 to Maria-Berta Valenti, women's and children's clothes specialist in Barcelona; 1890 seamstress to Suzanne *Talbot (Paris couture, milliner). 1902 est. modest millinery workshop at above address. Around 1909, introduced concept of mother-daughter collections, encouraging customer loyalty; first offering of men's collection 1926. *Iribe created Lanvin logo (possibly with involvement of *Rateau) 1922. Perfumes introduced 1923: first three trademarked 'Kara-Djenoun', 'My Sin' ('Mon Péché' in France), and 'Où Fleurit l'Oranger' ('Where the Orange Tree Blossoms'). 'My Sin' an international bestseller. Imaginative names – endearing, ambiguous, poetic, musical. Bottle designed and produced by *Brosse in 1923 – cubic clear glass, with black faceted stopper featuring intaglio logo on top – remains virtually unchanged. Another model, 'La Boule', designed by Rateau and produced *c.* 1925 by *Romesnil has been used for all Lanvin perfumes, in black-glass, clear-glass and Sèvres porcelain limited editions. Earliest powder-box model was lacquered papier-mâché replica of black boule. The Lanvin boule, with Iribe logo, is a masterpiece of design, but because of large-scale production its true significance is not always appreciated.

Lasco, Etablissements
6 cité Paradis, Paris
Trading company. Extensive exports to USA, Canada – luxury goods, *objets d'art*, fashions, perfumes. Often retained exclusivity for exported perfumes, such as *Jovoy 'Gardez-moi'.

Lasègue
8 rue de Reims, Maisons-Alfort (Seine)
Perfumes, cosmetics. Est. *c.* 1910 by Arthur Lasègue. Interesting graphics.

Laurent, Bona & Bicart
Boxes. Luxury production. Grand Prix 1925.

Lazell
Newburgh-on-Hudson, New York
Perfumes, cosmetics, toiletries. Est. *c.* 1870. 'As the Petals' line introduced *c.* 1910, displaying wonder-

ful drawing, dancing Salomé surrounded by veils. Later acquired by Max Factor.

Lebouvier, Blanche
3 rue Boudreau, Paris
Luxury fashions. Est. in 19th c. by Blanche Lebouvier. Grand Prix 1900. Business purchased by René Pacquet, furrier *c.* 1910. First perfume, 'Folle Maîtresse', introduced for Christmas 1925. Short-lived perfumes.

Lecomte, Germaine
9 avenue Matignon, Paris
Couture house. Est. 1920 by Germaine Lecomte as modest workshop. Became couture house 1924. Perfumes introduced 1946. 'Soir de Fête' presentation reflected evening-gown style in 1946 fashion collection.

Lederer, Hermann
Fancy articles. Speciality: metal compacts, representing valises, envelopes. Participated in 1937 exhibition.

Lefèbure & Cie
Glassworks, crystalworks. Est. 1806. In 19th c. and early 20th c. produced classic crystal bottles with superb quality brass or silver covers (*Delettrez, *Rigaud). *Volnay was an important client in the 1920s.

Léger, Fernand (1881–1955)
Painter. Designed *Revillon 'Cantilène' special edition 1948.

Legrain
9 rue Richepanse, Paris
Perfumes, cosmetics. Est. 1921 by Simon Moscovitz with associate Alzic Manole. Moscovitz later known as Simon Legrain or Isidore Legrain. Presentations sometimes luxurious and/or humorous.

Legrand, Hector
118 rue Henry-Litolff, Bois Colombes (Seine)
Perfumes, cosmetics, toiletries. Est. 1856. Proprietor in early 20th c. was J. Caron. Business should not be confused with L. *Legrand. Small luxury production. Spectacular presentation of 1920, 'Eglantine de la Reine' ('Queen's Wild Rose'), used 'tiara' bottle by *Lalique (designed in 1919 for René Lalique & Cie and known as No. 509 or 'Fraîcheur') with elaborate label and box.

Legrand, L.
11 place de la Madeleine, Paris
Perfumes, cosmetics, toiletries. Est. 1811 by L. Legrand after purchasing formulas (patented 1720) from descendants of Fargeon, perfumer to 10-year old Louis XV. Business purchased 1860 by Antonin Raynaud; succeeded by widow. Purchased by Armand Schul *c.* 1910. Later known as Société Centrale de la Parfumerie Française. In 19th c. perfumers to Napoleon III, British and Italian courts. Gold medal 1889. Grand Prix, 1900. Two major 19th-c. innovations: introduction in 1879 of

138 L. Legrand, 'Fin comme l'Ambre', 1913, Baccarat bottle no. 246, clear and frosted crystal, black patina on heads of lions, brass cap over inner stopper, and gilded label. H. 11.5 cm (4½ in.).

'Parfumerie Oriza' (first perfume 'line' – perfume, related cosmetics and toiletries under one name with co-ordinated graphics) so successful that company became known later as 'Oriza' or 'Oriza-Legrand'; and patent of 1887 for 'solid' perfumes, 'Essence Oriza Solidifiée', presented in wax form 1887. Luxury presentations, such as 1913 'Fin comme l'Ambre' ('Refined like Amber'). Acquired *Rosine perfumes 1930. (138)

Lelong, Lucien
16 avenue Matignon, Paris
Couture house. Est. by Lucien Lelong (1889–1958), son of a couturier. Quickly gained leading position. Perfumes introduced 1924 in very modern luxury presentations. Names consisted of letters ('A', 'B', 'C', and later 'J' and 'N') or clever phrases: 'Tout Lelong' ('All Lelong' – *tout le long* means 'all along'). Lelong, a talented sculptor and collector of *blanc de Chine* (white Chinese porcelain) had a passion for white. Later his white sculptural perfume presentations reflected these interests, as did the luxurious draperies by Jean-Michel Frank and the plasters by Alberto and Diego Giacometti used for the couture house. In 1930s produced extraordinary, humorous representations for US market: 'Ting-a-Ling' (with real bells), 'Gyroscope' (working model). Salon closed 1948.

Lemoine, G.
57 rue Saint-Lazare, Paris
Perfumes, cosmetics, toiletries. Est. by Georges Lemoine in mid-19th c. as Parfumerie du Globe. Pomade 'La Moscovite' a great success. Beautiful *Viard bottles 1920. Acquired by Lever Brothers 1950.

Lenglen, Suzanne (1899–1938)
French tennis player. Wimbledon champion, whose style inspired fashions, perfumes. *Cadolle perfumes named 'Après le Tennis' and 'Suzanne Lenglen' 1927.

Lengyel
11 East 16th Street, New York
Perfumes. Est. 1733 in St. Petersburg, Russia. Branches opened: Budapest (1917), Paris (1926), New York (1929). Some luxury presentations. (139)

139 Lengyel, 'Julika', 1928, possibly rare first limited edition. Bottle in clear and frosted glass with brown patina and gilded base and stopper. H. 11.7 cm (4⅝ in.).

Lenthéric
245 rue du Faubourg-Saint-Honoré, Paris
Milliner, fashions, beauty-hairdressing salons, toiletries, cosmetics, perfumes. Est. 1795 as millinery. In 19th c. fashion accessories added. From 1873 perfumes informally blended in store for sale. Guillaume Lenthéric, a hairdresser, est. 1885 the perfume-cosmetics company, La Parfumerie des Orchidées. Orchids – fashionable, uncommon, inspirational, imported flowers – were wonderful symbol for Lenthéric. Very large premises acquired 1885 at above address for millinery, perfumes, cosmetics and important beauty-hairdressing salon. Quickly became city's most famous salon. By 1900 branches had been opened in Deauville, Monte Carlo, Nice, Baden-Baden, London. Mme Lenthéric then well-

known as milliner; her hats and accessories for 'Le Tout Paris' endorsed by many famous actresses. With long fashion history and early perfume involvement, Lenthéric could claim to be first fashion house (although not first couturier) to introduce own perfumes – over 25 years before *Poiret. Also first beauty salon with own perfumes. Acquired by Velsch & Holtz c. 1910. Perfume presentations ranged from luxury to low-priced.

Lepape, Georges (1887–1971)
Painter, engraver, illustrator, costume and set designer for stage, films. Great artistic innovator. For over 30 years his aesthetic views influenced artists working in fashion, theatre, illustration, decorative arts, perfume presentations. Had long association with *Poiret, starting 1910. Worked for Ballets Russes, *La Gazette du Bon Ton, Femina, Vogue.* Illustrated many books. Designed posters, advertisements for *Arys, *Legrand, *d'Orsay, *Piver, possibly others. Worked primarily for *Rosine, Arys. Perhaps designed perfume presentations.

Leroux, A.
46 boulevard Magenta, Paris
Perfumes, cosmetics. Est. 1862. Products sold initially in hairdressing salons.

Lérys
9 boulevard Bonne Nouvelle, Paris
Perfumes, cosmetics. Est. 1921 by Léon Bellon. Interesting, often luxurious presentations. Etienne *Drian's 1920s drawings of 'The Parisian Woman' reproduced in all Lérys advertising.

Lesourd-Pivert
24 rue Albouy, Paris
Perfumes, cosmetics, toiletries. Est. 1876. Interesting presentations.

Lesquendieu
5 rue de la Tacherie, Paris
Toiletries, cosmetics, perfumes. Bossard-Lemaire (est. 1861) was acquired 1882 by J. Lesquendieu, whose name was adopted for company c. 1903. Interesting presentations in 1920s.

Leune
Glassworks. Creator, producer of perfume bottles, purse bottles. Director 1923–26 was Paul Daum (son, nephew of founders of Daum Frères glassworks). Daum produced glass pieces in Nancy, Leune did surface decoration in Paris, with Auguste Heiligenstein (1891–1976), master enameller, as artistic director. He designed some Leune bottles inspired by Ballets Russes and *Bakst – depicting dancing female nudes with light drapery, also reminiscent of Isadora Duncan. Leune purse bottles were designed with participation of *Pautot.

Lido, Les Parfums du
78 avenue des Champs-Elysées, Paris
Perfumes. Est. 1927 as Un Coin de Venise. Affiliated to Lido night club.

Linetti
Venice
Perfumes. Charming novelty presentations with Venetian themes.

Lionceau
110 rue Demours, Paris
Perfumes, cosmetics. Est. 1920 by Michel Schasseur. Generally luxury presentations. Large exports to USA. Acquired by S. S. Pierce, Boston-based food chain, 1922. *Demours, *Elesbé affiliated companies.

Lorenzy-Palanca
62 boulevard des Dames, Marseilles
Soaps, cosmetics, perfumes. Est. 19th c. by Jules Lorenzy. Major branches in Algiers, Oran, Nice, Toulon. Primarily soaps. Produced perfumes after 1900. Beautiful paper graphics, label designs. Bankrupt 1930. Name used subsequently by new company, Société Anonyme André Lorenzy.

Louis, R.
26 West 58th Street, New York
Perfumes, cosmetics, toiletries. Introduced 'The Finger Marcel', hair-waving preparation, 1926. The perfume 'Pense à Moi' ('Think of Me'), c. 1926, was presented in a simple bottle with silvered curls as

surface decoration, reflecting the company's hair-waving speciality.

Louiseboulanger
3 rue de Berri, Paris
Couture house. Est. 1923 by Louise Boulanger. Previously associated with *Chéruit, *Callot Sœurs. Jean Dunand decorated salons. Catered to small élite group (Marlene Dietrich was client). Only one perfume, 'Louberri' 1923. Closed 1939.

Lournay
4 rue de la Paix, Paris
Perfumes. Franco-American company est. c. 1900. 'Vivante' ('Alive'), luxury *Viard edition, 1923: three identical Grecian figures on bottle, like three film frames – portraying name 'Alive'. Low-priced to luxury presentations. Acquired by *Colgate 1945. (140)

140 Lournay, 'Vivante', 1923, designed by Julien Viard. Bottle in clear and frosted glass with brown patina. H. 16.5 cm (6½ in.).

Lubin
11 rue Royale, Paris
Perfumes, cosmetics, toiletries. Est. 1798 by Pierre-François Lubin (1774–1853) as Aux Armes de France. Claimed ownership and use of all the secret beauty formulas of French court. Success rapid and significant: in 19th c. became favourite supplier of most European royal courts. Félix-André Prot (1811–85) succeeded Lubin 1853. Company passed to his heirs 1885 and became Paul Prot & Cie c. 1900. Luxury to medium-priced presentations. Many avant-garde models, often displaying unusual features.

Luyna
22–24 rue Paix, Vincennes (Seine)
Perfumes, cosmetics. Est. 1830, subtitled 'Les Parfums des Princesses'. Supplied French aristocracy. Purchased by *Monpelas 1918. Luxury presentations.

Luzy, de
5 rue Ybry, Neuilly (Seine)
Perfumes, cosmetics. Est. 1917 by Progalia S.A.

Lydès
29 rue Auguste Bailly, Courbevoie (Seine)
Perfumes, cosmetics. Est. 1918 by Eugène Philippe Rodier. First perfume, 'Ambre des Pagodes', very successful. Name 'Lydès' did not appear on this presentation. Became well-known overnight. Worldwide exports. Luxury presentations.

Lydia
15 rue Royale, Paris
Perfumes. Active early 20th c. Luxury presentations. Daring names, e.g. 'Rien qu'une nuit' ('One night only'), 1928.

Lys d'Or, Les Parfums du
19–21 Préau aux Eaux-de-Vie, Paris
Perfumes. Est. 1921 by Maxime d'Hotman de Villiers. Perhaps affiliated to *Ybry. Produced luxury perfume sets (bottles, compact and vaporizer) for export only. Successful c. 1925. Production short-lived.

Lysogène, La Compagnie Française du
Perfume company. Only one known perfume, 'Rediviva', c. 1908.

Lytée
372 rue Saint-Honoré, Paris
Perfumes, cosmetics, toiletries. Est. in 19th c. by François Libisch. Gold medal 1900. Interesting presentations.

M

Maigrot, Henri (1857–?)
Caricaturist. Signed drawings 'Henriot' or 'Pif'. Director of *Charivari*. Designed first humorous advertising for perfumes: *Millot, 'Eau de Cologne Primiale'.

Malyne, Les Parfums de
Bar-sur-Loup (Alpes-Maritimes)
Perfumes. Est. c. 1925 by J. Seren. Charming presentations.

Manassé, Emilienne
6 cité Paradis, Paris
Perfumes. Est. 1925 by M. and Mme Manassé. Short-lived.

Maquet
Printers, engravers, publishers, paper. Est. 1841. Léon Tissier, proprietor in 1920s, employed many leading artists: *Arnoux, *Barbier, Belville, Besnard, *Brunelleschi, *Lepape, Valdo-Barbey, Willette. Created *Guerlain 'Poudre aux Ballons', *Martial et Armand packaging papers, many L. T. *Piver designs ('Trèfle Incarnat', 'Belflor' etc.), as well as paper fans and perfumed cards for *Rigaud and others.

Marbœuf & Cie
Boxes, labels, papers. Participated in 1925 exhibition. Clients included: *Cadolle ('Amour en Cage'), *Chanel, *Gabilla ('Hosségor'), *Vivaudou ('Narcisse de Chine'), *Rigaud ('Vers la Joie') and *Roger & Gallet sets.

Marceau, J. A.
16 rue Larrey, Paris
Perfumes, cosmetics. Franco-American-Canadian. Est. c. 1910 by Joseph-Alfred Marceau. 'Madoukâ' featured wonderful paper graphics, 'Ambre Noir', splendid *Dépinoix bottle.

Marcy, Les Parfums de
120 avenue des Champs-Elysées, Paris
Perfumes. Est. c. 1910, possibly by Lazare Bloch. First small factory at Les Lilas, later prestigious Champs-Elysées shop. After WW1 affiliated to Société Anonyme des Parfums Sidlay, with Paul Heymann as proprietor and true innovator. Many high-quality representational creations – 'Les Fleurs Miraculeuses', 'Le Bouquet Miraculeux', 'Le Collier Miraculeux'.

Mare, André (1885–1932)
Painter, designer of interiors, *objets d'art*, home accessories. With Louis *Süe est. La Compagnie des Arts Français.

Marganne & Degrèze
Glassworks. Previously known as Ed. Letexier & Cie. Created and produced unusual, high-quality bottles.

Marinello
36 avenue Hoche, Paris
Perfumes. Est. c. 1910 in La Crosse, Wisconsin. Later Franco-American. Some interesting presentations.

Marquay
45 avenue de l'Opéra, Paris
Perfumes. Following success of *Dorilly 'L'Elu' ('The Chosen One'), introduced in 1946, new company Marquay est. 1947 at same address as Dorilly at that time. Many luxury figural presentations.

Marquis
21 rue Le Peletier, Paris
Perfumes, cosmetics, toiletries. Active in 1920s, producing for other perfumers and under own name, primarily for export.

Martainneville
Glassworks. Headed by André Lesage. Le *Galion an important client in 1930s.

Martial et Armand
10 place Vendôme, Paris
Couture house. Est. 1907 by Martial and Armand, independent designers. Became very successful. Perfumes introduced 1924. In existence until 1950s.

Martin, Charles (1888–1934)
Draughtsman, illustrator. Worked for *Poiret, *Rosine, *La Gazette du Bon Ton*, *Femina* etc. For Lucien Vogel, Martin conceived style of early de *Vigny presentations and advertising.

Martin, Jean
Boxes. Luxury productions for *Bourjois, *Chanel.

Martine, Atelier
Design studio, school. *Poiret est. school for girls aged 12–15 in 1911, with the wife of the painter Paul Séruzier as headmistress. Girls were encouraged to find inspiration from nature – create without interference or criticism. Colourful, exuberant, youthful designs for fabrics, wallpaper, carpets, murals resulted. Works exhibited at Salon d'Automne, also in London, New York, German shops. Produced furniture, accessories, complete interiors designed by *Barbier, *Iribe, *Lepape, the painter Guy-Pierre, Fauconnet, etc. Designs for *Rosine and other perfumers (*Guyla).

Marty, André (1892–1974)
Illustrator, engraver, costume and set designer. Worked for major fashion magazines, and for *Poiret, *Rosine, *Raphaël.

Matchabelli, Prince
160 East 56th Street, New York
Perfumes, cosmetics, toiletries. Est. 1926 by Prince George Matchabelli (1885–1935), Russian émigré, with his wife, Princess Norina (actress – stage name Maria Carmi, leading lady in *The Miracle*). In 1924 Matchabelli had opened a small antiques shop, Le Rouge et le Noir, at 545 Madison Avenue. Name derived from Stendhal's novel – red for aristocracy (Matchabelli's origins), black for clergy (*The Miracle* a religious play). Perfumes were personally blended for clients. First three named perfumes: 'Princess Norina', 'Queen of Georgia', 'Ave Maria'. Distinctive crown-shaped bottles introduced 1928 – many sizes, luxury editions made in France; labels always on underside. Colour coding of bottles: initially 'Princess Norina', 'Queen of Georgia' (red); 'Ave Maria' (black). Later perfumes: 'Duchess of York' (spectacular periwinkle-blue opaline), 1934; 'Katherine the Great' (white), 1935; 'Beloved' (blue), 1940; 'Wind Song' (green), 1953; 'Added Attraction' (red), 1956. Matching cosmetics cases and sets with miniature crowns. Splendid Paris shop opened 1930s. Princess Marguerite Matchabelli succeeded as proprietor after his death.

Maubert
17 rue Lamartine, Lille
Perfumes, cosmetics, toiletries. Est. 1820. At first primarily soaps, later charming perfume presentations.

Maudy
7 rue Lilas, Colombes (Seine)
Perfumes. Est. 1928 by Adrienne Foy. Affiliated to de *Musset. Luxury, unusual presentations in 1920s.

Maugenest, André
Glassworks. Produced many important luxury bottles, mostly designed by R. Deverin; also produced some *Viard bottles. Bankrupt 1932.

Mau-Riel
Glassworks. Speciality: high-relief surface decorations for bottles, cream jars, perfume burners. Produced some *Viard models. *Dépinoix created and produced some models for Mau-Riel, marked with the latter's signature. Important client, *Ramsès.

Max, Fourrures
19 avenue Matignon, Paris
Furriers. Modest shop, est. by T. Max before 1900, which became Max-Auspitz c. 1905. Andrée Leroy (1880–1948), at first sales assistant and model, became stylist with M. Schmid as fur technician; business then known as Leroy et Schmid. From 1918 Andrée Leroy sole proprietor and designer. Business became Fourrures Max, offering superb avant-garde styles. Logo designed by *Benito and advertising conceived by *Draeger. Only perfumes – 'Parfum Max' – shown at 1925 exhibition, possibly only available to salon clients.

Merlet
50 rue de Paradis, Paris
Perfumes, cosmetics, toiletries. Est. c. 1900 by Maurice Merlet. Romantic names used for perfumes: 'Fleurs des Sables' ('Flowers of the Sands'), 'L'Heure des Etoiles' ('The Hour of the Stars'), 'Fée Blonde' ('Blond Fairy'). Charming 1920s presentations.

Métivet, Lucien (1863–?)
Caricaturist. Notable illustrator. Worked for *Le Rire*. Like *Maigrot, designed first humorous advertising for perfumes: *Millot, 'Eau de cologne Primiale'.

Miga
99 Zweierstraße, Zurich
Perfumes. Est. c. 1925 by Villy Frey. Luxury presentations.

Mignot-Boucher
19 rue Vivienne, Paris
Perfumes, cosmetics, toiletries. Est. 1818, became important in 19th c. Introduced 'Parfumerie Germandrée' line.

Millière, Maurice (1871–?)
Painter, draughtsman, engraver, illustrator. Drawings published in *La Vie Parisienne*, *Illustrated London News*. Created 'La Parisienne', charming, frivolous character. In 1920s designed advertisement for *Neige des Cevennes featuring ethereal, glowing portrait of 'La Parisienne'.

Milliot, G.
Labels, papers. Est. 1890. Clients: *Giraud, *Godet, *Gravier, *Lorenzy-Palanca. Luxury production.

Millot, F.
98 boulevard de Sébastopol, Paris
Perfumes, cosmetics, toiletries. Est. 1839 by Félix Millot. Quickly became successful, prestigious. Major exports worldwide. Egyptian court perfumer at end of 19th c. Participated in many 19th-c. exhibitions: prizes included gold medal 1900. Numerous and varied products; 19th-c. bestseller was 'La Pommade à la Graisse d'Ours' ('Pomade with Bear Fat'). Henri Desprez succeeded as proprietor. 'Crêpe de Chine', created 1925 by Jean *Desprez, became sustained bestseller. First prestigious company to use humorous advertising. Generally luxury avant-garde presentations.

Milou & Cie, Marius
Boxes. Important producer of paper, leather, textile boxes. Produced *Caron 'Narcisse Noir'.

Minncho
17 rue du Printemps, Les Lilas (Seine)
Perfumes. Est. 1925 by Paul Heymann. Charming novelties. Affiliated to de *Marcy. Short-lived.

Miro Dena
373 Fifth Avenue, New York
Perfumes. Est. c. 1900 by Mrs Frederick Hubbard in Syracuse, NY. Very successful in 1920s. French luxury presentations.

Moiret
58 rue Claude Bernard, Paris
Perfumes. Franco-American. Active 1920s.

Molinard Jeune/Molinard
52 boulevard Victor Hugo, Grasse
Perfumes, cosmetics, toiletries. Originally a small shop in Place du Cours-Honoré-Cresp, Grasse, est. 1849 by Molinard, a young perfumer and chemist, selling mostly perfumes made by others. Molinard, who was known as 'Le Parfumeur Provençal', was succeeded first by his son-in-law, then by his grandson. Company became known as Molinard Jeune. After WW1 the proprietors René Honorat and Henri Bénard opened a Paris branch and the company became the Société Bénard et Honorat. An elegant

shop was opened in 1930 at 21 rue Royale (same address as earlier *Ramsès shop). 'Concretas', wax-form perfume in charming Bakelite containers, introduced 1925. Company became Molinard 1938. Perfume presentations ranged from splendid to modest.

Molinelle
49 Roland Gardens, London
Perfumes. Est. 1928 by Stanley Frederick Coles. Many luxury presentations in 1930s.

Molyneux
5 rue Royale, Paris
Couture house. Est. 1919 by Edward Molyneux (1891–1974), Irish origins, London-born designer who trained at Lucile Ltd. Sober, classic fashions very successful. First 20th c. British couturier, working in Paris, able to impose British clothing taste. Introduced three perfumes in 1925, all with names associated with rue Royale addresses: '3' (Maxim's restaurant); 'Le Numéro Cinq' (current address); '14' (previous address). Because *Chanel had introduced her 'No. 5' in 1921, 'Le Numéro Cinq' was sold in USA as 'Le Parfum Connu' ('The Known Perfume'). Sober, streamlined presentations reflected fashion style. Salons closed 1950.

Monclair
152 boulevard de Saint-Cloud, Garches (Seine-et-Oise)
Perfumes. Est. 1945 by Léon Bellon (also founder of *Lérys). Charming presentations, e.g. 'Secret d'un Vieux Livre'.

Monna Vanna Ltd
120–122 rue Borghèse, Neuilly (Seine)
Perfumes. Est. 1910, name adopted from title of play by Maeterlinck. Originally British. Luxury presentations.

Monne
Paris, Cairo
Perfumes. Affiliated to *Ramsès and Orosdi-Back.

Monpelas
22–24 rue Paix, Vincennes (Seine)
Perfumes, cosmetics, toiletries. Est. 1830 by Louis-Constant Monpelas. Purchased by the Swiss company Steinfels Frères c. 1890. 'Malacéine' was powder bestseller. Beautiful paper graphics. Acquired *Luyna 1918.

Montespan
25 rue Bergère, Paris
Perfumes. Est. 1928 by Francis Crucq Fils Aîné, an important 19th-c. company. Generally featuring exquisite paper graphics, e.g. 'Joïda', 1945.

Morny, de
201 Regent Street, London
Perfumes. Est. 1910. Company used French names and presentations, was very successful in France. Elegant romantic advertising in *La Gazette du Bon Ton*. Very luxurious.

Moser, Koloman (1868–1918)
Austrian painter, illustrator, designer of *objets d'art*. Joint founder of Wiener Werkstätte 1903. Influenced fashion design, perfume presentations (*Poiret, *Thayaht).

Mossi, Laboratori
Italian toiletries, cosmetics. Exquisite graphics.

Mouilleron
2 quai Billancourt, Billancourt (Seine)
Perfumes, cosmetics. Est. 1819. Charming presentation 'Secret de Femme' c. 1910. Acquired by *Cottan c. 1935.

Mülhens & Kropff
Glockengasse 4711, Cologne
Perfumes, cosmetics, toiletries. Est. 1792 by Wilhelm Mülhens, who received formula for Johann Maria Farina's 'Aqua Mirabelis', later known as 'Eau de Cologne No. 4711' (name derived from business address); 'No. 4711' adopted for all company products. Family business.

Murano
Glass-making centre, Venice, comprising various glassworks on islands in the Lagoon. Famous since

pre-Renaissance era. Limited edition of GI. VI *Emme 'Insidia' produced by Venini 1945.

Mury
19 rue du Rocher, Paris
Perfumes, cosmetics, toiletries. Est. 1917, affiliated to Henri Muraour, an important essential oils company founded 1789 in North Africa, with branches in Algiers, Grasse and Paris. In 1920s became major international company with success of 'Narcisse Bleu'. Elegant presentations, later low-priced.

Musset, de
42 West 34th Street, New York
Perfumes. Franco-American, est. 1928 by Marcel Foy (former president of *Godet) namd after the poet Alfred de Musset. Luxury *Dépinoix creations. Short-lived.

Mÿon
11 place de la Madeleine, Paris
Perfumes. Est. 1928 by Morgan Farrell, in association with Simon Jaroslawski. Same address as that of furrier *Blondel, and (formerly) L. *Legrand. First luxury presentations in brightly coloured *Baccarat bottles, similar to *Ybry's style. After 1931 no interesting new presentations. Lesser-quality products sold until 1940s.

Myrurgia
239 Calle de Consejo de Ciento, Barcelona
Perfumes, cosmetics, toiletries. Long-established Spanish perfumer. *Viard created exclusive luxury bottles 1921–33, some produced by *Dépinoix. Boxes also French-made. Gold medal 1925 for 'Suspiro de Granada', perhaps the most splendid Spanish presentation.

N

Nancy, Cristalleries de
Glassworks. Est. 1920 by M. Bayet. Produced crystal, half-crystal and glass bottles in various colours. Surface decoration completed in own Paris specialized workshop. Known for 'omnibus' models – bottles in various colours with boxes and labels – always stocked. Major client *Rénaud. Stamp within circle 'Cristal Nancy', initials 'CN', cross of Lorraine; below 'France'. Bankrupt 1934.

Neige des Cevennes
12 rue Calmels, Paris
Perfumes, cosmetics, toiletries. Est. 1917 by Maurice Kahn. Excellent graphics.

Nesle Normandeuse, Verrerie de la
Glassworks. Est. 1882 by Félix Denin (also then du Courval director). From inception produced bottles exclusively. Remained family business; proprietor in 1930s was Denin's granddaughter, Elisabeth Evrard, who married Raymond Guignard (*Romesnil).

Nesly
40 rue d'Enghien, Paris
Perfumes. Est. c. 1910. Possibly affiliated to *Deslys. Luxury presentations.

Nice-Flore
54 route du Var, Nice
Leather goods, perfumes. Est. c. 1919 by Union Française de Parfumerie et de Maroquinerie. Charming presentations. *Dépinoix was a supplier.

Nildé
51 rue du Rocher, Paris
Perfumes, cosmetics. Est. 1914 by Charles Davis. Beautiful presentations.

Ninon, Parfumerie
31 rue du Quatre-Septembre, Paris
Perfumes, cosmetics, toiletries. Est. c. 1850 by Dr Leconte as Maison Leconte. Successful 'Ninon' line (named after Ninon de Lenclos, a 17th-c. beauty) introduced 1874. Later adopted as company name. Elegant presentations.

Nipola Co., The
St Paul, Minnesota
Perfumes. Introduced 'Lucky Lindy' (subtitled 'The Essence of Luck') in 1927 soon after Charles Lindbergh (familiarly known as Lindy) landed his

plane, the 'Spirit of St. Louis', outside Paris on 21 May. Lindbergh, Michigan-born, was brought up in Minnesota and considered it his home state, and Minnesota regarded him as a native son. Particularly charming miniatures. (141)

141 Nipola, 'Lucky Lindy', 1927, display unit with 18 bottles in clear glass with brass caps; display coloured blue, orange and white, h. overall 38.0 cm (15 in.); h. of bottles 6.8 cm (2⅝ in.).

Nissery
9-13 rue des Champs, Asnières (Seine)
Perfumes. Est. in 1921 by Jules-Joanin-Anatole Muraour. Company affiliated to *Mury. Elegant presentations.

Nogara
Grasse
Soap, perfumes. Est. 1902 by Louis-François Pélissier. Around 1910, major branch opened in Paris. Affiliated to *Pélissier-Aragon. Beautiful presentations using *Dépinoix bottles.

Norman, Merle
9130 Bellanca Avenue, Los Angeles, California
Cosmetics, perfumes. Est. 1931 by Merle Norman, with her nephew, Jack Boison Nethercutt, and his wife. 'Jolly Sin' of 1953 was a very original, thoughtfully co-ordinated presentation – cheerful, sophisticated luxury, typical of 1920s France, unlike anything created in USA in the 1950s. (142)

142 Merle Norman, 'Jolly Sin', 1953. H. 9.0 cm (3½ in.).

Nortier, G.
Labels. Est. 19th c. Acquired by A. Ponsot, long-established label manufacturer. Luxury production.

O

Odéon
12 rue de l'Ancienne-Comédie, Paris
Perfumes. Est. 1902 by Herphelin and Noilhan. Beautiful 1920s presentations.

Odlys
178 Grand-Rue, Maisons-Alfort (Seine)
Perfumes. Est. 1920 by Mme A. Chabert. First perfume: 'Pétales Argentés' ('Silvered Petals'). Luxury presentations. Short-lived.

Offenthal
24 rue de la Paix, Paris
Perfumes, cosmetics. Est. *c.* 1925. Interesting presentations. Bestseller 'Ce Soir ou Jamais' ('Tonight or Never'), included elaborate account of how Mme de Pompadour obtained power through seduction.

Oja
4 rue Ancelle, Neuilly (Seine)
Nail-care products. Est. 1910. Introduced first nail polish.

Orcel, Gilbert
5 rue du Cirque, Paris
Milliner. Est. 1938. Introduced perfumes 1954. 'Coup de Chapeau' ('Tip of the Hat') presented in beautiful sculptural *Brosse bottle. (143)

143 Gilbert Orcel, 'Coup de Chapeau', 1954, Brosse bottle, white opaque glass with gilding. H. 12.0 cm (4¾ in.).

Orsay, Count Gabriel Alfred Guillaume d'
(1801–52)
Artist. Excellent portrait painter, sculptor, arbiter of elegance. Quintessential 19th-c. dandy. Had close relationship with both the Earl of Blessington and his second wife, Marguerite. As 'cover' he married Lady Harriet Gardiner, 15-year old daughter of Lord Blessington by his first wife. After Lord Blessington's death in 1829, he lived with Lady Blessington until her death in 1849. Advertising claims by Parfums *d'Orsay that formulas originated with the Count and Lady Blessington were entirely baseless – neither had anything to do with perfume.

Orsay, Parfums d'
17 rue de la Paix, Paris
Perfumes, cosmetics, toiletries. Est. 1908 by well-capitalized investor group – Siegfried and Sally Berg (German), Leo Fink (Dutch; previously associated

144 D'Orsay, 'L'Elégance', 1923, design and bottle by René Lalique. Bottle in clear and frosted glass with brown patina, and gilded label on side; box black and white with gilding, lined with yellow satin. H. 9.5 cm (3¾ in.).

with *Boldoot) and M. Van Dyck (a naturalized French citizen). Selected d'Orsay name and coat of arms to create image of long-established, aristocratic, luxurious French company. Purchased castle as headquarters. Produced all perfumes and packaging. During WW1, when French government confiscated German business interests, company liquidated and reformed with French owners and management, with Gaston Monteux as new proprietor. Leo Fink later est. *Forvil. Company advertising featured Count d'Orsay as dandy, and perfume names reflected this image: 'Le Chevalier d'Orsay', 'Le Dandy', 'Milord', 'Comtesse d'Orsay', 'L'Elégance', etc. Luxury to medium-priced presentations. *Süe and *Mare decorated main shop at above address in magnificent, ornate Art Deco style. Süe also designed famous octagonal bottle – 'Ganika' (clear glass), 'Le Dandy' (black or clear glass). D'Orsay awarded 1925 Grand Prix. (144)

Osram
Electrical supplies. 'Osram' perfume bottle *c.* 1913 was in the shape of a light bulb; L. T. Piver 'Volt' of 1922 had similar bottle.

Ota
Paris
No facts known. Perfumes of 1929, in simulated-pearl presentations, may have involved Ota Polacek of *Cherigan.

Ouchy, Parfums d'
45 rue Laborde, Paris
Perfumes. Est. 1928 by Rodolphe Agranatt. Some beautiful presentations.

Oviatt
Los Angeles, California
Department store. Oviatt Building completed 1927. *Lalique created glass panels and 'Le Parfum des Anges' presentation of 1928 (both featuring Los Angeles city symbol).

P

Palmer
Cincinnati, Ohio
Perfumes, toiletries. Est. 1847 by Solon Palmer. Family business producing mainly low- to medium-priced presentations.

Paquin
3 rue de la Paix, Paris
Couture house. Est. 1890 by Jeanne Paquin (1869–1936), designer trained at *Rouff, and Isidore Paquin. Success came quickly, with major London branch. First designer to introduce black as elegant colour not associated with mourning: black garments trimmed with vivid colours (blue, red, green) and gold embroidery. Perfumes, cosmetics introduced 1939. Small black-glass bottles with gilded stoppers, each with a stone of a different colour: '9 x 9' (blue); 'Habit Rouge' ('Red Frock') (red); 'Espoir' ('Hope') (green) – relating to Paquin style and colours. *Bérard designed most Paquin advertising. Closed 1962.

Parfise
42 rue de Paradis, Paris
Perfumes, cosmetics. Created perfumes and presentations for other perfumers. After 1923 affiliated to *Grenoville. Owned Charny perfumes for exports.

Patou, Jean
7 rue Saint-Florentin, Paris
Couture house. Jean Patou (1875–1936) purchased Maison Parry 1912, adopted Patou name after WW1. Very successful avant-garde fashions – luxurious adaptation of sportswear using specially woven and dyed fabrics. *Süe and *Mare designed similar sophisticated salon interiors; perfume and cosmetics presentations were also designed by Süe.

Paul, Les Parfums de
366 Fifth Avenue, New York
Perfumes. Affiliated to Marques de *Elorza. Novelties, luxury presentations.

Pautot, M.
Sculptor, engraver, silversmith. Speciality: stopper covers, mostly silver for purse bottles by *Dépinoix and *Leune.

Payan, Honoré
33 boulevard Malesherbes, Paris
Originally from Grasse, affiliated to Payan & Bertrand (which had been established in 1854). In the 1920s the proprietor, Achard Carémil, introduced some superb presentations.

Pélissier-Aragon
Grasse
Essential oils, perfumes. E. Alziary est. small factory, Alziary Fils, 1850; became Alziary et Barbe 1863; Pélissier-Aragon from 1887. In 1924 Emile-André Pélissier coined appealing trade name Les Fontaines Parfumées, Grasse.

Perugia, André
11 rue du Faubourg-Saint-Honoré, Paris
Shoe designer. Originally from Nice, discovered by *Poiret. First show in Poiret's salons, 1921, received rave reviews. Designed all shoes for Poiret fashions. Style luxurious, delicate, intricate, extravagant. Perfumes 'Les Heures de Perugia' introduced 1927.

Peszyǹska, Louise
19 rue Auber, Paris
Corsets. Est. 19th c. by Louise Peszyǹska. Perfumes introduced 1929.

Peynet, Raymond (1908–)
Draughtsman, illustrator, stage designer. Achieved fame after WW2 with charming cartoons in French press. Designed advertising for *Schiaparelli's 'Succès Fou'.

Picard, A.
34 rue Sainte-Anne, Paris
Perfumes, cosmetics. Est. *c.* 1886 by Albert-Pierre Picard and H. Neyrac. Then known as A la Guirlande Fleurie. Superb graphics before 1914.

Pierre, Albert
Metalwork. Metal boxes (mostly aluminium); brass stopper covers. Clients: *Rigaud, *Roger & Gallet.

Piguet, Robert
Rond Point des Champs-Elysées, Paris
Couture house. Est. 1933 by Robert Piguet (1900–53). Perfumes introduced 1939. Closed 1951.

Pinaud, Ed.
18 place Vendôme, Paris
Perfumes, cosmetics, toiletries. Obscure beginnings in late 18th c. M. Besançon est. small shop 1810, later purchased by M. Legrand. Business acquired 1839 by Edouard Pinaud (1810–68), and shop renamed A la Corbeille Fleurie. Emile Meyer became partner 1852, business renamed Pinaud et Meyer and second shop, Parfumerie de la Noblesse, opened. Victor Klotz, Meyer's son-in-law, became partner 1872. Company became Victor Klotz et Cie 1905, later H. et G. Klotz. Family business until 1931. From 1840 products sold under Ed. Pinaud name. Business success led to appointment as perfumer to all European courts *c.* 1860. After participation at Vienna exhibition of 1873, Pinaud became household name. Participated in many 19th-c. exhibitions, awarded many prizes. Major exporter. Many 19th-c. Pinaud fakes are seen, mostly outside France. At the turn of century, the Ed. Pinaud building was completed in New York. Many perfume innovations.

Piver, L. T.
23 boulevard des Italiens, Paris
Perfumes, cosmetics, toiletries. Michel Adam attracted to perfumed gloves in Italy, studied perfume trade. Awarded title of 'Parfumeur-Gantier' 1769. Est. small shop between 1769 and 1774; its name, A la Reine des Fleurs, retained as company's subtitle. Succeeded by family members, Paul Guillaume Dissey and, in 1813, Louis-Toussaint Piver, whose name was adopted as company name. Alphonse Piver succeeded L. T. Piver. Participated in all major 19th-c. and 20th-c. exhibitions. *Süe and *Mare redesigned Piver shop in 1920s and Süe designed 'Rêve d'Or' presentation. Piver frequently a leader in new perfume designs, concepts.

Plassard, L.
17 rue du Quatre-Septembre, Paris
Perfumes, cosmetics. Est. 1815 as Demarson, later Demarson et Cie, Demarson-Chételat and Chételat et Cie. Exhibited regularly – 1819, 1839, 1844,

1849, 1855, 1867 and 1878 – under its various names; awarded many prizes. Louis Plassard purchased company 1894, renamed it L. Plassard. Some exceptional presentations before 1930, later examples less impressive.

Pléville
38 rue des Mathurins, Paris
Perfumes, cosmetics. Est. 1922 by Michel Pléville. 'Flamme de Gloire' ('Flame of Glory') celebrated Olympic Games of 1924, held in Paris. Luxury production. Affiliated to *Dalon.

Pochet et du Courval
Glassworks. François Le Vaillant est. La Verrerie du Courval in 1623. During 18th c. introduced perfume bottles, which became sole production in late 19th c. Pochet, est. 1780 as Deroche, was exclusive selling agent for du Courval. Pochet's heirs, the Colonna de Giovellina family, became glassmakers. Among imaginative models was *Guerlain 'Eau de Cologne Impériale'. Pochet et du Courval produced some *Viard models.

Poet
5812 Pine Street, Philadelphia, Pennsylvania
Perfumes. Est. c. 1925 by Estelle L. Poate. Luxury *Baccarat presentations. Short-lived.

Poiret, Paul
107 rue du Faubourg-Saint-Honoré, Paris
Couture house. Est. in 1903 by Paul Poiret (1879–1944) after working for Doucet, and *Worth. Married Denise Boulet, his muse, 1905. Introduced slim, elongated dress without corset ('Directoire' style) 1906. First Oriental fashions 1911 – also est. Ateliers *Martine, *Colin, and Parfums de *Rosine. Friends and colleagues included leading figures in the arts, theatre, fashion, literature and illustrators. Extremely successful 1910–20 but tried, unsuccessfully, to introduce his fashion creations in the USA when visiting after WW1. Totally against 'La Garçonne' fashions 1922; introduced folklore-inspired costumes. Due to increasing financial difficulties, gradually lost control of all businesses. Built three expensive barges for 1925 exhibition: *Amours* (displayed Martine, Rosine productions); *Délices* (restaurant); *Orgues* (daily fashion shows). Bankruptcy sale 1926. Couture house closed 1929. Unsuccessful from 1930 until his death. During this period he painted, recited poetry at parties, and was helped financially by friends.

Premet
8 place Vendôme, Paris
Couture house. Est. c. 1911 by Mme Premet, successful dressmaker. Mme Charlotte was the company's innovative director after 1918. Perfumes introduced 1924.

R

Raffy
21 rue Béranger, Paris
Perfumes. Est. c. 1918 by Marcel Raffy. American company for which Raffy sought to suggest French origins. Sued by French perfumers' association for having used a fictitious Paris address. Produced perfumes for export to USA.

Rallet
4 rue Berryer, Paris
Perfumes, cosmetics, toiletries. In 1842 Alphonse Rallet est. small shop in Moscow. Est. Russian perfume and soap industries, with exclusively French management. French employees created perfumes and presentations. 'Eau de Cologne Russe' of 1842 became bestseller. Supplied Russian, other Eastern European, and Asian courts. Participated in many international exhibitions. Awarded 48 first prizes, Grand Prix 1900. Expanded rapidly after being purchasd by *Chiris in 1898. By 1914 was considered giant Russian industry. Business nationalized 1917. Factories and branches closed and employees returned to France. Same management est. French company in Cannes with same formulas and employees. Produced identical perfumes, many presentations inscribed in French and Russian, some in Russian only. Acquired by *Coty 1926, but continued under Rallet name. After 1926, Rallet exported to Russia. From 1919, Rallet specialized in creating, producing perfumes for sale under other perfumers'

and couturiers' names (notably *Chanel 'No. 5', created by Ernest Beaux). Many original designs recorded as Rallet were actually produced for others. 'Polar Eau de Cologne', possibly introduced in 1930s, featured spectacular bottle. (145)

145 Rallet, 'Polar Eau de Cologne', possibly 1930s, sculptural bottle with glass cover over inner stopper. H. 19.5 cm (7⅝ in.).

Ramey
332 rue Saint-Honoré, Paris
Perfumes, cosmetics. Est. 1913 by Georges Herman as Laboratoires des Produits Radiacés. Some avant-garde creations.

Ramsès
30 rue d'Hauteville, Paris
Cosmetics, perfumes. Est. 1916 by M. de Bertalot with Orosdi-Back (successful perfume exporters, then managed by Léon Orosdi, heir of founder Emile Orosdi, who had made a fortune exporting *Bourjois products to the Orient). Became a major exporter to Africa and the Far East, with offices in Paris and Istanbul. Created luxurious Egyptian-style presentations. Opened sumptuous shop at 21 rue Royale, at corner of the rue du Faubourg-Saint-Honoré, with five monumental marble figures of pharaohs on the exterior. Façade was destroyed c. 1929 after the company had failed, following convictions in the Ernest *Coty affair. However, products of lower quality bearing the Ramsès name existed until 1940s.

Raphaël
3 avenue George V, Paris
Couture house. Est. 1930 by Raphaël Lopez. Specialized in tailored styles. Logo depicting Diana and faun designed by Marty 1936. Perfumes, introduced shortly afterwards, featured interesting one-word names.

Rateau, Armand Albert (1882–1938)
Interior designer. Work in Art Deco style included designs for Jeanne *Lanvin (furniture, entire decor for home and salons); also created masterpiece Lanvin boule.

Rauch, Madeleine de
37 rue Jean-Goujon, Paris
Couture house. Small workshop, The House of Friendship, est. 1928. Madeleine de Rauch and her sister (associate) were excellent golfers: in 1947 first perfume, 'Pitch', used golf motif.

Raymond, de
1 avenue de la Villa, Vincennes (Seine)
Perfumes, cosmetics, toiletries. Est. 1925 by Raymond Legrand. First perfume, 'Mimzy' became bestseller. Est. de *Seghers. Bankrupt 1932, but continued in USA under different management, with low-quality presentations.

Reboux
23 rue de la Paix, Paris
Milliner. Est. in 1865 by Caroline Reboux (1837–1927). Milliner to Empress Eugénie. Perfumes introduced 1928, names were simply colours: 'Noir' (black), 'Vert' (green), 'Rouge' (red), 'Jaune' (yellow).

Rénaud
45 rue de Montmorency, Paris
Perfumes, cosmetics, toiletries. Est. 1817. Generally low- to medium-priced presentations.

Renoir
20 rue de la Paix, Paris
Perfumes. Est. 1939. Also produced perfumes for others (*Piguet).

Rétonval
Glassworks in Vallée de la Bresle dating from 15th c. Purchased by Amédée Scobart 1875; by *Brosse 1929. Closed 1930.

Revillon Frères
42 rue La Boétie, Paris
Furriers. Est. by Louis-Victor Revillon 1839, with purchase of oldest Paris fur shop (François Givelet, est. 1723). Louis-Victor's father, Count d'Apreval, had taken Revillon name during French Revolution. Very successful in 19th c., with huge premises at 77–81 rue de Rivoli (site now occupied by La Samaritaine department store), and with London, and New York branches. Remained family business. Perfume company est. 1932, perfumes introduced 1934. Many beautiful presentations.

Rey, Honoré
Boxes. Speciality: leather-covered perfume boxes resembling jewelry boxes. Produced the box for 'Blue Lagoon' (c. 1919) and possibly boxes for other *Dubarry perfumes.

Ricci, Nina
39 avenue Montaigne, Paris
Couture house. Est. in 1932 by Nina Ricci (1883–1970; born Maria Nielli in Turin). Quickly became very successful. Nina Ricci was designer until 1954, her elegant, feminine style always flattering. After WW2 her son and successor, Robert Ricci, introduced perfumes, featuring *Bérard graphics and Marc *Lalique bottles.

Rigaud
16 rue de la Paix, Paris
Perfumes, cosmetics, toiletries. Est. 1854 by J.-B.-F. Rigaud, who was succeeded by his son Henri. Very successful with branches in London, Milan, Madrid, North and South America. Participated in 19th-c. exhibitions, awarded gold medals 1878, 1889, 1900. In 1853 the tea shop, La Porte Chinoise, located close to the first Rigaud shop (near the Théâtre du Palais-Royal and the Comédie Française) became a fashionable meeting place, increasing popular awareness of Oriental cultures, contributing to interest in Japonisme. Rigaud first to introduce names with Far Eastern associations: 'Melati de Chine', 'Kanaga-Osaka', 'Pagoda Flowers'. Famous Parisian actresses were among Rigaud clients – theatre-related perfume names included 'Actrices', 'Prince Igor', 'Mary Garden', 'Marthe Chenal', 'Geraldine Farrar'. Many luxury presentations.

Rimmel Ltd, Eugène
96 Strand, London
Perfumes, cosmetics, toiletries. Est. 1834 by two Frenchmen, Eugène Rimmel and his father (Lubin-trained perfumer). Splendid shops in London and Paris. All perfumes were produced in Grasse by the Rimmel family. Imaginative products included perfumed jewelry, gloves, fans, cards, calendars, etc. Very successful. At Great Exhibition of 1851 Rimmel's giant perfume fountain scented the entire hall. Perfumer to British, Spanish, French royal courts. Eugène Rimmel published *The Book of Perfumes* (1864), bestseller for years. Died 1887, was succeeded by two sons. Despite financial setbacks, company maintained luxury image, producing some extraordinary presentations, e.g. 'Art Moderne', 1925.

Rival
166 avenue de Neuilly, Neuilly (Seine)
Perfumes. Est. 1939 by Jean Clavelier.

Robertet & Cie, P.
Grasse
Essential oils. Est. 1850 by François Chauve. Acquired by P. Robertet 1875. Major producer of essential oils. Few beautiful presentations under own name.

Robj
3 cité d'Hauteville, Paris
Artistic bibelots. Est. by Lucien Willemetz in 1908. Produced small figurines, boxes, decanters, lamps, etc. First perfume 1924: 'Le Secret de Robj' (intended for perfume burners) became popular. Other perfumes followed, some created for other perfumers. Willemetz bankrupt 1933, but continued to produce as Robj.

Rochambeau
105 West 40th Street, New York
Perfumes. Franco-American company, est. 1923 by Xavier Rochambeau and Robert Coudert de Saint-Chament. Speciality: French-made medium- and low-priced novelties – small, fragile, toy-like, blown-glass bottles – for export to USA. Few survived. Affiliated to La *Gourde du Poète, whose style was similar.

Rochas, Marcel
12 avenue Matignon, Paris
Couture house. Est. in 1925 by Marcel Rochas (1902–54). Created 'wide shoulders look' in 1931 and *guêpière* (waspie), 1942. Perfumes introduced in 1926. His motto – 'Jeunesse, Simplicité, Personnalité' ('Youth, simplicity, personality') suited both fashions and perfumes: early names included: 'Air Jeune' ('Young Look') and 'Audace' ('Audacity'). *Poiret was friend and mentor. *Cocteau, *Bérard, *Fini inspired Rochas perfumes aesthetic. Published *1925–1950. Vingt-cinq Ans d'Elégance à Paris* (1951), a singular book registering, analyzing artistic, cultural, societal, fashion trends and events. Couture salons closed 1953.

Rodin
9 rue Auber, Paris
Perfumes. Est. 1946 by Norman S.A.R.L. Beautiful presentation for 'Saree'. Also sold as Norman 'Adoration'.

Roditi & Sons, D.
1 rue Ambroise-Thomas, Paris
Exporter of fancy goods. Exclusive agents for US department store Stix, Baer & Fuller, St. Louis. In 1926 introduced 'Raquel Meller' perfume named after Spanish singer (famous in Paris for her interpretations of 'La Violettera' while wearing a black-lace shawl). Enamelled decoration on bottle produced by *Lalique simulated this shawl design.

Roger & Gallet
38 rue d'Hauteville, Paris
Perfumes, cosmetics, toiletries. Est. 1862 by Armand Roger and Charles Gallet after acquisition of rights to Jean-Marie Farina eau de cologne. In late 17th c. in Italy, Jean-Paul Feminis, grocer-druggist, had formulated 'Aqua Mirabilis'. He then moved to Cologne, and was successful throughout Europe promoting its 'medicinal' properties. He was succeeded by three nephews, Farina brothers. In 1806, a descendant, Johann Maria Farina est. Paris company as Jean-Marie Farina. Formula now promoted for personal enhancement. Hugely successful – became perfumer to Napoleon I, later to French, British royal courts. Farina was succeeded in 1840 by Jacques Collas, colognes being exported worldwide. Roger & Gallet engaged in many lawsuits over the use of the Jean-Marie Farina name. Grand Prix 1889 exhibition. From late 19th c. many splendid presentations.

Romesnil, Verrerie de
Glassworks. Est. 1776 by Jean-Charles Libaude to produce plate glass. After many changes of management, d'Imbleval and Guignard families became proprietors 1898, succeeded by Guignard's son and grandson (Raymond). Perfume bottle production began in 19th c. Clients: *Gellé, *Guerlain, *Houbigant, *Pinaud, *Piver, etc.

Rosine, Les Parfums de
107 rue du Faubourg-Saint-Honoré, Paris
Perfumes, cosmetics, toiletries. Est. 1911 by *Poiret (first couturier to introduce own perfumes). Many important artists and illustrators worked for Rosine. Poiret lost financial control *c.* 1925. Business acquired in 1930 by Société Centrale de la Parfumerie Française (L. *Legrand), and managed by Mme. Nevarte Cordero. Most of the existing Rosine perfumes were produced until 1950s in standard presentations.

Rouff, L.
8 rue Royale, Paris
Couture house. Est. in 19th c. Perfumes introduced 1927, *Baccarat a supplier. Merged with *Drecoll 1929. Rouff perfumes available until 1940s. The couture house was renamed Maggy Rouff in 1930; perfumes under this name also available from 1930s.

Rubicon of Fifth Avenue
New York
Perfumes. Created 'Trylon' perfume for New York World's Fair, 1939.

Rubinstein, Helena
46 West 57th Street, New York
Beauty salons, perfumes, cosmetics, toiletries. Est. 1908 by Helena Rubinstein (1872–1965), born in Poland. After spending her youth in Australia, she opened beauty salons in Melbourne (1902), London (1908), Paris (1912), New York (1915). During WW1 promoted products in New York. Major international company, worldwide exports. First perfume 'Mahatma' ('The Great One') and 'Valaze' cosmetics line of 1915 introduced at 1925 exhibition; extraordinary gilded presentations awarded gold medal.

S

Saillard
Paper boxes, labels. Luxury production, including *Gaillard designs for *Violet.

Saint-Louis, Cristalleries de
Glassworks. Original glassworks est. 1767; crystal production introduced 1781. In early 20th c. major artists who designed bottles for Saint-Louis included Maurice Dufrêne, Marcel Goupy.

Salancy
21 rue des Abeilles, Tours
Perfumes, cosmetics. Est. 1913 by Henri Salmon and Henri Chancy (hence company name). Affiliated to Parfumerie Olga, Tours.

Salomé
8 place de l'Opéra, Paris
Perfumes, cosmetics, toiletries. Est. *c.* 1909 by Marius Cartier. Maurice Blanchet purchased business 1929, merged it with *Coryse and renamed it Coryse-Salomé. Affiliated to *Cartier.

Saumont, H.
Glassworks. Perfume bottles, many in opaque black or coloured glass. Clients included *d'Amboise, *Fragonard, *Gueldy, *Lionceau.

Sauzé Frères
25 rue d'Hauteville, Paris
Perfumes, cosmetics, toiletries. Obscure beginnings in Marseilles, 1822; later in Lyons, Paris. Family business: Etienne, Léopold, Maurice Sauzé. Artistic perfume posters produced *c.* 1900. 'Fleurs de Mousse' ('Moss Flowers') of 1905, which was presented in many different editions, became bestseller. (146)

146 Sauzé, 'Fleurs de Mousse', *c.* 1905, prototype bottle in gilded black glass, designed by Julien Viard, and prototype blue box. H. 8.8 cm (3½ in.).

Saville
Watford, Hertfordshire
Perfumes, cosmetics, toiletries. Created wonderful novelties in 1920s using Bakelite.

Schiaparelli
21 place Vendôme, Paris
Couture house. Est. 1928 by Elsa Schiaparelli (1890–1973), originally Italian. Her friends included Dada artists (Duchamp, Man Ray, Picabia, Tzara, *Cocteau), who influenced her style. Had first success with sports clothes, 1925. Original, imaginative designs. Soon became important *haute couture* designer: colourful, striking fashion fantasies fully developed by 1935. Befriended Surrealist artists. Surrealism became vocabulary for fashions, accessories. First perfume 'S' introduced 1929. In 1936 'Shocking' exhibited Surrealist style. Startling display consisted of glass replica, larger than life size, of the 'Shocking' dressmaker's dummy filled with 'Shocking' perfume bottles. *Bérard, Clément, *Cocteau, *Dali, *Dufy, Frank, *Peynet all worked for her. *Vertés designed most perfume advertising. Schiaparelli believed couturier perfumes should only be produced by active fashion designers. Salons closed during WW2, reopened 1945. Closed definitively 1954.

Schmied, François-Louis (1873–1941)
Illustrator, bookbinder. Redesigned famous *Bichara graphics in 1920s.

Schwander, Georges (1889–*c.* 1980)
Glass artist. Speciality: perfume bottles. Gold medal 1925. Joined *Brosse 1933.

Seghers, de
Paris, New York
Perfumes, cosmetics. Est. *c.* 1926 by de *Raymond.

Seguin et Aubert, Veuve H.
Boxes. Luxury production. Participated in 1925 exhibition.

Sennet et Cie
Printers, labels, graphic designers. Est. 1853 as H. Deschamps. One of most important producers of labels. Clients: *Erizma, *Gilot, *Isabey, *Lengyel, *Sauzé, *Vibert.

Sergy
30 bis, rue Bergère, Paris
Perfumes, cosmetics. Est. 1910 by A. Sergent (who had also est. *Gueldy after affiliation to *Amiot). Lower-price products. 'Billet Doux' ('Love Letter') of 1929 featured wonderful graphics.

Shiseido
Ginza, Tokyo
Perfumes, cosmetics, toiletries. Pharmacy est. 1872 by Dr Yushin Fukuhara. Introduced toothpaste 1888, later perfumes and cosmetics. Supplied Imperial family. After trip to Europe and USA, Fukuhara transformed pharmacy in 1900 to American-style drugstore (serving sodas and ice cream). Innovative flesh tone powder introduced 1906. In 1908 son, Shinzo Fukuhara, studied at Columbia College, New York, then spent time in Paris. Shinzo and two associates est. Shiseido Cosmetics 1927. Became extremely successful, with many branches, exporting to Western countries. Labels for cosmetics and soaps displayed extraordinary sophistication and understanding of Western aesthetics. While Japan's influence on Western art has been fully explored, little has been written about Western influence on Japanese culture; Shiseido certainly played a crucial role in bringing Western aesthetics to Japan.

Shulton
New York
Perfumes, cosmetics, toiletries. Est. 1934 by William Schultz. First perfume introduced 1937: 'Early American Old Spice' inspired by early American artefacts in the Metropolitan Museum, New York. Attractive miniature samples.

Sibeoni, Jacques
32 rue Bichat, Paris
Perfumes, cosmetics, toiletries. Active in early 20th c. Used Egyptian theme for presentations: 'Le Secret du Sphinx', 1913; 'Toute l'Egypte', 1917; 'Un Rêve sur le Nil', 1919, later sold to *Ramsès and *Monne.

Est. Les Parfums de Rivoz 1926. Bankrupt 1931, but continued to produce perfumes.

Silka
16 quai de la Mégisserie, Paris
Perfumes, cosmetics. Est. 1909 by Maurice Roussel (related to Parfumerie Roussel, est. 1852, producer of very successful 'Eau Gorlier' in 19th c.). Refined, sophisticated personality. Romantic, original perfume names. 1910s–20s striking, unusual luxury presentations.

Simon, Mario
Illustrator. Worked for *Martine, *Rosine, and possibly Elizabeth *Arden.

Société Française d'Orfèvrerie d'Art
Metalwork. Display stands for testers, samples, perfume burners. Clients: *Lubin, *Rigaud etc.

Société Parisienne de Verreries
Glassworks. In 1889 Louis de Beaune est. Paris glass trading company for perfume bottles produced by Vallée de la Bresle glassworks. Est. major London distribution centre. First major French perfume bottle exporter. SPV name adopted after trading company sold to Vallée de la Bresle glassworks group. After 1930 often worked with *Dépinoix, *Viard. Merged with Dépinoix 1936.(147)

147 Société Parisienne de Verreries, bottle no. 1911 (used for Bardin, 'Œillet Blanc'), and bottle no. 1912, both c. 1920. H. 11.5 cm (4½ in.); 7.2 cm (2⅞ in.).

Soliman, Ahmed
Cairo
Perfumes. Unusual luxury presentations in 1920s.

Süe, Louis (1875–1968)
Architect, painter, designer of *objets d'art*, interiors, home accessories. With *Mare est. La Compagnie des Arts Français in 1919. Süe also designed perfume presentations. Designs by Süe et Mare were inspired by French tradition and executed in luxurious, precious materials; they designed interiors for *d'Orsay, *Patou, *Piver shops.

Suzanne
5 rue du 29-Juillet, Paris
Perfumes. Est. 1925 by Suzanne Perichon. First perfume 'Le Secret de Suzanne', 1925. 'Tout de Suite' of 1938 featured an unusual presentation and was advertised in USA as 'Fragrance of Lightning' and 'Tempestuous Perfume'.

Suzy
5 rue de la Paix, Paris
Milliner. Est. 1921 by Mme Suzy. Perfumes, introduced 1939, featured unusual creations. Successful until 1960s.

T

Talbot, Suzanne
14 rue Royale, Paris
Milliner. Est. by J. Suzanne Talbot in late 19th c. (at first designed clothes and hats). Prestigious company, introduced perfumes 'J', 'S', 'T' c. 1924.

Thayaht, Ernesto (1893–?)
Italian painter, sculptor, engraver, medallist, goldsmith, illustrator, interior designer. Early Futurist. After 1918 worked in France, mostly for *Vionnet. Fashion illustrations showed clothes against backgrounds decomposed into basic geometric shapes, similar to Vionnet fashion technique. Designed outstanding Vionnet logo 1919, in which symmetry reflects that of Thayaht name – a palindrome.

Tissier
Glassworks. Est. 1761, also known as Verreries de Creil et de Quiquengrogne. Small luxury production.

Tokalon
7 rue Aubert, Paris
Perfumes, cosmetics, toiletries. Originally British known as To-Kalon, possibly est. before 1900 as chemical-pharmaceutical company. Produced laundry soaps. Important branch in Syracuse, NY. Francis B. Mastin became proprietor c. 1910. Company diversified into property as Société Immobilière Franco-Anglo-Américaine. Beautiful presentations, generally with extraordinary graphics. (148)

148 Tokalon, 'Pero' display for powder, c. 1920, black, red, white and gilded paper; h. overall 34.0 cm (13 ⅜ in.). Diameter of powder box in display 6.5 cm (2½ in.), of larger powder box at right 8.0 cm (3⅛ in.), of smaller box 5.8 cm (2¼ in.).

Tolmer et Cie
Printers, publishers, perfume graphics, advertising.

Tranoy, Paul
73 rue de la Malcence, Tourcoing
Soaps. Est. in 19th c. Superb graphics.

Tré-Jur
19 West 18th Street, New York
Perfumes, cosmetics, toiletries. Est. 1924 by Albert Mosheim. Opened Hamburg branch. Affiliated to *Varva. Tré-Jur spelled as French phonetic equivalent of 'treasure'. First figural bottles for 'Suivez Moi' depicted elegant 19th-c. woman holding a mirror. Sample sizes had simulated gemstones inlaid in caps.

V

Vaissier, Victor
4 place de l'Opéra, Paris
Soap, perfumes. Est. in 1869 by Antoine Vaissier in Roubaix as Savonnerie des Nations. Succeeded in 1888 by Victor Vaissier, who introduced perfumes. Superb graphics.

Valois, Rose
18 rue Royale, Paris
Milliner. Successor (in 1927) to Lewis, important 19th-c. milliner. First perfume 'L'Ambiance de Rose Valois', 1929. Original 1950s miniatures.

Valoy
8 rue Jacquart, Pantin (Seine)
Perfumes, cosmetics. Est. c. 1900 by Salomon Frères. Also known as Parfumerie Centrale. Superb graphics.

Vanderbilt, Lucretia
Fairfield, Connecticut
Perfumes, cosmetics, toiletries. Est. c. 1925 by McKesson & Robbins, a distributor of retail products. Advertised Lucretia Vanderbilt as 'The aristocrats of toiletries, Parisian in their characteristics, American in their perfection.' Some beautiful presentations.

Vantine's, A. A.
61 Hunters Point Avenue, Long Island City, NY, and Japan
Importer of oriental wares, perfumes, cosmetics, toiletries. Est. c. 1850. Perfumes sometimes presented in bottles in the form of oriental deities, the accompanying Japanese-made lacquered boxes being temple-shaped. Beautiful French-made bronze perfume burners. Company had American and Japanese headquarters.

Varrel, J. B.
94 rue du Faubourg-Poissonnière, Paris
Perfumes, cosmetics. Est. 1917 by Jean-Baptiste Varrel. Affiliated to de *Luzy. Beautiful graphics. Short-lived.

Varva
New York
Perfumes, cosmetics. Affiliated to *Tré-Jur.

Vases Parfums, Les
Nice and Paris
Perfumes. Est. 1923 by E. L. Raibaut. 'Florina' products in interesting animal-shaped bottles. (149)

149 Les Vases Parfums, unidentified perfume, c. 1923, Dépinoix bottle. H. 8.0 cm (3⅛ in.).

Véga
18 rue de Genas, Lyons
Perfumes. Est. c. 1910 by Jean Piot. Ornate luxury presentations, advertised as 'flacons et parfums d'art'. Small production.

Verger & Cie, Léopold
Lipstick, cosmetics cases. Luxury production using metal, galalith.

Verlayne
9 rue du Faubourg-Saint-Honoré, Paris
Perfumes. Est. 1944. Some luxury presentations.

Verreries et Ateliers d'Art, Les
Glassworks, labels, boxes, papers. Active 1920s, with Maurice Mathy as artistic director. Speciality: surface decoration (patinas, enamels, gilding). Produced for other glassworks.

Vertés, Marcel (1895–1961)
Engraver, illustrator. Noted for *Schiaparelli perfume advertising.

Viard, C. & J., & Viollet Le Duc
25 rue Chevalier-Désiré, Montreuil (Seine)
Major workshop, opened after 1918. Clovis Viard (1857–1927), sculptor (worked for Barbedienne foundry), was awarded gold medal 1900. His son Julien (1883–1938), also a sculptor, exhibited 1900–08 at Société des Artistes Français in decorative arts section and received many prizes. Awarded

Prix de Rome 1907. Business associate was Viollet Le Duc, a member of the great 19th-c. architect's family. Many creations signed 'J. Viard' in mould. Various glassworks produced Viard models, then returned them to Viard for finishing (surface recutting, polishing, patinas, enamels, gilding and stopper adjustment). Range of producers accounts for wide variation in quality of Viard-signed models, but quality of surface decoration always excellent. Viard produced moulds from drawings; many major glassworks commissioned production of difficult moulds, and application of surface decoration. Unique creative approach reflects background of sculptors. Bottles and stoppers designed as totally interdependent. Models very varied, from simple to elaborate figural designs. Introduced figural stopper featuring multicoloured patinated sculpture combined with decorated bottle acting as pedestal. Viard stoppers conveyed imagery of perfume names (notably oriental figures) and were markedly more delicate than related bottles. Many imitators missed significance of relative proportion of bottles and stoppers, achieving less artistic results. Non-figural models, mostly of soft geometric form, had smaller stoppers of a vaguely floral nature. Coloration was applied on acid-etched surfaces, facilitating absorption of patina (mostly organic watercolours) producing subtle transparency. Choice of surface colorations was determined by perfume colour, so enhancing presentation. After Clovis' death, Julien continued workshop. In 1938 company merged with primary producer, *Dépinoix. Other producers included: *Baccarat, *Bobin, *Maugenest, *Pochet, *Société Parisienne de Verreries. Clients included: *Gabilla, *Gueldy, *Isabey, *Lubin, *Ramsès, *Sauzé, *Volnay. The Viards were not well known to the public – company received trade-press coverage only – but were leading designers and innovators.

Vibert Frères
60 boulevard de Sébastopol, Paris
Perfumes, cosmetics, toiletries. Obscure beginnings in Lyons, 1772. Awarded Grand Prix, 1900. Remained family business until acquired by Lanquest Frères c. 1925. Producers of successful hair lotion 'Pétrole Hahn'. Charming perfume presentations; also created perfumes and luxury presentations for other companies.

Vidal
Italy
Perfumes. Charming figural presentations. Venetian themes.

Vieux Rouen
Glassworks. Est. in 1892 by Amédée Scobart (1842–1908), proprietor of *Rétonval, who later est. *Feuquières. Perfume bottle specialists. Scobart was succeeded by son Georges. Business acquired by *Brosse 1929.

Vigny, de
416 rue Saint-Honoré, Paris
Perfumes, cosmetics. Est. 1919 by Lucien Vogel with help of his brother Jacques, a perfumer (later associated with *Dana and *Molyneux, creating 'Le Numéro Cinq'). Company and products named de Vigny after the poet Alfred de Vigny. Company name changed to Les Parfums de Luxe SA 1921. At inception two distinct perfume personalities were introduced: the ethereal and the humorous. The former was conceived by Charles *Martin for advertising (primarily in *La Gazette du Bon Ton*) and for presentations using bottles designed by *Lalique; the latter, conceived by Michel de *Brunhoff, as seen in 'Golliwogg', 'Chick-Chick', 'Guili-Guili' and 'Be Lucky'. Awarded gold medal 1925. After 1929, without involvement of Vogel, Martin, Lalique and de Brunhoff, quality of designs for new presentations declined considerably. From c. 1933 de Vigny name was gradually simplified to Vigny.

Vinolia Ltd
37-38 Upper Thames Street, London
Soaps, perfumes. 19th-c. soap producers from Bebington, Cheshire. Perfumes possibly introduced in 1901. Some luxury presentations.

Violet
29 boulevard des Italiens, Paris
Perfumes, cosmetics, toiletries. Obscure beginnings 1810. First shop named A la Reine des Abeilles, (The Queen Bee) which became permanent com-

pany subtitle. Became Rehns & Cie in 1885. Participated in all 19th-c. exhibitions. In 1923 trademarked 'Veolay' for all exports to U.S.A., simulating English pronunciation of French name. Both spellings occur. Many luxury presentations. Awarded Grand Prix 1925 for *Gaillard designs.

Vionnet, Madeleine/Vionnet
50 avenue Montaigne, Paris
Couture house. Est. 1912 by Madeleine Vionnet (1876–1975), who had previously worked for Kate Reilly (London), *Callot and Doucet (Paris). She introduced collections without corsets (inspired by Isadora Duncan) for Doucet in 1907. Couture house closed during WW1, reopened 1919. Prestigious clientèle. Introduced avant-garde styles – deceptively simple, bias-cut, no ornamentation, allowing freedom of movement, using black or pale colours. Perfumes introduced 1924; only two presentations known, both expressing fashion philosophy. Salons closed 1939.

Vivaudou
15 rue Royale, Paris
Perfumes, cosmetics, toiletries. Franco-American. Est. 1915. by Victor Vivaudou Affiliated to *Delettrez, initial creator of Vivaudou products. Delettrez retained luxury image. Vivaudou produced medium- to low-priced presentations.

Viville
24 avenue de l'Opéra, Paris
Perfumes, cosmetics, toiletries. Est. 1892 when René-Albert Viville acquired Maison Camus, a company est. in 1836 by Ernest Camus. 19th-c. bestseller was 'Le Parfum des Femmes de France'. Firm acquired by *Yardley. Wide range of luxury to low-priced presentations.

Volnay
244 rue de Rivoli, Paris
Perfumes, cosmetics, toiletries. Est. 1919 by René Duval, who had previously worked for *Coty and est. Brahma, c. 1912, producing oriental-style presentations. Became very successful, with branches in London, Milan, Brussels, New York, South America and Australia. Produced for other perfumers (e.g. *Fontanis). Chose exotic, romantic, unusual perfume names, used eclectic styles. Innovative presentations with pearlized finish. Several *Lalique models, including 'Gri-Gri'.

Vuitton, Louis
70 avenue des Champs-Elysées, Paris
Luggage. Est. 1854 by Louis Vuitton. Creators of first practical, elegant steamer trunks, wardrobe trunks, stylish luggage. Became packer to Empress Eugénie. Awarded prize 1867. Perfumes officially introduced in 1927; two known luxury presentations.

W

Walska, Ganna
2 rue de la Paix, Paris
Perfumes. Est. 1927 by Ganna Walska, an untalented opera singer, notorious for highly publicized, acrimonious divorce. First perfume 'Divorçons' ('Let's Divorce'). Short-lived.

Weil
4 rue Sainte-Anne, Paris
Furriers. Family of luxury fur designers. Perfumes introduced 1927 as 'Parfums pour la fourrure'. Elegant presentations.

Wheaton Glass Co.
Glassworks. Est. 1890 by Dr Theodore Corson Wheaton, with purchase of existing pharmaceutical glass factory at Millville, New Jersey. Expanded considerably during WW1, when perfume-bottle production was suspended in Europe. Family business: in 1946 founder's grandson formed company to produce perfume bottles; he later merged the two Wheaton companies. Since the 1920s major clients included: *Arden, *Avon, *Carnegie, *Chess, *Lelong, *Matchabelli.

Willk, Alexandre
Manufacturer of Houpette 'Pli', unusual container with retractable powder puff. Primary client was *Molinard.

Wolff & Sohn, F.
Durlacher Allée 31, Karlsruhe
Perfumes, cosmetics, toiletries. Est. 1857. *Baccarat a supplier. Some luxury presentations.

Woodworth
392 Fifth Avenue, New York
Perfumes, cosmetics, toiletries. Est. 1854 in Rochester, NY, as Woodworth & Bunnel. Very successful, unusual for a company without the help of extensive advertising until 1928. Some French luxury presentations by *Dépinoix, *Viard.

Worth
7 rue de la Paix, Paris
Couture house. Est. 1858 by Charles Frederick Worth (1826–95), born and trained in England. Began designing dresses for his wife; admiration of others caused Worth to open fashion department in Paris fabric store where he worked after 1846. Became successful couturier, designing for Empress Eugénie and European royalty. Remained family business. Perfumes, introduced 1924, all in *Lalique presentations. Company sold 1946; salons closed 1954.

Wymot
25 rue Croix-Jordan, Lyons
Perfumes. Est. 1922 by Vincent Pierre. Small luxury production.

X

Xydès
9 rue Gounod, Paris
Perfumes. Originally a Portuguese company, est. in 1922 by Pierre-André Pignel. Luxury presentations. Short-lived.

Y

Yardley & Co. Ltd
8 New Bond Street, London
Perfumes, cosmetics, toiletries. Est. 1770 by Thomas Yardley. Lavender toilet water first bestseller. Drawing by Francis Wheatly reproduced on Yardley advertising and presentations was 'The Flower Sellers', from *The Cries of London* (1793). Became major international company. Acquired *Viville, then phased out that name.

Ybry
6 rue Ybry, Neuilly (Seine)
Perfumes, cosmetics. Est. 1925 by Simon Jaroslawski. Luxury presentations. Company experienced financial problems from inception. Shared advertising of 1927 showed fashionable Parisian woman smoking Osborn cigarette, using Ybry perfume (an unusual, possibly economical, concept). After 1930, quality and designs declined dramatically. Original French company bankrupt 1932, though Ybry name continued in existence until 1940s on lower-quality presentations.

Ysiane
38 rue d'Enghien, Paris
Perfumes, cosmetics. Est. c. 1925. Affiliated to La *Diaphane. Some charming presentations. Short-lived.

Z

Zenobia Ltd
Woodgate, Loughborough, Leicestershire
Perfumes, cosmetics, toiletries. Est. c. 1900.

Zofaly
59 rue Galilée, Paris
Perfumes. Est. c. 1930 by Jeanne Crespin in Montargis (Loiret). Charming presentations.

Bibliography

GENERAL WORKS

(a) The period before 1910
(including catalogues of major international exhibitions)

Borsi, Franco, and Ezio Godoli, *Paris 1900*, New York, 1977

Bourget, Paul, *Nouveaux Essais de Psychologie Contemporaine*, Paris, 1883

Brunhammer, Yvonne, *et al.*, *Art Nouveau Belgium France*, Houston, Texas, 1976

Champier, Victor, *Les Industries d'Art à l'Exposition Universelle de 1900* (2 vols.), Paris, 1902

Clair, Jean, *Sous la Direction de Vienne 1880–1938, L'Apocalypse Joyeuse*, Paris, 1986

Cooper-Hewitt Museum (various authors): *L'Art de Vivre, Decorative Arts and Design in France 1789–1989*, New York, 1989

Exposition Universelle de 1867 à Paris, Catalogue Général Publié par la Commission Impériale (3 vols.), Paris, 1867

Geffroy, Gustave, *Les Industries Artistiques Françaises et Etrangères à L'Exposition Universelle de 1900*, Paris, 1900

Grasset, Eugène, *Ornements Typographiques Paris 1880. La Plante et ses Applications Ornementales*, Paris, 1899

Great Exhibition of the Works of Industry of All Nations, 1851, Official Descriptive and Illustrated Catalogue (3 vols.), London, 1851

Madsen, Stephen Tschudi, *Sources of Art Nouveau*, New York, 1976

Marx, Roger, *L'Art Social*, Paris, 1913

Meige, Henri, *Charcot-Artiste*, Paris 1925

Montesquiou, Robert de, *Rapport du Comte Robert de Montesquiou sur le Musée Rétrospectif de la Classe 90 (Parfumerie) à l'Exposition Internationale de 1900*, Paris, 1900

Musée de la Mode et du Costume – Palais Galliera: *Femmes Fin de Siècle 1885–1895*, Paris, 1990

Pevsner, Nikolaus, and J.M. Richards, *The Anti-Rationalists*, New York, 1973

Picard, Alfred (ed.), *Rapport 1889, Exposition Universelle Internationale de 1889 à Paris*, Rapports du Jury International, Paris, 1891

Réunion des Musées Nationaux: *Le Temps Toulouse-Lautrec*, Paris, 1991

Silverman, Debora L., *Art Nouveau in Fin-de-Siècle France, Politics, Psychology and Style*, Berkeley, Los Angeles, London, 1989

Soriau, Paul, *La Suggestion dans l'Art*, Paris, 1893

Spillman, Jane Shadel, *Glass from World's Fairs 1851–1904*, Corning, N.Y., 1986

Vachon, Marius, *La Femme dans l'Art, Les Protectrices des Arts, Les Femmes Artistes*, Paris, 1893

West, Rebecca, *1900*, London, 1982

Wichmann, Siegfried, *Japonisme, The Japanese Influence on Western Art since 1858*, New York and London, 1985

(b) The period since 1910

Alexandrian, Sarane, *Surrealist Art*, London, 1970; reprinted 1985

The American Heritage History of the 20's and 30's, New York, 1970

Battersby, Martin, *The Decorative Thirties*, New York, 1971

Bayard, Emile, *Le Style Moderne*, Paris, 1961

Deshairs, Léon (ed.), *L'Art Français depuis Vingt Ans* (10 vols.), Paris, 1925

Encyclopédie des Arts Décoratifs et Industriels Modernes au XXème Siècle en Douze Volumes, Paris, 1925

Néret, Gilles, *The Arts of the Twenties*, New York, 1986

Time-Life Books: *This Fabulous Century: Sixty Years of American Life, Vol III, 1920–1930*, New York, 1969

Verne, H., and R. Chavance, *Pour Comprendre l'Art Décoratif en France*, Paris, 1925

Wilson, Richard Guy, Dianne H. Pilgrim and Dickran Tashjian, *The Machine Age in America 1918–1941*, New York, 1986

CLASSIFIED WORKS

Artists and Designers
(alphabetically by name of subject)

Guelingani, Franca, Celio Brunelleschi and Folco Lazzaroni Brunelleschi, *Umberto Brunelleschi*, New York, 1979

Erté [Romain de Tirtoff], *Things I Remember*, New York, 1975

Sanchez, Léopold Diego, *Jean-Michel Frank Adolphe Chanaux*, Paris, 1980

Gray, Christopher, *Sculpture and Ceramics of Paul Gauguin*, New York, 1980

Bachollet, Raymond, Daniel Bordet and Anne-Claude Lelieur, *Paul Iribe*, Paris, 1982

Mairie de Paris, *Paul Iribe, Précurseur de l'Art Déco*, Paris, 1983

Geffroy, Gustave, *René Lalique*, Paris, 1922

Marcilhac, Félix, *René Lalique 1860–1945 Maître-Verrier. Analyse de l'Œuvre et Catalogue Raisonné*, Paris, 1989

Utt, Mary Lou and Glenn, with Patricia Bayer, *Lalique Perfume Bottles*, New York, 1990, and London, 1991

San Lazzaro, G. di (ed.), *Hommage à Fernand Léger*, Paris, 1971

Lepape, Claude, and Thierry Defert, *From the Ballets Russes to Vogue, The Art of Georges Lepape*, London, 1984

Olivier-Vial, Frank, and François Rateau, *Armand Albert Rateau*, Paris, 1992

Theatre

Baer, Nancy Van Norman, *Theatre in Revolution, Russian Avant-Garde Stage Design 1913–1935*, New York and London, 1991

Latour, Geneviève, and Florence Claval, *Les Théâtres de Paris*, Paris, 1991

Pozharskaya, Militsa, and Tatiana Volodina, *The Art of The Ballets Russes, The Russian Seasons in Paris 1908-29*, London, 1990

Spencer, Charles, *Erté*, London, 1986

Spencer, Charles (with contributions by Philip Dyers and Martin Battersby), *The World of Sergei Diaghilev*, New York, 1979

Fashion: general

Martin, Richard, *Fashion and Surrealism*, New York, 1987, and London, 1988; paperback edition 1989

Milbank, Caroline Rennolds, *Couture, The Great Designers*, New York and London, 1985

Pickens, Mary Brooks, and Dora Loves Miller, *Dressmakers of France*, New York, 1956

Rochas, Marcel, *1925–1950. Vingt-cinq ans d'élégance à Paris*, Paris, 1951

Fashion and Designers
(alphabetically by name of subject)

Charles-Roux, Edmonde, *Chanel and her World*, New York, 1981

Daché, Lilly, *Talking Through My Hats*, New York, 1946

Musée des Arts de la Mode: *Hommage à Christian Dior 1947–1957* (exhibition catalogue), Paris, 1986

European Costume and Textiles including an Important Collection of Jeanne Lanvin Fashion Designs, Sotheby's sale catalogue, London, 19 September 1989

Etherington-Smith, Meredith, *Patou*, New York, 1983

Deslandres, Yvonne (with Dorothée Lalanne), *Poiret*, Paris, 1986

Musée de la Mode et du Costume, Palais Galliera: *Paul Poiret et Nicole Groult, Maîtres de la Mode Art Déco* (exhibition catalogue), Paris, 1986

Poiret, Paul, *Art et Phynance*, Paris, 1934

—, *En Habillant l'Epoque*, Paris, 1930

—, *Revenez-y*, Paris, 1932

Schiaparelli, Elsa, *Shocking Life*, New York, 1954

White, Palmer (with a foreword by Yves Saint-Laurent), *Elsa Schiaparelli: Empress of Paris Fashion*, London, 1986

Demornex, Jacqueline, *Vionnet*, New York, 1991

Marcilhac, Félix, Introduction to sale catalogue *Mobilier Art Déco Madeleine Vionnet Souvenirs de Jacques Doucet*, Paris, 31 May 1985

Glass

Bloch-Dermant, Janine, *L'Art du Verre en France 1860–1914*, Lausanne, 1974

—, *Le Verre en France d'Emile Gallé à nos jours*, Paris, 1983

Compagnie des Cristalleries de Baccarat: *Baccarat, Les Flacons à Parfum, The Perfume Bottles*, Paris, 1986

Jones-North, Jacquelyne Y., *Commercial Perfume Bottles*, West Chester, Pennsylvania, 1987

Perfume Industry

La Revue des Marques de la Parfumerie et de la Savonnerie: *La Parfumerie Française et l'Art dans la Présentation*, Paris, 1925

Perfumers

Colard, Grégoire (with a foreword by Michel Déon de l'Académie Française), *Le Charme Secret d'une Maison Parfumée – Caron*, Paris, 1984

Coradeschi, Sergio, *La Collezione Borsari 1870*, Milan, 1990

Fellous, Colette, *Guerlain*, Paris, 1987

Roger & Gallet, Parfumeurs et Créateurs (1806–1989), Bernay, 1987

PERIODICALS

General: Art and Design

Amour de l'Art, L'
Art Décoratif, L'
Art et Décoration
Art Vivant, L'
Renaissance de l'Art Français et des Industries de Luxe, La
Revue des Arts Décoratifs

Fashion

Art, Goût, Beauté
Femina
Gazette du Bon Ton, La
Jardin des Modes, Le
Vogue

Perfume Trade Publications

American Perfumer
Parfumerie Moderne, La
Revue des Marques de la Parfumerie et de la Savonnerie, La
Toilette

Theatre

Comœdia Illustré

206

Index